WASHINGTON GLADDEN'S CHURCH

WASHINGTON GLADDEN'S CHURCH

The Minister Who Made Modern American Protestantism

David Mislin

ROWMAN & LITTLEFIELD
Lanham • Boulder • New York • London

Published by Rowman & Littlefield
An imprint of The Rowman & Littlefield Publishing Group, Inc.
4501 Forbes Boulevard, Suite 200, Lanham, Maryland 20706
www.rowman.com

6 Tinworth Street, London SE11 5AL

Copyright © 2020 by The Rowman & Littlefield Publishing Group, Inc.

All rights reserved. No part of this book may be reproduced in any form or by any electronic or mechanical means, including information storage and retrieval systems, without written permission from the publisher, except by a reviewer who may quote passages in a review.

British Library Cataloguing in Publication Information Available

Library of Congress Cataloging-in-Publication Data

Names: Mislin, David
Title: Washington Gladden's Church : The Minister Who Made Modern American Protestantism
ISBN: 978-1-4422-6892-0 (cloth)
ISBN: 978-1-5381-5963-7 (pbk)
ISBN: 978-1-4422-6893-7 (electronic)

CONTENTS

Preface vii
Acknowledgments xiii

1 Observer 1
2 Survivor 21
3 Rebel 41
4 Journalist 61
5 Pastor 85
6 Reformer 105
7 Unifier 129
8 Critic 151

Afterword 173
Notes 175
Index 203
About the Author 211

PREFACE

Over the last few years, any time I've told someone that I'm writing a book about Washington Gladden, I've gotten one of two responses. From most people, I'm met with a simple "Who?" From a relatively small group of scholars—mostly historians of religion in the United States but a few more general historians of the late nineteenth and early twentieth centuries as well—I've received a different one-word response: "Why?" I've come to realize that both groups are essentially asking me the same question: Why should we care?

It's a fair question to ask. Washington Gladden was a straight, white, male Protestant minister who died over a century ago. He lived and worked in a very different culture. In his day, Protestant clergymen (and they were nearly always men) exerted a far greater influence on American society. People are right to wonder why such a historical figure matters today. As a society, we have recognized the importance of hearing diverse voices, including in the study of the past. The United States is now a religiously pluralistic and far more secular society. Besides, as my colleagues have reminded me, many scholars have written extensively on Gladden. Is another book about him necessary?[1]

At the simplest level, this book is necessary because Gladden was a hugely influential figure who deserves to be better known, and there are limits to what has been written about him. A half century before Billy Graham earned the title of "America's pastor," Gladden might well have laid claim to it. Late in his life, the editors of a popular periodical observed that "his actual pastorate extends over the whole United States."[2]

They were right. Gladden was not simply the pastor of a church, though he was quite successful in that role. He was a widely revered writer and lecturer. He helped to bring theological liberalism into the mainstream of American Protestantism, made commitments to social justice a key aspect of religious identity, and offered a sharp critique of many of his society's failures. Throughout his life he bridged the political and religious spheres, and he was unquestionably one of the leading public intellectuals of his day. His career included a stint as religious editor of a major newspaper and a term on the city council of Columbus, Ohio. He published dozens of articles in the most-read periodicals of the time, and he wrote over thirty books.

While Gladden's influence and stature highlight his importance in his own time, he has additional significance in ours. The issues that confronted the United States during his life confront Americans again today. Gladden lived and worked amid growing economic inequality. A wealthy elite grew ever richer (and ostentatiously so) while the vast majority of people slid downward. Large-scale corporations, a relatively new phenomenon, amassed greater and greater power and exerted an ever-larger influence on US politics. The political culture of his day was marked by extreme partisan rancor, with people's votes determined more by identity than by policy. The nation was plagued by anti-immigrant fervor, which often morphed into attacks on the primary religious minority of the day, Roman Catholics. And as the United States grew increasingly engaged on the world stage, it embraced a policy of imperialism and was drawn into overseas military conflicts.

Nor were things better within churches. The rise of agnosticism and atheism had created a generation of young Americans who were skeptical of the claims of Christianity. In particular, religious faith seemed increasingly at odds with the demonstrated facts of science and history. At the same time, churches and ministers clung to outdated codes of morality and standards of behavior, which made them seem irrelevant in a rapidly changing world.

In short, the problems of the early twenty-first century are the same problems that Gladden faced over a century ago.

Therein lays Gladden's particular significance, and the reason why his life and work is worth revisiting now. An elusive goal in recent years has been the cultivation of a "religious left" to counterbalance the political and cultural influence of the Christian right in the United States. Gladden was instrumental in creating a vibrant religious left during his lifetime. The Social Gospel movement, which he was critical in shaping, united mainline Protestants of various denominations, sometimes in cooperation with Catholics and Jews. Together, they combatted economic inequality, advocated for the poor and working class, and battled political corruption.

Moreover, Gladden's religious liberalism offered a faith that evolved with the times. He urged the reinterpretation of older beliefs in light of new scientific knowledge, and he insisted that moral values needed to be reconsidered as social norms changed. Though some particular circumstances certainly differ, Gladden's message offers a starting point for a template for a modern religious left.

Or, more accurately, he offers a template for a religious center-left. One of the defining characteristics of Gladden's outlook was its expansiveness. Perhaps because he had grown up in an evangelical family, Gladden never became overly dogmatic in his religious liberalism. Indeed, he was at times described as a "conservative liberal." He worked to create broad coalitions of politically engaged Christians, even if they did not all share the same theological outlook. His efforts proved successful. Many churches and denominations found themselves rejuvenated with the message of theological liberalism, and Gladden's wedding of religious and political commitments led to meaningful changes in social policy, especially on issues of workers' rights and government oversight. Gladden serves as a model of a reformer who worked within existing institutions and brought significant changes to them.

At the same time, Gladden's life also presents a cautionary tale for those who seek to challenge the religious and political status quo. For all the innovative aspects of his work, Gladden remained wedded to many conventional ideas of his era. His political and religious thought was significantly influenced by women, yet he failed to appreciate women's demand for greater political and social equality. Gladden sharply criticized racial discrimination, yet he could not escape partially blaming African Americans for the rise of Jim Crow segregation. While he vehemently opposed anti-Catholic nativism and the anti-immigrant propaganda that accompanied it, he at times denigrated immigrants and called for restrictions on naturalization rights.

Gladden had the personal capital to take stronger stands on these issues without losing public support. Had he done so, he might well have built support for progressive causes that would have brought greater changes to American life. But the conservative side of the conservative liberal sometimes exerted too much influence.

Thus, Gladden exemplified a potential peril for the broad coalition of a religious center-left that he helped to create. While often successful in meeting many of his goals, Gladden never fully lived up to the ideals that he espoused. He hewed close to the middle, and thus never developed the transformative coalition that he might have created. More problematic in the long term, because of its emphasis on gradual change and respectability, the religious message Gladden offered was easily co-opted and stripped of its more critical elements in the years after his death.

For those Americans who today seek to cultivate a religious left, there are important lessons in Gladden's successes. He was an unapologetically religious person who wedded his faith to a commitment to progressive politics. He moved effortlessly among the worlds of church, government, and journalism. But there are also lessons in his failures. For someone who espoused a critical vision for society, Gladden was quite comfortable with the world as it was.

A truly successful religious left would embrace Gladden's broad-mindedness and commitment to weaving together spiritual, social, and political commitments. Its members would, however, subject their culture to more sustained critique than he managed to do.

A few words about this book are in order at the outset. As I've noted, there is no shortage of existing scholarship on Gladden, not least of which is Jacob Dorn's masterful biography, *Washington Gladden: Prophet of the Social Gospel*. While this book is something of a biography, I have no pretentions of matching Dorn's exhaustive treatment of Gladden's life. Dorn provides a level of insight and detail—especially into Gladden's later life—that I have not even attempted to duplicate here. Nor would I claim that this book represents a full treatment of US religious history during Gladden's lifetime.

Rather, my goal is to illuminate key aspects of Gladden's professional and intellectual life: his youth and education, his early career struggles, his rebellious streak as a young pastor, his work as a professional journalist, as well as his later development as a pastor, reformer, voice for unity, and social critic. My focus is primarily on the ideas Gladden espoused and his efforts to put them into action. To the extent that personal relationships and events in his life shaped those ideas, I have explored them. But I have not examined every aspect of his work in detail. For example, in chapter 7, I discuss at some length Gladden's determined effort to break down denominational barriers among Protestants by fostering a spirit of cooperation. But I spend little time talking about a failed effort to merge three Protestant denominations. Although the attempted merger occupied an enormous amount of his time (and accounts for a considerable portion of his archived correspondence), it ultimately proved insignificant compared to his other contributions to the ecumenical movement.

I have also attempted here to do something that other scholars of Gladden have not. Following Dorn's lead, nearly all writers on Gladden have devoted disproportionate attention to the second half of his life—that is, to the years after his move to Columbus, Ohio, at the age of forty-six. The reasons for doing so are understandable. While the early part of his career was marked by professional uncertainty, in his later years Gladden achieved his greatest public stature. More practically, the bulk of his archival materials—letters, sermons, and articles—are dated after his move to Columbus.

The downside of this approach is that it treats the first half of Gladden's life as a mere prologue to what came later. A careful evaluation of sources, however, reveals that he arrived at many of his religious and political commitments early in life. By his mid-thirties, an observer later noted, Gladden was already writing "the plain-spoken, hard-hitting editorials that laid the groundwork for his later books."[3]

Thus, I have tried to strike a greater balance, even with less robust source material, by exploring all of the periods of Gladden's life equally. I have focused particularly on his four years as religious editor of the *Independent*, which afforded him a considerable platform early in his career. In so doing, I hope to convey the significant influence of early friends and acquaintances on his later views.

More importantly, I show that his linked commitments to religious liberalism and progressive politics—the things that make Gladden's message most resonant in the modern world—characterized nearly his entire life.

ACKNOWLEDGMENTS

It goes without saying that one incurs a large number of debts in writing a book, even a relatively modest one such as this. First and foremost, I am grateful to the many colleagues who read drafts of chapters, discussed ideas with me, or responded to elements of the manuscript at conferences. Andrew Ballou, Margaret Bendroth, Catherine Brekus, Heath Carter, Chris Evans, Sara Georgini, David Holland, Elizabeth Jemison, and Paul Putz all offered valuable feedback. Many of the ideas explored here had their origins in my doctoral dissertation, and I remain grateful to my advisor, Jon Roberts, and my committee members, Brooke Blower, Charles Capper, David Hempton, and Bruce Schulman. Paul Harvey reviewed the manuscript, and I am appreciative of his feedback.

My work on this project was greatly aided by archivists and librarians, most notably Matthew Benz at the Ohio History Connection, who helped me negotiate the shifting sands of the Gladden collection.

I am grateful to Jon Sisk, my editor at Rowman & Littlefield, who took interest in this project and helped shepherd it to completion. An important venue for testing ideas for this project has been *The Conversation*. I am thankful for that platform, and especially for Kalpana Jain's tireless editing of my work there.

In the early days of this project, I received an e-mail from Jacob Dorn, the author of the definitive biography on Gladden. He read my work and provided kind, thoughtful feedback. I was saddened by news of his death in 2017 and regretted that we never met in person.

The Intellectual Heritage Program at Temple University has served as my academic home for the duration of this project. Joseph Schwartz, Daniel Berman, Dustin Kidd, Emily Carlin, and Douglas Greenfield have provided the tools necessary for my continued professional development. I am especially thankful for the colleagues who inspire me with their skill as scholars and teachers: Elizabeth Hayes Alvarez, Genevieve Amaral, Jessie Iwata, Rob Rabiee, Natasha Rossi, Sheryl Sawin, Elizabeth Sunflower, and Naomi Taback.

Most importantly, I am grateful to my family: my mother Kim Mislin Cran, who in addition to her love and encouragement is a minister who embodies the best of the Social Gospel tradition. I am also grateful to my in-laws, Carol Bragg, Jerry Elmer, and Anita, Joshua, and Rebecca Kestin, for their ongoing support of this project. I remain indebted to John and Susan Russell for years of encouragement. This book would never have been finished were it not for my spouse, Jonathan, who did more than his share of dishes and laundry as I completed the manuscript. Our son, Benjamin, who arrived halfway through the writing process, contributed more to this project than he realizes. I only regret that this manuscript kept me away from him far too often.

I

OBSERVER

At first glance, there was nothing unusual in the letter from Lewis Matson that reached Washington Gladden late in June 1855. The two young men corresponded regularly. They had grown up together in Owego, New York, where Gladden remained while Matson began his studies at Yale. Matson's letters reported the mundane details of life in New Haven: his struggles with his roommate, the hard work of studying, and his longing for the familiar environment of his hometown.[1]

But this letter was different. "Don't be enraged, Gladden," Matson wrote, "because now and then I make a slight, incidental allusion to your circumstances, in 'romantic' life." What followed was anything but a few incidental allusions. Matson mentioned three women by name, suggesting that Gladden had simultaneously carried on relationships with them all. Matson saved his most cutting remarks for his discussion of the third, whose name was Flora and who held particular interest for Matson: "Next time you are with her all alone upon the sofa (in the dark) with arms around her waist, with her hand tightly pressed in your own, remind her that I am still alive." While his friend was away at college, Gladden had apparently made moves on his love interest.

Such behavior, Matson continued, was the norm for his friend. "When I am with her (if you will ever permit me to be)," Matson continued, "I will remind her of your fickle disposition, of how many young hearts have been broken even in the act of being laid upon the altar of your love." He concluded by telling Gladden not to complain that "you haven't time to marry Annette as you want to and then spend three quarters of your time at Miss Branch's house . . . or at Flora's."[2]

Matson was correct that this was not atypical for Gladden. When a cousin announced his interest in a young woman, he noted that she was a "real good . . . Christian girl" and not one of Gladden's "fancy flirts." Another of Gladden's friends chastised him for badly treating a "poor girl" who had "bestowed her heart" on him.[3]

Nor was Gladden unique among his circle of friends in this way. They regaled him with their own accounts of flirtatious encounters with the apparent expectation that he would approve. A cousin recounted a ride to a church event in which he went in a wagon with "nine girls," and because it was so full "I had to take one of the girls on my lap . . . a nice little bird she is." The trip home was just as fun for Daniels: "I sat between Lydia Gildman (my favorite) and Miss Vaughn. I had an arm around each one and if I ever enjoyed a ride of 2-1/2 miles it was that night." Another friend who taught school boasted that his "kingdom" included four young ladies, "of 16 and upward (not very far upward)" who were "quite pretty, a couple of them especially so."[4]

Contrary to modern stereotypes of nineteenth-century prudishness, this behavior was about as normal for adolescents in the 1850s as it is now. While his youthful actions might appear unseemly for a man who would become a nationally respected, beloved clergyman, his adolescent relationships are important for understanding the man and the minister Gladden would become. For Gladden, religion was inseparable from the rest of life, and that was true even at an early age. The women with whom he flirted were also the women who influenced his ideas about faith, human nature, and the meaning of life. Friends and rivals alike shaped his understanding of Christian belief at the same time they taught him about sex and romance.

In fact, much in Gladden's early life contributed to his future path as a minister, social reformer, and critic. His tumultuous childhood provided a broad set of experiences that cultivated his empathy for people in a wide range of circumstances. An early internship with a newspaper inspired a love of writing and journalism. Perhaps most importantly, living in a religiously and politically vibrant community on the eve of the Civil War ensured that faith and civic responsibility would forever be linked in Gladden's mind.

Solomon Washington Gladden was born in February 1836 in Potts Grove, a tiny hamlet situated between the two branches of the Susquehanna River amid the rolling hills and farmland of north-central Pennsylvania. He was named after his father, though to differentiate himself he went by Washington from an early age (early on, he adopted the nickname "Wash," and, for a select few friends, "Tony").

The Gladden family was a case study in downward mobility. Several generations back, around the time of the American Revolution, the family enjoyed a reasonably high level of social status. But that had gradually diminished, and they reached their nadir with Washington Gladden's father. Solomon suffered from poor health and became a teacher rather than entering a trade that required manual labor. Like many of his generation, he left his native New England in the hopes of finding success by joining the push westward through New York State. In 1833, Solomon married one of his former students, Amanda Daniels. The two moved south to Pennsylvania, which had recently announced a plan to establish a state-funded school system and seemed to promise better opportunities. Solomon became the head of Potts Grove's school, while Amanda took work in a nearby town to make ends meet. Three years later, they gave birth to their first child, Washington. They enjoyed a relatively happy life in Pennsylvania and soon had a second child, George.[5]

Tragedy struck not long after. Just before Washington's sixth birthday, Solomon Gladden contracted an intestinal illness. Amanda and Washington were on a trip, but they managed to reach home just before Solomon died. The experience remained with Gladden throughout his life. Nearly seven decades later, he recalled his father as a "nearly constant companion" in his early childhood. He also remembered the immense grief that accompanied the loss. "The droning, dreadful days at a neighbor's while we waited for the funeral" dragged on without end. For some time after, there were "many nights that I cried myself to sleep."[6]

The loss of a parent was difficult enough; what followed was even worse. The family's finances had been precarious when Solomon was alive. Despite her best efforts, Amanda Gladden proved unable to care for Washington and his now two-year-old brother. She made the difficult decision to separate the family.

For a time, Gladden lived with his paternal grandparents in Springfield, Massachusetts. The trip there introduced him to the "tortures of travel." He later remembered that "the roads were rough, the inns primitive, the weather often harsh." He traveled for nearly 250 miles "numb and cramped" in a carriage with a man, woman, and baby—people he barely knew—and "a round cheese-box next to the dashboard, that held the provisions for the journey and served as a seat for me."[7]

Gladden recalled his time in New England as a happy one, but the arrangement did not last. He returned to his mother's hometown of Owego, New York. He did not live with his mother, though. Amanda had remarried while he was in Springfield and would soon have two additional children by her second husband. Instead, Gladden lived with his uncle, Ebenezer Daniels, who had offered Gladden an apprenticeship on the family farm.[8]

Owego sits on New York's southern border near Binghamton, and in the decades before the Civil War it boasted a population of roughly eight thousand people. Though hardly a bustling metropolis, it served as a major economic hub for the region. The gently rolling hills to the north of the village provided a rich supply of timber. At the town's docks, lumber would be loaded onto barges. These would float down the Susquehanna, eventually reaching the Chesapeake. Grain and livestock also passed through the town en route from western New York farms to the larger cities of the mid-Atlantic. Because of its prime location, Owego enjoyed considerable growth and prosperity during Gladden's childhood. Those years witnessed the construction of a ritzy hotel described as "the most magnificent building between New York and Lake Erie." For the rest of his life, Gladden considered Owego his home. In his later years, long after he moved away, he purchased a home there to return to every summer.[9]

Owego's wealth did not extend to the Daniels family, or, by extension, to Gladden. The family lived in a "poor little farmhouse" on their forty acres of land outside of town. Gladden's childhood consisted of working the farm and attending the town's public school during the off-season. He also went to church—a lot. No other family "was in its pew as many Sundays of the year as ours," he recalled. In typical nineteenth-century fashion, the Presbyterian church the Daniels family attended had both a morning and an evening service. Dutiful Christians attended both. With insufficient time to return to the farm between the services, Sunday was given entirely to church. Services started and ended the day (each having a sermon that often lasted more than an hour) with a midday activity in the nicer weather of sitting in the church cemetery and enjoying meals of "doughnuts and apples."[10]

His family's intense religiosity did not initially set Gladden on the path toward ministry. Rather, he became interested in journalism, and in 1852 he had his first experience in the field. The sixteen-year-old was offered an apprenticeship at the *Owego Gazette*, one of the town's two newspapers. The position required that he live with the paper's editor. Though the accommodation was not luxurious, the move allowed Gladden to end his stay at the Daniels farm and move into the comparatively bustling center of Owego.[11]

The apprenticeship introduced Gladden to a booming field. Nineteenth-century Americans loved newspapers, and the nation boasted the highest readership of news anywhere in the world. Even a small town like Owego could expect to have at least one weekly paper that provided ample advertising space for the town's businesses along with a mix of local, regional, and national news. Importantly, the *Gazette* initiated Gladden to the world of politics as well. The media landscape of the nineteenth century in many ways resembled the twenty-first century world of partisan online news. Newspapers of the pre–Civil War era often received funding from a political party and in return dutifully gave favorable coverage to that party. Even those newspapers that were not funded by a party still reflected the views of their editors.[12]

Political affiliation put Gladden at odds with his employer. The Daniels family, like most devout Northern Protestants of the day, belonged to the Whig Party. In many respects, they were the quintessential Whigs: deeply religious farmers who embraced the party's moralistic message of thrift, temperance, and devoutness. By contrast, the *Owego Gazette*'s publisher was a Democrat who was quite active in local politics.[13]

In reality, these partisan divisions amounted to little at this particular moment in US life. Historically, the major divergence between the two parties had been the role of the federal government, with Whigs supporting a more active state. But during the 1840s, Democrats had championed territorial expansion that added Texas, California, and Oregon, and they came to support more government involvement to develop and improve the acquired regions. Meanwhile, both parties encompassed a range of positions on the question of slavery. It would be several years before Democrats became synonymous with southern slave states. In this time of transition in US politics, Gladden had little substantive disagreement with the views of his employer.[14]

While the apprenticeship introduced the adolescent Gladden to the heady worlds of journalism and politics, working at the *Gazette* provided a more basic education as well. It offered "a large opportunity for the study of human nature." As he later recalled, "All kinds of causes sought the advocacy of the paper; all sorts of cranks demanded a hearing; advice of every description was sought and volunteered, and personal grievances and bereavements were always knocking for admission to its columns."[15]

Gladden was not exaggerating. The *Gazette*'s contents give lie to any conceptions of nineteenth-century culture as one of restraint and privacy. The paper printed seemingly every heart-wrenching story it could find. Sentimental reflections on death appeared frequently, such as one by an Owego citizen about his daughter's illness. Her sickness progressed "with increasing virulence, until groans and bitter lamentations are extorted from her agonized frame," and these were relieved only by her death. The account spared little detail of the grief that followed. "Her seat at the breakfast table is vacant, her plate is unwittingly placed for her," the girl's father recounted in the paper. "No more do we hear her repeat her morning and evening prayers. Her incessant prattle about her school, her lessons, her teachers . . . has ceased forever."[16]

Other reports in the *Gazette* contained titillating accounts of the macabre. Suicides were a frequent subject. One article told of a man known to be "subject to fits of mental aberration" who had hanged himself, leaving his "wife and a large family of children to mourn." Murders were another popular topic. One issue reported on a Pennsylvania woman (also suffering from "mental aberration") who "administered poison to . . . her husband, three children, and a servant," and then left them all to die.[17]

If one wished to find an environment that would introduce a future clergyman to the widest range of human emotion and experience, the *Owego Gazette* was quite ideal. Gladden excelled at the work there. By the end of his first year, he oversaw all of the paper's local news coverage. Soon, however, a new opportunity presented itself. A local minister saw unfulfilled intellectual potential in Gladden. The clergyman encouraged him to enroll at Owego Academy. The school promised "both mental and moral direction" and offered free courses to young men and women who agreed to teach school for a period of time. Gladden took that offer and enrolled in the academy.[18]

As he cultivated the love of journalism and the interest in politics that would shape his future career, Gladden forged a number of close friendships that would be equally important. Many of these developed into lasting relationships that directed the course of his life and influenced his views on a range of subjects.

The most significant of these relationships was with the woman who would eventually become his wife. Jennie Cohoon, whose family had moved to Owego a few years earlier, was a fellow student at Owego Academy. By the autumn of 1857, the two seemed seriously involved. Lewis Matson wrote of Jennie in a letter, and snidely noted, seemingly in reference to her, that Gladden's "affections . . . are concentrated only upon one" person. The two became engaged the next year.[19]

Despite their earlier tiff about Gladden's treatment of women, he and Matson sustained their friendship. The two often discussed issues of religion, faith, and human nature. In these letters a divergence started to emerge between Gladden's outlook and the views of his more traditionally pious friend. "The world is full of all sorts of trials and misfortune, shin bruises and heart aches, and according to my notion is all a fleeting show," Matson wrote, quickly adding "but you think differently." Even at the age of twenty, Gladden had begun to espouse a more optimistic outlook about humanity than many of his peers.[20]

At least as judged by the volume of saved correspondence, one of Gladden's deepest friendships at this point in his life was with a young woman named Hattie Hamilton. When she first met Gladden, Hamilton was a preceptress at Owego Academy, though she later moved north to take a similar position at the Ladies Institute of Auburn, New York.[21]

Hamilton's letters conveyed a bold, carefree personality. When her work frustrated her, she strove to "go on cheerfully, doing what is required." She lived life to the fullest, such as when on a fishing trip with friends she was "perfectly reckless" and waded through a cold mountain lake "regardless of consequences." She frequently made cutting observations, telling Gladden that a "seedy old bachelor" was to marry a widow lady. Hamilton wondered whether "he will say 'pshaw!' to her so often as he does to his horse." Even Gladden could not escape from her pointed quips. After asking for a lock of his hair, she added, "You will think I am a selfish sort of a girl, dear Wash, to ask for some of your hair when you have so little."[22]

Not surprisingly, Hamilton's fiery personality drew mixed reactions from those who met her. On the one hand, she charmed many people, especially young men. The first time he met her, Matson confessed to Gladden how easily he could "have been deep in love with her." On the other hand, a potential suitor rejected her for being "coarse, vulgar, and unrefined." Despite the bluntness that some found off-putting, Gladden and Hamilton sustained a friendship for years.[23]

In fact, every historian who has studied Gladden's life has puzzled over the precise nature of his relationship with Hamilton. Their correspondence was often quite flirtatious, even by the emotive standards of nineteenth-century writing. She used phrases like "my dear, darling Wash" to refer to him. She described a visit together as a "delightful dream" in which she had "seen you, conversed with you, and even kissed you." She often expressed her hope for additional times together, where "we would talk just as long as we pleased; and kiss each other just as often, too." Such exchanges have prompted historians to speculate that Hamilton was yet another woman with whom Gladden was romantically entangled in his early adulthood. One scholar has gone so far as to suggest a love triangle that created an enormous dilemma for Gladden: Should he marry the free-spirited, fun, modern Hattie, or—as he did—choose the quiet, safe, conventional Jennie Cohoon? It was a choice between "Victorian respectability and sensual gratification."[24]

But there are equally strong reasons for doubting that Hamilton and Gladden saw their relationship as a serious romantic one. For one thing, she recognized the budding relationship between Washington and Jennie. Hamilton referred to Cohoon in one letter as "Mrs. G. in perspective." In another she wrote, "I rejoice with you" knowing that he had "seen 'Jennie with the light-brown hair'" and noted, in a seeming reference to an eventual marriage, that she "wondered what calculations you were making for about four years from now." Given that all three had many overlapping acquaintances in small-town Owego, it is difficult to imagine that Hamilton was unaware of Gladden and Cohoon's relationship.[25]

Moreover, viewing Hamilton simply as a jilted lover ignores the fact that she was equally direct with Gladden about her own romantic interests in other men. She wrote to Gladden about someone she liked very much and asked if he would "be at all jealous if I should give him a place in my heart next to yours." She likewise announced her intention to find a love interest among Gladden's class of college students and asked him to "speak a good word for me" to them.[26]

Given the ambiguity of Hamilton's letters to Gladden and the lack of surviving correspondence from him to her, the exact nature of their relationship remains unknown. The safest interpretation—and the most likely one—is to accept her assessment that they were close friends. She expressed gratitude that their correspondence resulted in "strengthening our mutual friendship." Indeed, perhaps the best characterization of their relationship was Hamilton's description of Gladden as "a perfect treasure of a brother."[27]

Treating Hamilton primarily as a romantic interest also obscures the crucial fact that Gladden seemed to view her as an intellectual peer. The two discussed religion often. Hamilton was deeply religious and was concerned not only for her own spiritual well-being but for those around her. But whereas others in Gladden's social circle, such as Lewis Matson, tended to be pessimistic in outlook, Hattie Hamilton was more cheery in her religious views. She eagerly reported the "joyful news" that a couple that previously "never felt any interest" had "both recently been converted," which she viewed as something that could and should happen to everyone.[28]

Hamilton repeatedly emphasized her conviction that being a good Christian meant making the world a better place. Christians were not to be religious by abandoning their daily routine. Rather, they could enact their faith in the course of daily existence. "The duties of life demand our attention and we cannot serve God faithfully unless we perform them," she wrote. She also urged doing so with a "light heart." She lamented the tendency of young adults to become "grave and sober" when faced with the realities of life, insisting that happiness made it easier to "do more good" during the "one life" people had to lead.[29]

In advocating this perspective, Hamilton cited the influence of Henry Ward Beecher. As one of the most famous ministers of the day,

Beecher espoused an optimistic view that Christian faith could be integrated into life and work in the world. In their letters to one another, Hamilton and Gladden discussed Beecher's writings. She cited Beecher as the source of her conviction that "we may mingle our love for God with everything we do." The belief that Christians could link their faith to all aspects of life became a core tenet of Gladden's religious thought. Such sentiments pervaded Hamilton's correspondence. While hardly the sole source of these ideas, she was a key advocate for their value at a formative time in Gladden's life.[30]

Despite their considerable correspondence, Gladden and Hamilton saw relatively little of each other, especially after he entered Williams College in the fall of 1856. His strong academic record, achieved in upper-level courses at Owego Academy, allowed him to enroll as a sophomore. This allowed the twenty-year-old Gladden to undertake a three-year course of study.[31]

In the mid-1850s, Williams was far from the prestigious liberals arts college that it would become by the end of Gladden's life. The institution, Gladden noted in his memoir, had "modest pretentions" when he enrolled. There were only nine faculty members and just over two hundred students. As was typical of American colleges of the day, its curriculum was fixed. All students took the same courses. They could choose whether they wanted to take German and French, and that was the only choice allowed in four years of study.[32]

While the old-fashioned nature of Williams in the 1850s made for a rigid curriculum, the smallness of the college allowed students close contact with faculty. As Gladden observed, "The personal contact with the instructors" was better "than the methods of instruction." Two of his professors, John Bascom and Mark Hopkins, strongly influenced his future thought.[33]

Gladden spoke particularly highly of Bascom, who taught rhetoric at Williams and would later become the president of the University of Wisconsin. Unfortunately, Bascom published little on religion during his tenure at Williams. In his writing in subsequent years, Bascom articulated many of the same ideas that would define Gladden's religious thought, which suggests he influenced his student. Bascom offered a broad-minded message and was highly critical of Christians who refused to work together simply because of "some difference in doctrine."

In Bascom's view, God did not give identical messages to everyone. "God teaches one man one thing, and another another, drawing life alike out of each lesson," he wrote. The belief in the value of diverse opinions, limited though it was to Protestant Christianity, became a central element of Gladden's religious thought.[34]

The influence of Hopkins on Gladden was equally pronounced. Gladden recalled the college president as being "one of the four or five great teachers that America has produced," and, despite the tendency of students to "spy out inconsistencies and weaknesses" in their professors, the Williams student body was "always singularly unanimous and enthusiastic in its loyalty to the great president." Other assessments were equally glowing. A tribute at the time of Hopkins's retirement noted that the Williams president was "ranked among the best writers and preachers of his time," and he had "exerted an extraordinary personal influence" over all his students.[35]

As college president, Hopkins enjoyed the privilege of teaching the senior class courses in philosophy and ethics. The lectures that he delivered to Gladden's class no longer exist, but we have a good idea of their content. In 1858, the year Gladden would have taken his course, Hopkins began revising his lectures on moral philosophy. Hopkins published these lectures on ethics three years later. That volume reveals his thought on religion, morality, and human nature at the time he taught Gladden.

Three ideas that recurred through the lectures would also become central to Gladden's own thought, and we can reasonably surmise that Hopkins had a hand in developing them. Specifically, the professor emphasized an optimistic view of human nature, the importance of the social aspect of human life, and the need for practical morality that was relevant to ordinary life experiences.

Despite his reputation of being cut from an older cloth of dour clergy, Hopkins expressed optimism about human nature throughout his lectures. He argued that humans were essentially hardwired for good. "Towards the supreme good there must have been some constitutional impulse," he declared. This capacity came directly from a kindly God. "He wishes for our good," noted Hopkins, and had "expressed that wish in giving us the capacity . . . for its gratification." This was not a cold, distant deity. Rather, God and humanity were bound up together in the need or desire for human goodness. "The very end of God in the whole will be defeated if his creatures decline the good for which they were made."[36]

Fortunately, in Hopkins's view, humanity was not only good but also had the capacity for continued improvement. He took humanity's "interest in science for its own sake" as evidence "that we have an affinity with higher natures." In the specific realm of moral knowledge, humans not only had aspirations but potential as well. "There is that in every man which may, and ought to make him a competent judge" of moral science.[37]

This focus on individual capacity did not mean that Hopkins viewed religion and morality primarily in individual terms. On the contrary, he criticized the "selfish theory of morals" that claimed people did good only out of their own interest. He believed that humans were fundamentally social beings and that "society is the natural sphere of man." Humans, declared Hopkins, also had innate sympathy for one another. Consequently, whenever people attempted to do good, they by necessity had to "promote the good of others." Personal goodness was not a zero-sum phenomenon whereby one person's gain was another's loss. "The more there is of it . . . in any one," Hopkins observed, "the more material and ground must there be for the happiness of others." Being a Christian, therefore, meant being as concerned for others and for society as a whole as it did being worried about oneself.[38]

If society was so important, Christians could not ignore the morally laden political and social issues of the day. In 1858, that meant addressing slavery. "Men are born free," he proclaimed, and "the whole nature . . . rebels against unjust restraint." He offered a litany of intolerable features of slavery. The work that was responsible for adding value to property was not paid for, he argued, echoing the increasingly popular free labor ideology. Families, which in Hopkins's mind were the cornerstone of society, could be broken apart on a whim. Finally, slavery "interferes with the rights of the intellect" by keeping slaves from "learning to read the word of God."[39]

Hopkins's views on slavery suggested a kind of pragmatism. Though he rejected the institution in principle, his objections to it concerned slavery's practical effects. This pragmatic approach to morality characterized the college president's approach to other issues as well. With regard to food and drink—the excessive enjoyment of which was a subject of concern for moralists of the day—Hopkins observed that they should be enjoyed in moderation. "The proper notion of temperance . . . is not an abstinence from any particular thing, but such a control of all the appetites as will result in the greatest power and activity both of body and of mind," he wrote. Even for alcoholic beverages, his concern was with results. Alcohol did nothing to improve the greater good of society, and the desire for more and more "brought many gifted men to the verge of destruction before they were aware of it."[40]

Thus, during his senior year coursework at Williams, Gladden was exposed to many of the ideas of morality that would come to define his religious liberalism. The belief in human goodness and humanity's potential for improvement, the belief in the centrality of concern for the social, and a view of morality that focused more on practical results and less on inherent right and wrong would all become hallmarks of the message Gladden popularized.

Gladden pushed himself extremely hard in college, often to the point of illness and exhaustion. A cousin noted that both he and Gladden were "driven to the utmost extremity by hard study." He added, however, that he made the effort to "take time to have some hours of pleasure," whereas Gladden did not. Gladden's mother urged him to "be careful of your health," noting that he had already learned that "without health you cannot accomplish any thing of importance in your studies."[41]

There was more to college than study, even for a diligent student like Gladden. Without the extracurricular activities like sports and athletics that would become commonplace on US campuses by the end of the nineteenth century, "the intellectual life was a larger concern" in Gladden's college years. The main activity for students was participation in one of the college's two literary societies. These groups met weekly for sessions where students debated one another and presented original poetry, speeches, and essays.[42]

The emphasis on writing and speaking pushed Gladden to hone the skills he had developed writing for the *Owego Gazette*. He contributed regularly to the *Williams Quarterly* and in his senior year became one of its editors. Most of Gladden's contributions were fairly trite attempts at humor, featuring characters such as "the Reverent Total D. Pravity." He also wrote poetry, some of which he sent back to family in Owego. His mother praised his writing but added—in a comment that hinted at

Gladden's rising estimation of himself—the she hoped he would not allow himself "to be puffed up with such things."[43]

The writing led to other opportunities. Gladden's involvement with the Williams student journal led to his appointment as college reporter for the *Republican* newspaper in nearby Springfield. This position fostered two other influential relationships. The first was with the paper's publisher, Samuel Bowles. In the years and decades that followed, Bowles would be an enthusiastic champion of Gladden's writing and provide a home for his work.[44]

The second relationship was with the poet Nancie Priest, another woman who would influence Gladden's emerging political and religious thought. How the two initially came into contact is unclear. The likeliest explanation seems to be that she read one of his stories in a newspaper during his senior year at Williams and wrote to him. Despite their lengthy correspondence, the two seem never to have met in person.

Priest and Gladden were the same age. But while he attended college, she lacked even a high school education and worked in a paper mill to support her family, a not-atypical reality for a young, single woman in the mid-nineteenth century. During her short breaks in the grueling workday at the mill, she wrote poetry. One of her published works, "Over the River," received wide acclaim. Poetry might have been the impetus for her friendship with Gladden; the two bonded, among other things, over their mutual appreciation for Tennyson. As with Hattie Hamilton, Gladden's correspondence with Priest at times had romantic undertones. But it was far from one-dimensional. The correspondence offered a vehicle for both to examine their ideas about religion and politics.[45]

Also like Hamilton, Nancie Priest displayed considerable self-confidence. But whereas Hamilton was ebullient, Priest was quiet and introspective, or, as she put it, "exceedingly diffident, or awkward." But that did not bother her. "I have given up trying to think exactly like other people," she wrote. She noted her lack of desire to engage with "ignorant people who are content to remain so." She also boasted of her decision not "to place every body on my list of particular friends," even though the result was that she was "usually called 'proud.'"[46]

This independence carried into Priest's religious thought. "I am connected with no church," she wrote, and had "never made a profession of faith in Christ." Yet this did not reflect a rejection of Christianity. On the contrary, she viewed "the Bible as the only true guide to happiness." The problem was with churches. Religious institutions were so full of "useless members" who did not live up to the teachings of faith that she had "no desire to swell the number." She also criticized the clergy for emphasizing a negative, pessimistic message. "Don't you know," she asked Gladden, "that ministers are expected to look and act as if their sole employment was to meditate upon and mourn over the 'total depravity' of the human race."[47]

Echoing Hamilton and Hopkins, Priest insisted that religious faith must be paired with actions in life. She blasted the hypocrisy she found endemic in many Christian communities. "God requires of us the service of the heart and hands instead of the 'lip service' which many people seem to imagine all that is necessary," she wrote. To avoid such hypocrisy in herself, Priest accepted that she might be wrong in her religious opinions. She urged Gladden to tell her any time "you think me in an error" in her religious thought. She promised "to receive your opinions in the same spirit of kindness . . . whether they agree with my own or not."[48]

On political issues, specifically the matter of slavery, Priest went further than Gladden's other friends and mentors at college. She was adamant that religious conviction demanded urgent action in the public sphere. Whereas Hamilton spoke in general terms about bringing faith into daily life and Hopkins lectured against slavery in pragmatic terms, Priest embraced an urgent campaign against slaveholding. "How any one can pretend to be a Christian and at the same time defend or even excuse and palliate the great national sin of slavery is a perfect mystery to me," she wrote.[49]

In Priest's view, the problem wasn't just economic, nor was it limited to slaves and slaveholders. Rather, the system corrupted everyone who came into contact with it. She lamented the case of a family member who had grown up in New England but moved to a slave state. There, this relative had adopted the attitude that people "who are obliged to work for a living" were "entirely beneath us" and began to champion the merits of slavery. Priest's views on slavery anticipated Gladden's later outlook on other ills in society. When the social system became corrupted, it was impossible for individuals—even good individuals—to avoid becoming corrupted along with it.[50]

Thus the urgent need for all Christians to take action by combatting slavery. Gladden clearly agreed with Priest. The two noted their shared support for the newly formed Republican Party, which had been established a few years earlier to prevent the spread of slavery to the western territories and had replaced the defunct Whig Party to which Gladden's family had previously belonged. To what extent Gladden supported the complete abolition of slavery in these years is unclear. In his memoir, he described the 1850s as the turning point when the nation realized "that the time had come to put an end to slavery." But the Republican Party's aims were more limited, and Gladden had little to say at the time about ending slavery in southern states.[51]

Though the two only corresponded for a couple of years and Gladden did not acknowledge her influence (Priest herself died at a young age about a decade later), it is impossible to read Nancie Priest's letters without recognizing how they conveyed nearly all of the themes that would become central to Gladden's religious message. Her open-mindedness in religious matters and willingness to be convinced of a competing view, sense that church members and clergy were trapped in a rut of hypocrisy, conviction that Christian faith should be enacted in everyday life, and belief that Christians should take a moral stand on divisive political issues rather than avoiding them all found a champion in Gladden. If Priest was not the source of some of these ideas, she was, like Hamilton, at the very least a kindred spirit who helped Gladden refine and articulate his central beliefs.

In one of her letters, Priest complimented Gladden's sense of humor and teased him that "you will never do for a minister, if you don't conquer your propensity for fun-making." She was acknowledging a very real development. By the end of college, Gladden had become intrigued by the prospect of becoming a clergyman, a possibility he had entertained at various times throughout his adolescence. He considered enrolling at Union Seminary in New York to undertake formal training for the ministry, but ultimately decided against it. Gladden also briefly considered heading to Kentucky, but that, too, came to naught, in part because of the legality of slavery there.[52]

Instead, he returned to Owego. A recommendation from a professor at Williams noted that Gladden possessed "considerable experience in teaching" and was "eminently successful in this calling." Despite the proclamation of a childhood friend of his "future so bright" thanks to his education and his talents, it initially seemed that Gladden's life after college would be exactly the same as it would have been had he not gone to Williams: teaching school in small-town upstate New York. He did not find this a bright future, however. "Schoolmastering," he recalled discovering, "was not my trade." While he enjoyed the act of teaching, "the constant nervous strain wore upon me." He grew concerned whether the job would pay enough for him to achieve his goal of undertaking graduate study.[53]

Things changed quickly, thanks to the arrival in Owego of a young man with whom Gladden was already acquainted but would become a lifelong friend. Moses Tyler had just graduated from Andover Seminary and had been hired to become pastor of the town's Congregationalist church. He arrived the same month that Gladden returned from Massachusetts, and coincidentally, both men took rooms at Mrs. Peck's, a well-appointed boarding house in Owego. (While Tyler appreciated the boarding house, he thought less of the town, describing it as a "dismal village, whose name begins with a letter resembling the bung-hole of a barrel"—a view that likely explains why he remained there for only two years.)[54]

Gladden and Tyler found they had common views on religion, politics, and the interplay between the two. Both claimed to be influenced by Henry Ward Beecher. Tyler also shared Gladden's antislavery commitments; indeed, he was even more vehement in expressing them. At Yale, Tyler had gained widespread admiration—and had outraged students from the South—by single-handedly committing the college's senior class to raising the funds to provide a rifle for a group of abolitionists bound for Kansas. "At all the tables, in every knot of students, for three days the topic of debate and profanity has been your humble servant," Tyler gleefully reported to his father at the time. A few years later, when he reached Owego, he had grown all the more committed in these views.[55]

The young minister encouraged Gladden to pursue the ministry. Tyler allowed Gladden to deliver a sermon at Owego's Congregational Church. Soon after, the clergyman arranged a more regular preaching opportunity for Gladden at a small church in LeRaysville, Pennsylvania, twenty miles south of Owego. The congregation struggled with low attendance and poor finances. Church leaders hoped that a religious revival would improve their fortunes. Gladden, newly licensed to preach and eager to do so, happily obliged, and he launched an eight-week series of nearly daily services: five on weekdays and two on Sundays. He himself preached for almost all of them. The effort was successful. In his memoir, Gladden recalled a "considerable addition to the membership of the church," a fact supported by observers at the time. "I was very much pleased by the account of your work," a friend noted, adding that it was "better than I had faith to expect."[56]

The good results in LeRaysville led to several churches offering Gladden the position of minister. He accepted the pastorate of the First Congregational Methodist Church in Brooklyn. The city offered a nonprofessional advantage as well: Jennie Cohoon, his fiancée, had moved there. Gladden arrived in Brooklyn in the spring of 1860. He married Jennie that December in his own church. The two would enjoy nearly fifty years of marriage, and although Gladden mentioned her in his writing infrequently, they seemed to be quite happy.[57]

In 1855, Washington Gladden had been an adrift nineteen-year-old in small-town New York. Having lost his father at a young age and been separated from his mother, his options in life seemed limited to remaining in Owego and working as a teacher. His friendships seemed imperiled by childish behavior in romantic matters. Five years later, Gladden held a degree from Williams and a prestigious job in Brooklyn. And he was married to Jennie, the woman he had long wanted to wed.

The intervening years were quite formative. By the time he began his first pastorate in Brooklyn, his intellectual engagement with mentors like Mark Hopkins and John Bascom, friends like Moses Tyler and Hattie Hamilton, and correspondents like Nancie Priest had helped Gladden lay the foundations of his religious and political outlook. He integrated faith commitments into the rest of life, held an optimistic view of human potential, and demanded urgent, immediate action on the issue of slavery. Gladden's commitment to all of these views would deepen in the years ahead.

In other respects, the move to Brooklyn brought a close to aspects of Gladden's early life. Many of the friendships that were so influential during his late teens and early twenties would wane. In the years ahead, his contact with Matson, Priest, and Hamilton would decline. His romantic dalliances (or any record of them) would also end with his marriage.

Gladden's ties with his family also grew strained in the years ahead. His correspondence with his cousins in the Daniels family diminished, and letters from his mother suggest their relationship frayed. Gladden avoided making visits home to Owego, on one occasion failing to make a promised trip, leaving Amanda "sick with disappointment." The young minister seemed to want to put as much distance as possible between himself and Owego.[58]

But the losses did not appear to weigh heavily on Gladden as 1860 drew to a close. Rather, he focused on the many positives: a new wife, a promising job, and, equally important for someone whose religious and political views strongly emphasized the abolition of slavery, the election of the nation's first Republican president, Abraham Lincoln. For both Gladden and the nation, it seemed that anything was possible.

Those hopes would soon come crashing down.

2

SURVIVOR

The battlefields of Virginia were a miserable place to be in the "sultry and dry" early summer days of 1864, with the Civil War raging well into its fourth year. Yet Gladden was there. After a visit to the war zone, where he "slept in the front line one night when the rebels made a charge," he settled into the task of caring for wounded soldiers in the hospitals at Union Army headquarters at City Point. Gladden had volunteered with the Christian Commission, a group established by the YMCA, which functioned as a de facto chaplaincy corp. Its members provided religious guidance alongside practical assistance to soldiers, especially the sick and injured. This was no small task in a war where illness killed twice as many soldiers as died in combat, and where inevitable death from injuries was slow. City Point bore witness to this grim reality. The settlement had sprung from nothing and rapidly had grown into "a city of eight or ten thousand sick and wounded men."[1]

Gladden's work consisted of caring for the wounded soldiers, including some captured Confederate troops. He read to them, found whatever supplies he could bring to them, and took dictation of their letters home. Writing the words of these men, many of whom would never again see their loved ones, proved especially poignant. It was a crucial task. In a culture that believed a good death to be one that happened at home with family, these letters offered a modicum of comfort and closure to soldiers and their families.[2]

The suffering he saw on the battlefield and at City Point, Gladden confided at the time, "will be remembered as long as I remember anything." He was right. The memories proved powerful a half-century later when he recalled that those weeks "were a rather important part of my educational opportunity." During his work near the front lines, he learned "things which are not taught in the theological seminary."[3]

This observation about learning things not taught in theological school spoke to many aspects of Gladden's life and ministry in the early 1860s. In fact, he had not even gone to seminary. While his Williams College degree had earned him his first pastorate, it quickly became apparent that his lack of additional training left him at a comparative disadvantage.

The early 1860s witnessed Gladden's struggle to secure his professional footing. Unable to find the time to undertake much additional education save a few courses here and there, he adapted to circumstance. Trial and error in ministry, combined with opportunities like that afforded at City Point, gradually led him to articulate his religious convictions with greater confidence.

This personal struggle occurred, of course, against the backdrop of a national crisis. Even if he had tried, Gladden could not have ignored the effects of the Civil War. The conflict affected the New York region economically. Violent protests against the war struck close to home. And, ultimately, the conflict touched the Gladden family. Indeed, it was a family tragedy that drove Gladden to northern Virginia in the summer of 1864. Like most Americans of his generation, the Civil War represented a monumental event in Gladden's life. It shaped his political and religious views, and he viewed subsequent national events in light of it.[4]

As much as the early 1860s were a painful time for Gladden, they also proved to be professionally and intellectually formative years. He parlayed his lack of theological training into an asset by combining it with his experience. The result was a practical, relevant religious message. Gladden also reevaluated his understanding of being a Christian in light of the doubt and uncertainty brought by the Civil War. In so doing, he began to move away from his evangelical roots and toward the modern, progressive voice he would become.

Following the move from Owego, there were few signs of the difficulties ahead, and Gladden delighted in his new life in Brooklyn. Washington and Jennie settled in at 202 Dean Street in the city's Boerum Hill neighborhood, which had developed over the previous two decades.

The family grew, with the arrival of their first child, a daughter named Alice, in 1861.[5]

Gladden enjoyed Brooklyn. Though he later lamented that Dean Street was the favored route of market wagons, "the din of whose wheels on the cobblestone pavements began soon after midnight and never ceased," he reported to Moses Tyler his "pleasant time, reading, writing, tramping, visiting," as he settled into married and family life in a large city.[6]

In 1860, Brooklyn was, at least by nineteenth-century standards, a bustling metropolis. The city was home to 275,000 people (it was still an independent municipality and would not join with New York City until 1898), and much of its development remained close to the East River. The eastward sprawl outward on Long Island was in its earliest days. At the time of his arrival, Gladden later recalled, Brooklyn still "had not quite outgrown its bucolic traditions." But for a twenty-four-year-old who had grown up in rural New York and attended college in the Berkshires, the city was still "a thing stupendous and overpowering, a mighty monster, with portentous energies." He was struck by "the sense of its power to absorb human personalities and to shape human destinies," a recollection likely shaped by the fact that Gladden was completely overwhelmed by his first job.[7]

Part of what gave Gladden this perception about Brooklyn was its proximity to Manhattan, which was the nation's mightiest economic monster. As one historian has observed, by 1860 New York was the "spider in the web of the American economy," and that economy had boomed for much of the 1850s. The region was a center of trade and banking, and it boasted a burgeoning manufacturing sector as well. With the city's growth, it had taken on an air of "incomprehensible chaos." Even from the opposite bank of the East River, Gladden could not ignore the fact that he now lived in the most powerful metropolitan area in the country.[8]

Initially, Gladden was as delighted by his church as he was by the city. He reported improvements in attendance, the crowd on one Sunday being "nearly twice as large" as the week before. He received encouragement from his family that everything would continue to go smoothly for the young minister. "I cannot doubt," a cousin wrote to him, "that [God] has called you to make known the riches of his grace through the preaching of the gospel." All of Gladden's life—including failures such as his unsuccessful stint as a schoolteacher immediately after graduating from Williams—seemed to illustrate "a kind Providence" pushing him toward the ministry. Even in his first sermons, the cousin continued, "Your heart seemed to burn within you while you talked of the way in which the Lord God led you."[9]

Observations like these, though made with loving intentions, highlighted the pressure to succeed that Gladden faced in his first pastorate. But the young minister quickly recognized the obstacles in his way. He admitted to Tyler that he had no "means of judging" if he would "continue to enjoy these blessings." He also worried that, despite the growth in attendance, there was considerable empty space in his sanctuary. He was right to worry. Less than a year after starting in Brooklyn, Gladden was out of a job.[10]

The pastorate failed for several reasons. First, Gladden lacked the training needed to meet the challenge of preaching in a large city with many competing churches. Competition was the operative concept. By the mid-nineteenth century, clergy could no longer assume that each pastorate would be a long one. To remain in a church, ministers had to prove themselves successful, drawing large congregations (and ideally affluent ones). Preachers who did not succeed at doing so soon found themselves looking for a new pulpit.[11]

Gladden's one previous professional success had been in LeRaysville, a small rural town with few competing churches and ministers. By contrast, Brooklyn—known in the late nineteenth century as the "city of churches"—was home to some of the most famous preachers in the United States. Each Sunday, Gladden competed with men like Henry Ward Beecher, whose books he had read and discussed with Hattie Hamilton. Beecher and other Brooklyn ministers were household names across the country. They enjoyed wide renown for their sophisticated theological knowledge and oratorical skill.[12]

By contrast, Gladden was—in his own words—an "untrained boy." He had been granted license to preach just before his short stint in LeRaysville. But the examination to receive it had not been, at least according to his later admission, "a shining example of theological proficiency." Even if Gladden was being unduly harsh on his younger self, the fact remained that with his lack of experience he paled in comparison to the refined, seasoned preachers of Brooklyn. The stakes were all the higher, because church membership in the New York area was often a sign of social status. Gladden's lack of fame meant not only smaller congregations, but less financially advantaged ones as well.[13]

Gladden's woes were compounded by the fact that his church itself was quite dysfunctional. Its very name, the First Congregational Methodist Church, highlighted its problems. The church had originally been part of the Methodist denomination. In Methodism, a bishop appoints the pastors of churches. Some years earlier, however, this church had objected to a bishop's choice and in response had left the denomination. They added "Congregational" to the name, signaling their newly declared autonomy to choose their own ministers. Changing denominations did little to fix the church's actual problems, though. Its real issues were "a small membership," few "men of substance" at a time when church's reputations often rested on the prestige of their congregants, and, most troubling, "an enormous debt incurred in the erection of its edifice."[14]

Dealing with these factors would have been a tall order for any minister, but they were made worse by factors outside Gladden's control. New York, and Brooklyn with it, faced an economic crisis following the outbreak of the Civil War. Much of the region's economy depended on trade and commerce with Southern states. New York's merchants served as the middlemen between Southern farmers and the industrialists in the North and in Europe who produced finished goods with the raw materials. With the eruption of conflict, "business was at a standstill." People hoarded their money and certainly did not give it to churches. Even worse, whatever upsurge in religious feeling the war might eventually bring was not apparent in its early days. Instead, what existed was a state of shock. "This unwonted excitement did not prove conducive to the growth of churches," Gladden recalled. "The congregations dwindled, the Sunday-schools were decimated, the whole work of the church seemed to have come to a sudden pause."[15]

Were Gladden the minister of one of Brooklyn's larger, more financially stable churches, he might have been able to weather the storm, as the region's economy rebounded within a year. But neither he nor his church was up to the task. He found himself "struggling with conditions that were hopeless." By the middle of 1861, the church's financial reserves had dwindled and Gladden perceived that "the wolf was looking in" at his door. Saddled with a failing church and lacking the skills to compete with the celebrity clergy all around him, Gladden began to suffer the same health difficulties that had plagued him at Williams. After experiencing what he later described as a "nervous collapse" that left him in a "crippled position," he resigned from his first job.[16]

Retreating from the mighty monster of Brooklyn, Gladden found a new opportunity. The First Congregational Church of Morrisania, a few miles to the north, invited him to become its pastor. In the twentieth century, Morrisania would gain notoriety as one of the neighborhoods demolished by Robert Moses to make way for the Cross-Bronx Expressway, and as one of the hotbeds of drug use, gang violence, and arson that plagued the city in the 1970s. A century earlier, though, it was a quiet suburb of "country lanes, with no noise of wheels or whistles." It offered "time to work in our gardens, and birds and bees and butterflies filling the air with life and color and music." Most importantly, while it allowed Gladden to reach "the heart of the metropolis" within an hour, he was now "far enough from the madding crowd to escape the nervous wear and tear."[17]

While the move a few miles north brought Gladden to a more pleasant environment, it did little to ease his personal and professional difficulties. The family—which now included a new boy, Frederick, who was born in 1863—struggled with poor health. The baby, Gladden later reported, was sick continually in his first year.[18]

Nor were the struggles confined to the nuclear family. Gladden's mother wrote a series of letters recounting the plight of the family back in Owego. "I am in a desperate condition for I cannot work and have nothing ahead," Amanda wrote to her son. She recognized "that you will not be much better off," but nevertheless asking him to send whatever money he could.[19]

That was difficult for him to do because Gladden's new church suffered from the same financial problems as the one he had just left. The pastor's salary was low, and it quickly became apparent that it would not support a growing family. Two years into this job, Gladden offered his resignation. His letter noted that his "greatest sorrow" was that he had not "accomplished more" and expressed his "wish and prayer" that the church would "find another pastor worthier and more successful than myself." The overwrought nature of Gladden's tone suggests that he was perhaps being overly dramatic in the interest of securing a better position for himself. But such feelings were not to be unexpected; he had been a minister for three years and had still not enjoyed meaningful professional success.[20]

Unlike his Brooklyn congregation, the Morrisania church rallied to keep Gladden. They raised his salary to $1500 per year, with a promised increase to $1800 when circumstances allowed (between $40,000 and $50,000 in contemporary money), which constituted a doubling of the family's income. The weekly congregation averaged between 200 and 300, and it was "growing very healthily." Gladden noted that "my people were never so completely excited among each other, and in me, as they are at present." Most exciting for the young minister, the church had constructed a new building, which one local clergyman had described as the most "tasteful church edifice in New York or its vicinity." The increased attendance made "the church look quite full."[21]

Moses Tyler, who at this point was living in England, cheered his friend's good fortune. At last Gladden had "a great and powerful church, to be an honor to yourself and a blessing to all." The increased stability also afforded Gladden some small opportunities to continue his education. He enrolled in a few classes at Union Seminary. This was a far cry from the advanced degree he had hoped to pursue, but it gave him additional knowledge of theology and biblical studies.[22]

By late 1863, Gladden seemed contented. He told Tyler that he was "less likely to leave now than ever before." The family's fortunes appeared to be on the upswing as well. Both children were at last thriving, and Jennie had not enjoyed "such good health since we were married as during the last year."[23]

All of these struggles occurred against the backdrop of the Civil War. Although New York was far from the war's major battlefields, the conflict affected the city and the surrounding region deeply. Even as Gladden's personal fortunes began to improve, national life remained grim in ways that affected him personally.

New Yorkers had a particularly conflicted response to the war. Because of their economic ties with the South, many of the city's leading citizens spent the late 1850s seeking reconciliation with Southern states, though for pragmatic reasons of business more than out of genuine support for slavery. Gladden recalled that until the attack on Fort Sumter, the loyalty of most residents seemed to rest more with the South than the North. One historian has noted that many New Yorkers perceived the election of Abraham Lincoln and the South's move toward secession as "their most devastating political defeat," and they worked tirelessly to dissuade Southern states from leaving the Union. That his neighbors ultimately supported the Northern cause reflected, in Gladden's words, a conversion whose "suddenness quite eclipsed that of Saul" in the Bible.[24]

In fact, New York's conversion was neither as sudden nor as absolute as Paul's transformation in the New Testament. While New Yorkers certainly wanted the Union to win, many simply desired a return to the antebellum status quo. A large number opposed efforts to make the conflict about ending slavery. The Democratic governor of New York State, Horatio Seymour, remained a critic of Abraham Lincoln. Seymour denounced the wartime draft and emancipation in the strongest terms. A major newspaper, the *New York World*, urged compromise with the South. A small group of residents—though one that included the city's mayor, Fernando Wood—proposed that New York should withdraw from the Union and declare itself a free city. (Wood remained critical of the war for its duration; after being elected to Congress in 1862 he emerged as one of the leading opponents of the Thirteenth Amendment, which abolished slavery.)[25]

These debates went beyond words as opposition to the war spurred outright violence. In the summer of 1863, riots erupted in New York. The immediate spark was the draft, which remained unpopular with, as Gladden later described them, "large elements of imperfectly Americanized immigrants," primarily recently migrated working-class Irish. Though the desire to avoid conscription was certainly an impetus, deeper issues were at play as well. For years, New York had experienced tension between lower-class, white immigrants and African Americans who competed for the diminished number of low-paying jobs available in the wartime economy. The month before the riot, African American replacement workers had been brought in under police guard to take over for striking white longshoremen. Tempers ran high thereafter.[26]

When violence erupted in mid-July, rioters had three types of targets. The first was any facility associated with the federal government, especially the draft office. Second were elite institutions associated with members of the upper class who were perceived as supporting the war. Pro-Republican newspapers offered an especially attractive target in this regard, and the *New York Tribune*'s first floor was destroyed by fire. But rioters targeted wealthy businesses more generally and indiscriminately. Third, and most disturbingly, rioters targeted any and all African Americans. Black New Yorkers were beaten and lynched, homes were destroyed, and an orphanage for African American children was burned to the ground. All told, 105 people died in what remains the second deadliest riot in US history. It took five days and the arrival of twenty thousand troops in the city before order was restored.[27]

The riot left Gladden and his neighbors in Morrisania shaken. For once, their suburb did not feel a safe distance from the nearby metropolis. He recalled that as "the lawless elements were let loose," even from his home, "the horizon was lurid with conflagrations." Fearing for their own property, the suburb's residents organized a patrol to guard against potential rioting. The image of an urban riot stayed with Gladden. He cast it in epic terms as an "eruption of savagery" that "disfigured our civilization." His choice of terms is notable; whereas African Americans might be cast as savages in the terms of the day, Gladden ascribed the term to the actions of the white New Yorkers that attacked them. As was true for other members of the New York elite, the riot left him with a lasting anxiety that class division might breed violence and chaos in the nation's cities.[28]

Gladden's interest in the war had sources other than his immediate environment. He remained personally opposed to slavery. He was guided in this conviction by mentors like Mark Hopkins and friends like Moses Tyler and Nancie Priest. Henry Ward Beecher, whose writings influenced Gladden in college, similarly opposed the expansion of slavery in the 1850s. With the outbreak of war, Brooklyn's most famous minister became the foremost religious defender of the Union cause.[29]

More importantly, Gladden had a personal stake in the conflict, as he knew men injured and killed on the battlefields. Late in 1862, he wrote to Moses Tyler to share the "sad news" that a mutual acquaintance from Owego had died at Antietam, killed "by the explosion of a shell whilst engaged in prayer over one of his men who had already been mortally wounded." The man's death forced Gladden to make sense of seemingly senseless carnage. "Wasn't it a glorious death," he wrote to Tyler, befitting a "noble, earnest, faithful godly man!" Finding meaning in such deaths was a common response during the Civil War.

But even as Gladden emphasized that there was "nothing but rejoicing" for the deceased, his response suggested a more conflicted reaction. Reflecting the more complex emotions that underlay celebrations of the war dead, Gladden also acknowledged his "tears for those who have been bereft by his loss" and his wish of "vengeance for those who murdered him."[30]

Later in his life, Gladden would increasingly become troubled by the emotional cost of war. But in the early 1860s, he buried such concerns in popular sentiment. Deaths in combat, especially those that had some element of heroism to them, should be celebrated and not mourned.[31]

This outlook likely comforted Gladden as the war progressed and his own relatives enlisted in the army. His younger half-brother, LeRoy, did well for himself. He received public acclamation when he removed the body of his commanding officer from a battlefield while under fire. Gladden praised him as "a brave boy, and a splendid soldier," and boasted of the acclaim that his half-brother received.[32]

LeRoy was far luckier than Gladden's younger brother, George, who vanished during the Battle of Cold Harbor in the late spring of 1864. This battle came at one of the bleakest points in the war for the Union cause. With the presidential election approaching, Confederate forces adopted a strategy of attrition. The goal was to run up the Union death toll to sap morale and cost Lincoln his bid for reelection. Southerners hoped that a Democratic president would end the war and negotiate for peace. Gone were the large, epic battles like Gettysburg. In their place were constant skirmishes that anticipated the seemingly endless trench combat of World War I. Union casualties mounted. Cold Harbor was among the bleakest of these battles. Soldiers themselves were rightly pessimistic, and some pinned identification to the uniform before the battle. Even without the personal significance, Gladden spoke for most Northerners when he remembered that the battle of Cold Harbor "sent our hopes down to zero."[33]

George, who like his half-brother LeRoy belonged to the 8th New York Heavy Artillery, was severely wounded on June 3, the bloodiest day of the nearly two-week battle. Initial reports indicated that George "was shot just as he mounted the rebel breastworks." He fell in between the armies, so as to be "under fire" from "our own men and the rebels too." He was too far from his own troops and had "called out to the rebels for God's sake to help him . . . and they reached out and drew him inside of their works." That was the last anyone heard of George Gladden.[34]

Gladden set out for Virginia as soon as word reached him about his brother, but there was little more to learn. The regiment was pushed back almost immediately after George's injury, which meant there was little hope of anyone coming to his aid. Gladden's consolation, expressed with wartime bitterness, was that because his brother was "badly wounded, probably mortally," George "did not suffer long in the hands of those southern wretches, whose tender mercies are cruel."[35]

The Gladden family joined the large ranks of Americans who received no certainty about the fate of their loved ones presumed to have died. Forty percent of soldiers killed during the Civil War were not identified. Moreover, even when the army did identify its dead, no formal mechanism existed for relaying that information to families. Such tasks were among the many filled by volunteers in the Christian Commission. Ironically, the month after George's death, Congress finally passed a law giving the federal government oversight of recording deaths and burial sites. But even this policy remained more of a theory than a practice for the war's duration.[36]

Even without news on George's fate, Gladden was still committed to the Christian Commission and to City Point. On arriving, he immediately faced the reality of the war: a mass of soldiers who "had been marching for days," were "grimy with dust and perspiration," and whose "clothing had evidently been reduced to the minimum." Over the next two weeks he would care for them at the expense of his own health. Gladden managed to return to New York, but he faced "a sullen fight of two months with a slow fever" before he recovered from what he believed to be malaria.[37]

Despite the death of his brother, his own suffering, and the mass trauma that the nation endured, Gladden never lost faith in the Union cause. He derived no small satisfaction from the Confederacy's surrender in April 1865. "The sacrifices we have made are not in vain," he declared. "That recompenses us for all our losses." That he could hold such a view even in the wake of a family member's death speaks to Gladden's moral commitment to ending slavery and his investment in the Union cause.[38]

Though they lacked a personal connection, the death of President Abraham Lincoln a few days after the Confederate surrender also affected Gladden deeply. He had respected the future president from the time he first appeared in national politics during the late 1850s. Election night in 1860 had been a thrilling moment for him, an event he remembered long after.[39]

For Gladden, Lincoln's significance lay in the way that the president linked the nation's political and religious values. The election of 1860 represented nothing short of a "political revolution" that "registered an ethical advance in the American people." Specifically, they "had been drawn to the question, 'Who is my neighbor?' and they had learned to answer it more nearly in the sense of the good Samaritan." That watershed election proved for Gladden that the American people had become capable of viewing African Americans not as slaves who were property but as neighbors worthy of compassion and respect. Everything that followed—the war, the Emancipation Proclamation, and, eventually, the ratification of the Thirteenth, Fourteenth, and Fifteenth Amendments—reflected this changed perspective.[40]

This transformation in public opinion suggested something more fundamental about human nature: people and societies could change for the better. "The notion that human nature is a fixed quantity" and "that men always act from the same motives" had been undermined by the broad transformation of the American electorate during the 1850s. Perhaps echoing his college mentor, Mark Hopkins, Gladden insisted that ethics could be improved. What was needed was the "prophet and the moral teacher" to guide the way. He viewed Abraham Lincoln as such a figure.[41]

In Gladden's view, Lincoln was "the man who could meet a great emergency" with "wisdom and courage and gentleness." He maintained this view despite shifting Union fortunes during the war. As was true for many Americans, the assassination of "our best beloved President" a mere week after the war ended badly shook Gladden. "I heard loud voices in the street in front of my house when I arose, and hastily dressing I descended to the front porch," he reported. Stepping outside, he found his gardener, "tears running down his cheeks, and his eyes flashing vengeance." It was a "day ever to be remembered by the generations of countrymen for its unalterable grief and horror and indignation." Gladden was far from alone in this experience. As the train carrying Lincoln's body back to Springfield, Illinois, made its way through cities throughout the northeast, enormous crowds of heartbroken citizens gathered. In New York, so many people wished to view it that enterprising property-owners charged rent along the route.[42]

The Civil War thus ended on a horribly tragic note. It was all the more necessary to justify five years of events that left hundreds of thousands of Americans dead, including Gladden's younger brother and the nation's beloved president, whom Gladden had considered a modern prophet. Ultimately, Gladden joined his fellow citizens in justifying the war on the grounds that it ended slavery.

In later years, Gladden grew more cynical about the war's necessity. By the time he published his memoir nearly fifty years later, he wished that the nation's leaders might have made different choices and prevented four years of carnage. Still, even then, he conceded, "Perhaps the conflict was irrepressible, and had to be fought out. Perhaps the vast infidelity of the nation in harboring slavery—a crime in which both sections were implicated—had to be atoned for by the frightful retribution of the Civil War." This was a bleak assessment at odds with Gladden's later rejection of theologies of retribution and mass punishment. But perhaps it was the natural conclusion to be drawn after a war that killed so many Americans, including the president in whom he had invested so much hope.[43]

Even as he tempered his assessment of the war, Gladden never abandoned the optimistic conclusions he drew from it. This was true for many of his generation who emphasized the instances of heroism, perseverance, and resilience demonstrated in the conflict. For Gladden, it was all this and more. The Civil War confirmed his optimism that people could reform themselves ethically and transform society for the better as a result. This outlook became especially apparent in his later characterization of the war. "The suppression of the rebellion, the preservation of the Union," he wrote, "was not only our business, it was our religion." This characterization was crucial. Political and military actions for the right cause were inherently religious.[44]

While Gladden maintained his optimism about human nature through his personal struggles and the national crisis of the early 1860s, other aspects of his religious thought evolved. With a limited body of theological knowledge to drawn on, his sermons were by necessity quite practical in nature. But instead of apologizing for this approach to preaching, he grew to embrace it.

Gladden's inability to undertake meaningful advanced study remained a source of major disappointment. When he moved to Brooklyn, he had been "fondly counting" on beginning graduate study at Union Theological Seminary. Though he was delighted when his workload in Morrisania allowed him to take a few classes there, he found that the daily tasks of church work left "no space for systematic study." The country's most noted ministers had graduate degrees from Union, or Yale, or Princeton, and Gladden's lack of training set him apart from his elite colleagues. He felt this inadequacy especially keenly in the New York area, which was home to so many of the nation's best-known clergymen. Even worse, the profession itself had lost some of its luster, as the law and medicine supplanted the ministry as the fields that guaranteed elite status. In a profession of declining stature, Gladden could not even claim to be among the best.[45]

In letters to friends, Gladden revealed a growing insecurity about his reputation. He was nearing his thirtieth birthday, and he had not made the name for himself that he hoped. This occasionally caused him to lash out in frustration. Once, his former professor Mark Hopkins had to dissuade him from being "over sensitive" and making a large issue out of a perceived slight. Likewise, Moses Tyler counseled Gladden not to give in to worry. "Let us not be discouraged. Of all the great reputations in America very few of them were achieved when their possessors were at our time of life," he wrote. "Our turns will come by and by." While Gladden certainly found increasing professional success as the 1860s progressed, his lack of a graduate degree and his early career setbacks seemed to haunt him.[46]

Yet, instead of just wallowing, Gladden played to his strengths with growing confidence. He confessed to Tyler that his preaching "is of a very practical cast as yet. I am not quite ready yet to come out with my system of theology,—so I preach about things that I do understand." This was an accurate assessment of his early sermons, which portrayed theological questions in straightforward terms and urged direct action in the world.[47]

In the ideas they presented, Gladden's sermons from Brooklyn and Morrisania emphasized core Christian concepts in a simple manner with little intellectual nuance. He identified the central mission of

Christianity as "a warfare against evil," but for him evil was not a complicated concept. Rather, it represented "insubordination and resistance to divine authority." This was the essence of sin, and the specifics of the insubordination and resistance mattered little.[48]

Gladden similarly distilled the nature of God and Jesus in basic terms. He rejected conceptions of the universe as a mechanistic creation (the God-as-clockmaker idea popularized in the late 1700s), insisting that "this universe is not a cunningly devised piece of mechanism, wound up by the Creator to run till the day of judgment." Rather, the divine being's energy was "immanent in nature," and every human being was "all the while, in very deed, in the hands of God." Gladden did not feel obligated to explain how he reconciled this conception with his equally strong belief in human free will. For him, it was enough to acknowledge both.[49]

As he emphasized the involvement of God in the natural world, Gladden also focused on Jesus's humanity. Jesus possessed no special advantages of divine power during his time on earth. "He was here in the world as a man among men,—to bear all their burdens, humiliations, sorrows; to fight the battles they must fight; to face the hard questions that confront them; to live among them," he preached. The lesson of Jesus's life was not that he was special or different. Rather, he was "an example to us" of humanity's moral capacity and the ethical heights that any person could achieve.[50]

All of this spoke to the central point of Gladden's practical message: People had the moral capacity and the ethical obligation to work to transform the world. "You cannot have any very strong desires for the well being of another, unless you exert yourself in some way," he preached. It was not sufficient to expect miraculous intervention that negated the need of human action. "I have worked pretty hard for my living thus far, and I expect to do so as long as I live. If I should sit stolidly down, expecting that my life would be sustained without labor, I should deserve to starve," he told his congregants. The same logic applied to all realms of human activity.[51]

From the perspective of theology, none of these messages were especially sophisticated. Gladden avoided explaining how evil existed in the natural world if God was immanent in it, and he sidestepped vexing questions of the relationship between the human and divine in Jesus's being.

Yet this was a message that resonated in the context. An immanent God was one who had not abandoned humanity, even with its capacity for war and destruction. And the ethical obligation to action justified the enormous sacrifices that the Civil War demanded of Americans.

Indeed, this message would resonate with churchgoers long after the Confederate surrender. In the years that followed, Gladden unapologetically embraced the practical character of his religious message. He saved many of the sermons he preached in his first pastorates and reused them (with some revision) throughout his career. Rather than merely defending his own style he urged other ministers to adopt it as well. He attacked as "poorly qualified" those ministers who were "utterly unskilled in the questions of practical living." One was not "qualified to be a pastor" without "that knowledge of human nature and its needs which can only be gained by a close and sympathetic study of the individuals of his own congregation."[52]

Gladden did not deny the importance of intellectual development, but he saw it as just one ingredient of successful ministry. In a combination of genuine conviction and a rationalization of his own course in life, he suggested that American clergyman had become too aloof in the realm of theology. Being a good minister required deep, sympathetic understanding of ordinary churchgoers.

There was another important development in Gladden's religious thought during this period, though it was subtle and he himself was slow to acknowledge it. In his first pastorates, Gladden began to doubt the efficiency of religious revivals. In taking this step, he rejected not only the popular form of Protestant Christianity in the nineteenth-century United States but also one that had deep personal significance for him.

Owego sat on the edge of the "burned-over district," a region of upstate New York that experienced so many religious revivals during the Second Great Awakening of the 1830s and 1840s that contemporary observers likened it to land scorched by wildfire. At revival services, people gathered to hear fiery preachers like Charles Finney, who grandstanded "like a lawyer arguing a case before a court and jury" and told of the "glories or terrors of the world to come," depending on whether a person was saved or damned.[53] These services often had a highly emotional component. Gladden himself recalled one where "men and women were prostrate on the floor, groaning and screaming frantically; some were trying to pray; some were shouting 'Glory!' the excitement and confusion were indescribable."

These services held special emotional significance for Gladden. Attending a revival with him was one of his most powerful memories of the father who died early in his childhood. He remembered vividly the way "there were tears in his eyes, but the expression on his countenance was one of intense pain." Moreover, many of his close friends and family found personal meaning in revivals. His childhood friend Lewis Matson spoke highly of revivals and the conversions they brought, and Gladden's mother likewise viewed them as the height of religious experience.[54]

Yet, despite his personal history with them, Gladden shied away from revivals in his ministry. He was not the first to do so. The Congregationalist minister and theologian Horace Bushnell, whose work Gladden had read since college, had published his widely read *Christian Nurture* in 1847. In it, Bushnell advocated the gradual cultivation of religious conviction in children as they grew to adulthood, rather than expecting a sudden transformation that revivalists promised. Many others in Gladden's generation similarly questioned the value of the revivals that had been so important to their parents.[55]

Bushnell's influence on Gladden's thought is apparent from the earliest sermons he preached. "Christian growth is a gradual progression—beginning with a small grain of truth . . . and reaching perfection as the end of a long course of development," he told a congregation in early 1860. He contrasted this interpretation with the "commonly held" but erroneous belief in an "instantaneous metamorphosis" that made someone into a Christian.[56]

In Gladden's view, the particular problem of revivals was that they forced an in-or-out mentality. This demand alienated good people from church by making them believe they were unworthy. Nancie Priest alerted him to the perils of this mind-set. "Sometimes I doubt my being in reality a christian," she wrote. "I pray to be kept from deceiving myself with a false hope." In Gladden's view, people like Priest who thoughtfully reflected on their faith and their lives were the very people who most belonged in churches. But the all-or-nothing demands of revivals pushed them away. The more he reflected on it, the more Gladden recognized that outlooks like Priest's were the norm. "How many of us have attained," he asked, anything resembling "perfect faith?" His answer: not everyone.[57]

More pragmatically, Gladden doubted the effectiveness of revivals. Reflecting on his own apparently successful ones at LeRaysville, he recognized that even there the positive results were not from any special element of those services. They had a more mundane source: his efforts to reach out to community members and invite them to church. "Far more was done in the daily personal contact with the old and young" than through the revival services. But such contact could be accomplished in any number of ways. Special, dramatic services set apart from the ordinary life of the church were not necessary. In fact, they might represent an impediment to cultivating healthy religious lives.[58]

In the years ahead, Gladden would sharpen his critique of revivals, though he would occasionally find an "evangelist in this field with whom I can cooperate." But his general rejection of them sprung from the same source as his practical religious message. Faith was something woven into the ordinary moments of everyday life and activity. It was not a subject of special concern reserved for particular moments. This would, more and more, become the heart of Gladden's vision.[59]

By the middle of the 1860s, both Washington Gladden and the nation at large were in new places. The country, torn apart by years of contentious debate over slavery and ultimately Civil War, was reunited. It was a moment of national rebirth, though the shape the reunited country would take over the next few years remained to be seen. But it was nevertheless a time of optimism in Gladden's intellectual circles. A year after the war ended, Henry Ward Beecher wrote to Gladden that while some laws still needed to change, "the freedmen are doing well" and "only a few tainted spots in the South send up a bad odor." He proclaimed the time of political and military conflict over for good, believing that "moral forces" and evangelization would transform the former Confederacy. Few observers recognized just how obstinate white Southerners would prove to be, how apathetic Northerners would quickly become, and how much work would be required to truly remake the nation.[60]

Meanwhile, Gladden's early professional anxiety had given way to a newfound confidence in his vocation as a minister. He had found his voice as a preacher and had begun to wed religious and political issues. He soon received external validation of his growing professional success. Late in 1865, Gladden traveled to Massachusetts to attend a service at his alma mater commemorating the end of the Civil War. He was one of the speakers, and among those in the audience were members of the Congregational Church of nearby North Adams. Having been favorably impressed by Gladden's remarks, they contacted him soon after and asked him to be their new minister. He agreed. In March 1866, a month after his thirtieth birthday, Gladden returned to the mountains of western Massachusetts where he had spent his formative college years. "It was surely good for me," he observed, "to get away from the rush and roar of the metropolis and feed my soul for a little space upon the strength of these steadfast hills."[61]

3

REBEL

Life in North Adams was good. "No young preacher could have asked for anything better," Gladden recalled. His new church had "no financial problems" and paid him $2,000 per year, which gave the family greater financial comfort than they'd had in New York. Additionally, the congregation gifted him a bonus of $1,000 during his third year. The extra money was helpful as the Gladden family continued to grow. A third child, Helen, was born around the time of the family's move to North Adams in 1866. The following year a son, George (named after Gladden's brother who was killed in the Civil War), completed the family.[1]

Gladden also found the North Adams pastorate intellectually fulfilling. It brought the professional success that had eluded him in New York. Soon after moving to the Berkshires, he reported to Moses Tyler that "it has been a good year for me. I think I have learned something; and I hope I have accomplished something." With what was becoming something of a characteristic mix of self-congratulation and posturing for his long-standing friend, Gladden noted, "My own church is the cream of the population, and my congregation is increasing in intelligence as well as in numbers—by which I mean to say that the additions to it are mainly from the more intellectual classes." His reports back to Owego conveyed a similar sense of prospering in his work. The Daniels family expressed delight at hearing "of your success in North Adams."[2]

In the late 1860s, North Adams was a town of just under ten thousand people. Its economy was driven by small-scale industry, including mills for cotton and wool. The owners of these businesses had done well for themselves financially. But the town's residents had a strong cooperative spirit, and citizens participated in local government as equals. Gladden found that ministry in a village allowed a greater role in the life of the community than he had been afforded in Morrisania. "In the suburb of a great city there is so little social contact that there can be no common life," he mused; "neighbors do not know one another; the cultivation of local interests and enthusiasms is almost impossible." By contrast, a vibrant sense of common purpose existed in North Adams. Gladden quickly found that he was not just minister to his own church, but rather was "speaking to the whole community."[3]

Thus, his new pastorate offered Gladden the chance to be more than a religious leader. He could influence the civic life of the town more broadly. His tenure in North Adams allowed Gladden to take on the role of a public intellectual whose opinions carried weight in ever-expanding circles.

Being a minister in such a setting also posed challenges, which Tyler frankly acknowledged. "A small country town is intrinsically vile, a den of gossip, a nursery of small souls. I could live in a small town in any other capacity than the clerical," he wrote. Still, with suffering came reward. The job might, Tyler joked, benefit his friend in the long run. "A high place in heaven should be awarded to all parsons in country villages," and from that perspective, he told Gladden, "you will join the favored company of the martyrs, on the top benches above."[4]

At many moments in his North Adams pastorate, Gladden probably felt like a martyr. But he usually had only himself to blame for this. As he entered his thirties in this new position, two of Gladden's defining personality traits came to the surface: a deep commitment to strongly held principles, combined with a lingering sense of inadequacy that pushed him to engage in troublesome self-promotion.

The confluence of these characteristics led Gladden to forcefully espouse a range of views that defied conventional opinions. He vocally embraced the liberal theology of Horace Bushnell, believing that it offered the most accurate conception of the nature of Jesus's mission for humanity. In so doing he alienated himself from colleagues and risked his pastorate soon after his arrival. He also urged churches to revisit their assumptions about morality, using a debate about recreational activities to encourage a larger reconsideration of whether or not activities should be considered immoral just because people had always thought them to be bad. Finally, in the first of many such instances in his career, Gladden waded into a contentious local debate involving local businessmen, striking laborers, and replacement workers who were Chinese immigrants. This put him at the center of a growing national debate about labor issues and immigration. His outspokenness on these issues involved personal risk, but it also brought considerable reward. Gladden's stature, both in North Adams and beyond, rose significantly during the late 1860s.

From the outset of his ministry in North Adams, Gladden started to establish himself as a public intellectual. He began writing for the *Independent*, a Congregationalist newspaper based in New York. This began his "close and constant" relationship with the press, something he had "long coveted" but which had proved elusive in the first years of his ministry. He also began to lecture on subjects of popular interest. Notices in the local newspaper heralded him as a "modern prophet of social life" who had achieved "flattering success upon the platform as well as in the pulpit, being a fine speaker as well as a vigorous and easy writer."[5]

One such series of lectures, described as "lively and judicious," formed the basis of Gladden's first book, *Plain Thoughts on the Art of Living*. Compared to his later work, these lectures were fairly trite restatements of popular opinion. A central theme was the importance and almost sacred role of the middle-class family and home in the United States, which he deemed "the sources of its national life." He observed, "If they are pure and peaceful, the nation will be prosperous and powerful." This was a common view in the 1860s. Gladden's straightforward espousal of it lacked his later insight into the larger social forces that put a stable home out of the reach of many.[6]

The rest of the lectures were full of similar platitudes. "Good habits are not easily formed, but bad habits do not require much cultivation," he proclaimed, again ignoring the effect of broader social forces on behavior. He urged his audiences to "form the habit of doing good with your money," suggesting individual, local charity as a panacea to major ills like poverty. Gladden even showed a tendency to be moralistic on seemingly trivial points. He accused young people of giving "too much time and thought to your sports." He also declared staying up late at night to be "an outrage upon nature" and "simply and wholly abominable." By conveying such sentiments, Gladden parroted the popular views of the day about the importance of individual effort and self-discipline.[7]

Nevertheless, despite its indulgence in conventional wisdom, *Plain Thoughts* contained a few innovations in Gladden's thought that signaled its future direction. With more than a hint of autobiography, he diagnosed an increasingly common problem of his era: a sense of meaninglessness in modern life. "Thousands live and die without any fixed purpose," he lamented. While he worried about the impact of this phenomenon on everyone who experienced it, he was especially concerned about how it affected the wealthy. "A rich young man without an avocation is a greater nuisance in society than the sturdy beggar," Gladden observed. At this stage of his career, he had few solutions. He suggested people simply choose the work they enjoyed best. But in noting the increasing sense of alienation, he had begun to recognize a problem that would weigh more heavily on his mind in the years ahead. So, too, the conviction that the wealthy possessed far more power to cause social harm than the poor would take an ever-greater place in his thought.[8]

Moreover, despite his moralizing, Gladden recognized that government could not enforce good morals. This, too, signaled an important development. He urged audiences to "be always vigilant and positive friends of morality" and not to rely on official institutions. "Laws and officers can do nothing, unless there is a public sentiment to give them force," he observed. This position would put Gladden increasingly at odds with a growing number of Christians who sought to use the power of government to ensure public morality. Within a few years, Anthony Comstock would succeed in persuading Congress to pass sweeping obscenity laws. These would prevent the advertisement and distribution of a wide range of materials, including those that provided information on sex, contraception, and abortion. Though Gladden held a conventional moral code, this expansion of state power to oversee morals represented an unwelcome intrusion of government into people's lives.[9]

Gladden's final innovation in *Plain Thoughts* was to argue for the contingent nature of certain values. Noting that different behavior would be deemed appropriate in different religious settings, he urged his audience "to understand that there is and can be no fixed standard of good manners." This was not an embrace of relativism in morality, but it did suggest his awareness that morals and values were not absolute.[10]

This was a crucial realization. It led Gladden to espouse the belief that all convictions—not just morals but religious and theological ideas as well—might need to evolve. In the years ahead, he would develop this idea to a fuller conclusion.

As he lectured and wrote on a wide range of topics, Gladden found North Adams to be a community that was "much less set in its ways than the average New England town." Its residents were "hospitable to fresh thinking" and "not afraid of the truth even if it was new truth." Some innovations were welcomed. Soon after his arrival, he pioneered a new order of worship at his church, which met with enthusiastic approval.[11]

Gladden's embrace of new theological ideas, however, prompted controversy. One year after his arrival, the time came for him to be formally installed as the church's minister. In typical practice, other Congregationalist clergy from nearby towns would attend the installation service, and a noted preacher would deliver the sermon. For that honor, Gladden chose a man who had become his intellectual hero: Horace Bushnell, the retired pastor of the North Congregational Church of Hartford, Connecticut. Gladden's suspicion of revivals and emphasis on the humanity of Jesus, themes he had embraced in Brooklyn and Morrisania, reflected Bushnell's influence. By the time Gladden arrived in North Adams, he ardently supported the Connecticut theologian. "I've got to be a Bushnellite," Gladden wrote to Moses Tyler, "and shall avow his heresy about the atonement if it breaks my neck."[12]

Though Gladden was often overly dramatic, in this case his assessment of the risk was accurate. Bushnell frequently drew the label of heretic. Associating with the elder clergyman did, in fact, put Gladden at risk for having his neck broken, at least in the professional sense. That same year, at least one minister in the United States was denied ordination by his local colleagues because he accepted Bushnell's views.[13]

Bushnell was about three decades older than Gladden, and he had trained at the Yale Divinity School, which in the early nineteenth century was a bastion of Congregationalist orthodoxy. By the 1840s, Bushnell had strayed quite far from the dominant orthodoxy. Beyond criticizing revival culture, he embraced a more progressive understanding of theology. He described Christian doctrines as poetry and metaphor, and he believed that human understanding of God evolved as Christians worked through competing, overlapping metaphors. In other words, Christian belief could and should progress and change as each generation gained new knowledge.[14]

Bushnell's greatest innovation was his theology of the atonement; that is, how Christians should understand the nature and purpose of Jesus's death. Historically, American Protestants had interpreted the atonement in two ways. The first, and older, interpretation was that humanity had incurred a debt of evil through its sinfulness. Only the death of God's innocent son could pay such a debt. A second interpretation, which emerged in the eighteenth century and grew in popularity during the nineteenth, suggested that the atonement was necessary for moral order. If the universe had a consistent system of morality, someone had to pay the price for humanity's sins. Jesus needed to die, proponents of this argument suggested, to ensure the preservation of the moral order.[15]

Bushnell offered a third view, and this was the interpretation of the atonement that Gladden embraced. Jesus's death was not intended as payment for any sins; rather, it was meant to inspire humans to better behavior. By demonstrating selfless sacrifice, Jesus showed just what moral and ethical heights humans might achieve.[16]

The hallmark of Bushnell's religious thought was this high view of human potential. But while this appealed to people like Gladden, critics saw it as an outright rejection of core Christian beliefs. The specter of heresy charges hung over Bushnell's head. In the early 1850s his church withdrew from the local association of Congregationalists to prevent charges being brought against him. By the time Gladden arrived in North Adams, the fury against Bushnell himself had cooled as the theologian was an old man "with broken health" and in "disabled condition."[17]

While the retired Bushnell no longer faced intense scrutiny, embracing his ideas could derail the careers of younger ministers. When Gladden invited the elder theologian to give his installation sermon, Bushnell expressed concern. He would not accept the invitation until he was convinced that his young colleague "understood and are able to take responsibility for what may come."[18] A very real possibility existed that other Congregationalists in the vicinity of North Adams would refuse to allow Gladden's installation, which in turn would jeopardize his newfound professional and financial stability.

With what was becoming his characteristic mix of obstinacy and confidence, Gladden expressed far less concern than Bushnell did. "It is possible that they will refuse to install me," he told Moses Tyler, "but if they do I shall tell them lovingly to go to Halifax." Theological integrity mattered more than the approval of his colleagues. "I'm going to be honest through and through, and I haven't any fears that the good Lord will not take care of me."[19]

Gladden's optimism was well placed. In Tyler's words, he "sailed through the hell-gate of an ecclesiastical council" at which he was thoroughly questioned by colleagues about his theological views. Bushnell preached at the installation, which went ahead as planned. In the process, Bushnell traveled to North Adams early and spent a week with Gladden and his family. "Those were great days," Gladden recalled, "talking of things visible and invisible, meditating upon the mysteries of the heavens above and the earth beneath."[20]

Their time together confirmed Gladden's view of Bushnell as "the greatest theological genius of the American church in the nineteenth century." It also reinforced Gladden's commitment to Bushnell's views. Liberal theology, Gladden had come to believe, not only captured the true spirit of Christianity but offered the added benefit of particularly appealing to the modern American mind-set in several important ways.[21]

First, by shifting the understanding of Jesus's death, Bushnell's theology recast God as a more compassionate being while highlighting the horrors that judgmental, closed-minded people could inflict. Jesus "did not come to suffer, he came to save," Gladden wrote. The execution of God's son ceased to be understood as a necessary step demanded by unbending divine justice. Rather, it became a horrifying object lesson of what happened when "bigots" got hold of a "blameless and beneficent" person. God was not a cold-hearted arbiter. Rather, Jesus's death revealed God's compassion by illustrating to humanity "how much [God] is willing to do and suffer to save them from sin and death." Such a perspective resonated in a broader culture that increasingly emphasized compassion and humanitarianism.[22]

Gladden also appreciated that Bushnell's theology shifted the focus of Christianity away from nuanced theological statements and toward simple belief. "Instead of being called to preach certain formulas about Christ," ministers were freed "to preach Christ himself." Complex dogmas gave way to a simple message that made Jesus's life and teaching the core of Christian belief.[23]

This was the message Gladden had adopted out of necessity in the early years of his ministry, but now he recognized its inherent value. His deeper engagement with Bushnell gave intellectual justification to continue applying "the pragmatic test" to his message. Doctrinal commitments and theological formulations seemed less important. As his tenure in North Adams progressed, Gladden urged greater attention to "common-sense and common charity." He also argued that the practical standard of how people lived their lives was a better metric for evaluating them than the beliefs they espoused were. "Good men are commonly wiser than their theories," he observed, adding "we must not judge our fellow-men solely by the doctrines they teach."[24]

The greatest—and also the simplest—benefit that Gladden found was that Bushnell's theology made him happy rather than sad. This seemed a beneficial thing for religious views to do. "This truth has brought to me joy and inspiration," he wrote, whereas other theologies brought "trouble and darkness." Because of this happiness, he would not abandon his new outlook, even to win the approval "of my brethren in Christ." He urged other members of the clergy to do the same. His message for those hounded for accepting Bushnell's teaching was to invoke the Gospel of Matthew: "If they persecute you in one city, flee to another!"[25]

Of course, this was easy for Gladden to say. He had already weathered whatever controversy faced him. But other ministers were not so lucky. In a pattern that would continue for the rest of his career, those that didn't fare as well reached out to Gladden for counsel or just for a sympathetic audience. One minister noted that he had embraced Bushnell's view of the atonement. Personally, this had been a triumph. "I rejoice in a fullness of light where once I endured a gloomy mist," he wrote. Professionally, the story was different. What Gladden feared in North Adams had happened to this man: The local council of Congregationalists refused to support his ministry, claiming that he held erroneous views about the atonement. Nor did his own congregation come to his defense. They allowed him to stay on temporarily, but the church's lay leaders issued a statement "mourning for [his] error."[26]

Support for Bushnell's theology came with real risk. But Gladden's security in North Adams allowed him to emerge as a staunch defender of this new outlook among the rising generation of clergy.

Gladden's embrace of Bushnell's ideas caused small ripples of controversy, but discussions of theology were sufficiently esoteric to avoid igniting a major debate. Around the same time, though, Gladden jumped headlong into another contentious issue that attracted wider interest. The young minister began to speak publicly on "amusements," and, specifically, what forms of relaxation and entertainment were appropriate for Christians.

While the amusement debate was significant in and of itself, it became a proxy for larger questions: Were morals absolute and unchanging, or should they be modified as society's standards changed? And, if moral values were subject to reinterpretation, was the same true for other aspects of Christian belief? A small debate about recreational activities provided the first basis for Gladden's assertion that standards of morality should be reviewed and adjusted.

The impetus for Gladden's interest in the subject was a debate concerning a new YMCA facility in North Adams. Organizers proposed allowing games of checkers, chess, and backgammon to be played in the building. Gladden supported the proposal, believing it to be modest in its aims. But he was "in a small minority" in his support. "All my brethren in the ministry very positively disagreed with me," he recalled. They found it "highly dangerous to allow worldly amusements of any kind to be practiced in a place for whose management the churches were responsible." More generally, his colleagues believed that recreation was at odds with religion. "A truly converted man needed no diversions," they argued, because "the joys of religion alone should satisfy the soul." In the common view, living a godly life and working to improve the world provided all the recreation that a good Christian required.[27]

Early in 1867, Gladden addressed the amusement issue in the *Independent*. A notable shift in opinion had occurred, he wrote. Whereas the Puritans had "peremptorily forbidden" recreational activities, Christians of his own time had restricted a more limited number of activities and had "taken an attitude of indifference" toward the rest. The time had come for a further shift.[28]

Gladden went beyond this neutral position and wholeheartedly affirmed the positive value of recreation. "The play impulse is implanted in the human nature by God himself," he suggested. "The need of recreation" was one "we never outgrow." Churches needed to stop "divorcing" the desire to relax and play "from religion." It's time to show that "Christian people believe in play as heartily as worldly people do" and that the desire for recreation "is no more sinful than the appetite for food."[29]

Gladden's views about morality and amusements spoke to his larger conviction that happiness and fun need not be at odds with religion, and that Christians should integrate faith into the rest of life. When a nearby group of Protestants voted to ban games like dominoes in their recreational hall, Gladden blasted the decision. He argued that it reflected a "bald asceticism . . . as far as possible removed from a true Christianity." In his view, such people held a warped view of Christian life. They believed that religion was something "for the closet, and the prayer-circle, and the inquiry meeting" and that it had no place in "the daily experiences of life" like games and recreation.[30]

By contrast, Gladden argued that "Christianity has to do with the whole of life" and "should be mixed with our thought and activity." In this way "every pleasure" and "every pastime" could have religious significance. Gladden argued that it was possible to accept any activity as compatible with Christianity—even a game of checkers—so long as it "tends to elevate and bless mankind."[31]

Gladden did not limit himself to generalities but instead embraced particular activities long denounced by Christian ministers. He rejected "the old doctrine of the sinfulness of dancing," arguing that many forms of it constituted "a healthful recreation." He also complained about the hypocrisy shown in the criticism of amusements. Many of the "innocent games" denounced by clergy were "found in most Christian homes."[32]

Not only did Gladden affirm recreational activities as beneficial for Christians, but, more controversially, he also insisted that they belonged in churches. Instead of just complaining that games happened in places of dubious morals, Christians should offer an alternative. "The drinking saloons and the dens of infamy are the only places where amusement is furnished free," he wrote, to many young people. Rather than lamenting the situation, churches should work to break "the monopoly of the business of furnishing amusement" that had been held by "the Devil and his angels." Gladden urged the establishment of a central facility with a gymnasium, bowling alley, billiard tables, and facilities for "chess, checkers, backgammon, dominoes, and such quiet games."[33]

Beyond his message about incorporating religion with the rest of life, Gladden's position on amusements had significant implications about morality. First, he rejected common arguments that some recreational activities inevitably led to bad behavior. Suggestions of a slippery slope carried little weight with him. "There is no bond of logic, no affinity of nature," he wrote, "between billiards and drinking; nor between dancing and dissipation." The fact that "the amusements in question are almost uniformly associated with evil," was "the fault of Christian people" who fabricated connections. He urged his fellow Christians to stop repeating arguments that were unsupported by fact to justify preexisting assumptions about morality.[34]

Second, Gladden refuted the popular view that moral standards should be set to protect those with the weakest self-restraint. Many ministers sought to prohibit certain activities "because the morally weak may be led into injurious excesses." While he was concerned for such people, Gladden denied that all people needed to follow rules specifically designed for those "with weak consciences." Whether or not an activity was good or bad for an individual depended on whether it caused harm to that particular person. Something should not be deemed immoral for everyone just because it led certain people to behave poorly.[35]

In making this case, Gladden rejected the popular belief that people lacked self-control and were bound to sink into morally suspect behavior. "They tell you that you have no control over yourselves," he noted to his readers. The conventional wisdom was that "if you once get a taste of these forbidden amusements, you will rush into all manner of injurious excesses." By contrast, Gladden's message combined self-control with the more optimistic view of human nature he had held since college. "This gospel of imbecility has been preached long enough," he declared. "You have been diligently persuaded to believe that you are puppets in the hands of circumstance; that you can make no effectual resistance against the seductions of frivolity." When ministers preached this "abominable doctrine," they denied people's capacity for moral judgment and restraint. More troublingly, they precluded Christians from finding enjoyment in life.[36]

Third, and most significantly, Gladden used the particular case of amusements to suggest the need to periodically reconsider the standards of morality. When moral values were perpetuated without evaluation, they existed without a basis. "If I should tell you . . . that dominoes and backgammon and base-ball and skating are innocent amusements, and should forbid cards and billiards and bowling and dancing, I could not give you a single reason for my counsel," he declared. But such arguments persisted through the force of unchecked conventional wisdom.[37]

This line of argument "made a sensation." Some clergy rushed to Gladden's defense. Horace Bushnell, who was already supportive of Gladden, declared the younger minister's article on amusements to be "the best and happiest statement of that question I have seen." Another correspondent cheered the work as providing "the highest service in the community around you."[38]

But given that many Protestant clergy did, as he acknowledged, "proclaim the carnality of cards, and the bad influence of billiards, and the danger of dancing," Gladden drew considerable ire. His fellow ministers in North Adams subjected him "to a sharp cross-examination." In the *Independent*, Theodore Cuyler, a well-known preacher in Brooklyn, rejected Gladden's pragmatic assertion that amusements could be judged on how they affected each individual. Cuyler insisted that dancing, for example, "must be judged by its aggregate influence." He declared that given the choice "I would instantly say, Let the whole thing be swept out of existence" because "its evils infinitely overbalance the occasional recreation found under exceptional circumstances." Likewise, Cuyler argued, "if no man handles cards, there will be no gamblers at the card-table."[39]

Of the many who disagreed, none did so more fervently than an anonymous clergyman who adopted the name "Clericus" and blasted Gladden in a series of letters. "If Christ incarnate were to visit your house, about this time, it would be either to reprove you or enlighten you," this author wrote. "A minister of the gospel, talking about regulating dancing and card-play and the like. Why not preach that lechery and gambling be regulated," he observed, emphasizing the common view that such activities were irreconcilable with Christianity. This correspondent's major criticism was Gladden's endorsement of certain kinds of dancing. "I have never yet had under my supervision," Clericus wrote, "a person fond of dancing who was not also hollow-headed, and hollow-hearted." Dancing had even caused church members to go astray. The writer's conclusion indicated just how seriously this issue was taken. The minister who affirmed recreational activities "had better be on his knees before God. Shame on him! For he has no more right to advocate amusements than has Christ or the apostles."[40]

Gladden's writings on amusements inspired debate within his own family, though they responded less vehemently than Clericus did. His uncle Ebenezer Daniels noted that "we have been led to think seriously on this subject." This was true for Gladden's teenage cousin, who "has been accustomed to hear me speak of [Gladden] in the highest terms as a son as a scholar and as a Christian." It appeared that the family was not entirely persuaded by their cousin's position. Yet, even Ebenezer's conclusion that "I am not going to say that you are not [right]" suggested that Gladden's perspective had begun to win support even among his devout evangelical relatives.[41]

The force of the critique that Gladden faced, combined with the fact that those skeptical of him ranged from family members to famous clergy, highlights how contentious the issue of amusements proved to be. Gladden's determination to grant Christians access to them certainly reflected a deeply held belief in the value of reevaluating moral standards. But Clericus identified another motive as well. Gladden's articles "have caused me to think of you . . . as having but little humility, but an inordinate desire to be popular with the world," he wrote. Given Gladden's anxieties about his reputation, there was likely some truth to this assessment. The amusement debate granted the young minister the national attention he craved.[42]

Besides, whatever repercussions Gladden's reputation suffered proved short-lived. In the long run, his perspective won. By the end of his career, it was common practice for YMCAs to provide for "the play impulse" and give many opportunities for "innocent and healthy recreations." Gladden got more immediate revenge in North Adams. Soon after the debate about the YMCA, his most outspoken opponent, who "maintained that all sport is sinful and that true piety has no place in it for any other enjoyments other than those which are purely religions," was revealed to be engaged in scandalous recreational activities of his own. This minister "eloped with a young woman of his congregation" and "feigned suicide by drowning, in order to cover his flight to a distant state." In the wake of such a scandal, checkers seemed insignificant.[43]

Several years into Gladden's tenure in North Adams, the town faced a serious conflict that highlighted broader issues engulfing the nation. What began as a small strike grew into a contentious debate over class, labor rights, and immigration.

When he arrived in town, Gladden idealized North Adams as a harmonious community devoid of class division, despite the presence of industry in it. At town meetings "prosperous manufacturers were not disposed to put on airs, nor were their neighbors overmuch inclined to defer to them," he recalled. "Nothing resembling a social stratification" existed. This was perhaps not exactly true, given Gladden's own boast that his church's membership consisted of the elite segments of the community. Still, sufficiently little social polarization existed such that it was possible for social events to encompass a full cross-section of the town. Gladden recalled a party that was attended by "not only capitalists and merchants and professional people, but working mechanics and clerks and operatives of the mill of which the host was the owner."[44]

Beneath this tranquil surface, class divisions were quite present in the Berkshire town. One hint came in Gladden's growing awareness that church members appeared more concerned with showing off their status than fostering a welcoming spirit. In considering his congregants' concern for their appearances, he found many grounds for complaint. For one thing, "instead of joining in the song, or the prayer," he wrote, "the worshiper will be making eager observation of the various styles of dress exhibited, and plotting the purchase or the manufacture of new adornments."[45]

Far worse than distracted congregants were absent ones. The greatest problem with "Sunday overdressing" was that "it keeps the poor away from the churches." The reality was that people who could afford only "the plainest and coarsest attire" did not feel welcome or comfortable in churches where wealthy members showed off expensive clothes. The result was that churches were divided along class lines. "The places where the rich and the poor meet together bowing before the Lord," he lamented, "are almost unknown."[46]

This was a crucial observation. It marked one of Gladden's earliest public acknowledgments that churches were not harmonious places that transcended socioeconomic divisions in the community. Rather, they reflected—and perhaps even exacerbated—those divisions.

If class polarization in churches hinted at growing social division, the labor dispute that shook North Adams offered outright proof of it. For several years, a prolonged wage dispute had resulted in alternating states of "open or suppressed war" between the owners and manufacturers of a shoe factory, which was one of the major employers in the town. But in 1870, employees went on strike. When owners hired replacement workers, the strikers persuaded these replacements not to cross the picket lines. Then the owners brought in Chinese workers from California. This significantly enflamed tensions, although in Gladden's telling of the story, the curiosity of the strikers, who had never seen a Chinese person, is what prevented any violence. "Nobody wanted to miss" the sight of the of the strikebreakers for "long enough to stoop for a brickbat." Though the strike lasted for some months, it ended "without bloodshed."[47]

The arrival of Chinese workers turned North Adams, observers noted at the time, into "the banner town in all the country east of San Francisco for Asiatic novelties." More significantly, it forced Gladden to grapple with several major issues becoming prevalent in American life. The first was immigration, and particularly the growing population of Chinese migrants, who were deemed by many white Americans to be incapable of assimilating and a burden on society.[48]

According to Gladden, North Adams's reaction to the arrival of the Chinese was mixed, but less uniformly hostile than that of other communities. Some residents were "full of fears," but others proved "ready to give the strangers hearty welcome." Gladden appears to have been in the latter group. He visited the rooms where the Chinese workers lodged and reported that he found them to be "free from all vices" and "respectful and orderly in their behavior." He had great hope that they would learn English, and, in a reflection of both his optimism about their moral state and the extent to which he remained wedded to his own religious perspective, that they would convert to Christianity.[49]

While Gladden conceded that their lack of Christianity allowed these Chinese migrants to be cast in the terminology of the day as "heathens" and "heretics," he drew a firm line at a word commonly used against them: barbarian. He reminded his readers that China boasted an advanced civilization when Europeans were "offering human sacrifices upon the altars of their gods." But one did not even need to study history. "To any one who is permitted to see them in the street from day to day, as we see them in North Adams, it is evident enough that they are far from being savages."[50]

Gladden's defense of the Chinese on the grounds of their morality was atypical enough for a white, Protestant clergyman. But he went further, undercutting the economic arguments used to justify discrimination against them. Though he employed the term "coolie," which connoted an unfree laborer, Gladden nevertheless pushed back against the characterization of the Chinese workers as something akin to slaves. Rather, he insisted that they were "on precisely the same footing" with others who came in search of work. If the people of North Adams were going to welcome "emigrants from all parts of the world," they could not "refuse our hospitality to these industrious and thrifty strangers" from China.[51]

Gladden also challenged the claim, which has recurred about different immigrant groups at various points in US history, that the Chinese were willing to work for lower wages than native-born Americans, and thus would permanently drive wages down. On the contrary, he predicted that before long the Chinese workers would "want higher wages." The ultimate "effect of this immigration" would therefore be much less harmful than feared. To defend this point, he invoked the experience of the Irish immigrants who had come to the United States two decades earlier—the very immigrants who were among the most critical of the Chinese. He reminded them that the same statements made about the Chinese were made about them: They were called "degraded creatures" who "dwelt in shanties" and because they were "content to work for fifty cents a day, would crush 'American labor to pauperism.'"[52]

Gladden's efforts prevented an outbreak of violence and contributed to an early—though quite imperfect—attempt to celebrate multiculturalism. Early in 1871, the migrant workers held a dinner in celebration of the Chinese New Year and invited their Sunday School teachers and members of the clergy. Gladden was one of the featured speakers. Despite a characterization of the event as "unmarred by any Americanisms except in those who attended," Americans dominated the evening. The only speakers were white public figures, and even the menu consisted "mostly of American dishes, cooked by the Chinese themselves."[53]

Still, quite imperfect though it was, this effort marked a significant departure from the response Chinese immigrants encountered elsewhere in the United States, especially in California. Protestants there had similarly attempted to establish Sunday Schools, but popular opinion was far less supportive of the effort. White Californians held that the Chinese were so morally degraded that they should be barred from entering the state. Indeed, opposition to Chinese immigration was the one issue that transcended the partisan divide between Democrats and Republicans in California. For all the cultural chauvinism in the response of Gladden and the citizens of North Adams, it was a far cry from the vehement anti-immigrant sentiments expressed elsewhere.[54]

With the strike resolved, most of the Chinese workers returned to California, though some remained in North Adams. Still, their brief presence gave Gladden a firsthand perspective on the effects of Asian migration, and immigration more broadly, as the issue came to occupy a central place in American political discourse. His lasting conclusion from the episode seemed to be confidence that goodwill toward immigrants would encourage assimilation and prevent upheaval. Though his subsequent remembrances of these events were less charitable in their depiction of the Chinese workers than his writings at the time—a reflection, perhaps, of the anti-Asian sentiment that grew during the late nineteenth century—he nevertheless continued to affirm what happened in North Adams as "an encouraging instance of the absorbent power of good sense and good will in an American community." Attacks on immigrants accomplished far less than embracing them, he argued.[55]

Separate from the immigration issue, the strike forced Gladden to consider the changing relationships between workers and employers. He had begun to consider this question amid the tensions in North Adams that predated the workers' walkout. Like much of his thinking early in the career, his views were simplistic and tended to reflect conventional wisdom. He denounced people who used "rapacity and dishonesty" to gain wealth, or who demonstrated "wanton disregard of the interests of other people." Gladden believed the Golden Rule to be sufficient to combat such tendencies. Following its admonition to "do unto others" would restrain business owners from charging too much for goods or services. It would likewise keep consumers from seeking to acquire products for less than a fair price.[56]

Gladden demonstrated correspondingly little sympathy for workers' grievances. In considering social problems related to work, he was far more concerned by laziness and apathy than he was by unfair treatment of laborers. "Those who do not work have no right to play," he insisted, noting also that "a large share of the crime and poverty about us can be traced back to the objectless lives of the criminals and paupers."[57]

The peaceful resolution of the shoemakers' strike confirmed Gladden's view that such simple measures would prevent disharmony. The decade ahead would undermine this conviction. The 1870 strike in North Adams foreshadowed a long period of upheaval in the United States, and the difficulties to come would not be resolved as painlessly.

That turbulence remained in the future, however, and for the moment Gladden basked in the triumph. His pastorate was successful and he had attained national recognition as a religious and moral voice. His growing stature led to several offers of pastorates with higher salaries from churches in bigger cities. But Gladden was reluctant to leave a ministry that observers noted was "one of unusual pleasantness and prosperity."[58]

The beginning of 1871 brought an opportunity that was too good to pass up. In early January, Gladden was offered the position of religious editor of the *Independent*, the same New York–based newspaper to which he had contributed for several years and which had helped to heighten his stature. The terms offered by Henry Bowen, the journal's new publisher, were financially attractive: a starting salary of $3,000 per year that would increase to $4,000 by his fourth year. But the appeal was not merely financial. Bowen emphasized the national readership of the paper. "There is no such in field in the world as we offer," he promised. Gladden agreed and quickly accepted the offer.[59]

Gladden's friends and acquaintances cheered his decision because of the influence he would now exert. Moses Tyler predicted that "the new career now opened to you will be one of great honor, usefulness, and satisfaction; and will greatly enlarge your reputation." Another friend noted that the *Independent* was "doing more than any other human agency among us for the cause of Christianity." Sam Bowles of the *Springfield Republican*, who had known Gladden since his days at Williams College, had long thought the young minister was better suited to newspaper work. "You know the press is a great deal bigger field than the pulpit," Bowles wrote, adding that he "felt that it was your proper arena," and "been confident you would go to it sooner or later." Bowles was especially pleased by where Gladden was going. "The *Independent* is one of the best places, not only to make fame but to wield power, in all American journalism."[60]

Bowles's newspaper acknowledged the sadness of Gladden's congregation: "It is rather hard on the North Adams people, when they thought they were secure in the possession of the pastor of their choice, to have the dream so sadly broken." But the paper publicly stated Bowles's private views on the matter. The *Independent* offered "a position of more extended responsibility and usefulness" than any single pulpit did, and Gladden was right to take it.[61]

The response from Gladden's long-standing friends like Tyler suggests the way that Gladden was thinking about his work and career. While he was concerned with spreading the message of Christianity to a large audience, which was a central goal of a paper like the *Independent*, he also was concerned with his own reputation. The prospect of shaping the religious coverage of a newspaper with tens of thousands of subscribers offered Gladden a chance to build his own name in a way that preaching did not. He recognized he would "have under my survey the entire field of religious thought and action."[62]

There was a problem, however. Even as they congratulated him about his new position, Gladden's friends warned him about his new employer, Henry Bowen. Tyler noted that Bowen "grievously hurt my feelings by his conduct in a recent business transaction" and implied that this was because Bowen had done something unscrupulous. Tyler wrote that he wasn't sure how his friend would "get along with that same H.C.B." Sam Bowles echoed concerns about Bowen's ethics. "To one, who is as fastidious as I am in journalism, there would be a great deal of discomfort in working with, and especially under, Bowen." Even Gladden had reservations that business concerns might trump editorial policy at the paper.[63]

Still, the benefits of the new position outweighed any potential costs. While the warnings about Bowen were prescient, that would not become apparent for several years. For the moment, Gladden felt secure in his decision to leave North Adams. Though he would enjoy the opportunity to return to his church occasionally as a guest preacher, Gladden, along with Jennie and their four growing children, were on their way back to New York.[64]

4

JOURNALIST

New York had changed a lot in five years.

More than any other city, New York embodied the new direction of American life. The city was huge. Anticipating the urbanization that would characterize national life in the late nineteenth century, New York had already grown to around one million people. That meant that another two hundred thousand people had poured into the city since Gladden first arrived a decade earlier. New York was now indisputably the nation's leading city. The centralization of the banking industry in the city following the Civil War confirmed its status as the economic hub of the United States, and it was increasingly the center of intellectual and cultural life as well.[1]

But as the city grew richer, many of its residents grew poorer. New York was the place where the country's growing gulf between the very rich and the very poor was most obvious. While the wealthy lived amid rising prosperity, the number of poor and working-class residents grew rapidly. Half of the city's residents lived in cramped, unsafe housing that one historian has described as a "fetid sink of misery." The city had the highest death rate of any municipality in Europe or the United States.[2]

The expanding gap between the rich and poor manifested itself in the city's physical spaces. As real estate prices skyrocketed, wealthier residents increasingly segregated themselves in nicer neighborhoods where they enjoyed the full benefits of developing urban infrastructure. These New Yorkers also grew more comfortable with their status, and ostentatious displays of wealth became socially acceptable. As Gladden later described it, this "was a dark period in the life of the nation," when "the worship of Mammon had begun to assume that ascendency over the mind of the nation which was destined to become so portentous" in the years ahead.[3]

As would be the case in many US cities in the early twenty-first century, the middle ground between the very rich and the very poor was rapidly vanishing. It was becoming "more difficult for citizens of the respectable middle class to live in the city. New York is growing to be a congeries of millionaires and paupers, a plutocracy floating on the surface of a proletariat," noted one observer in the early 1870s. It seemed like the wealthy lived in a world apart, with little concern for the common good. In the minds of many, "the very wealthy class, caring little for anything but their own material comfort and gain, won't attend to municipal affairs." Gladden attributed this to greed. Rich people were "so intent upon private gain that they find no room in their lives for any concern about the commonwealth."[4]

While this state of affairs would influence Gladden's political outlook, it also had practical consequences. The absence of affordable middle-class housing meant that despite the location of the *Independent*'s offices on Park Place in lower Manhattan, the family chose to again live in Brooklyn. The distance from home meant being far away from the family, which compounded the long hours required by the job.[5]

In large part because of this rampant inequality, the city was also a powder keg, which Gladden repeatedly observed firsthand. Soon after his return in 1871, the city erupted in riots. A parade organized to celebrate the anniversary of Britain's conquest of Ireland provoked violence between the city's Catholic and Protestant residents. When the dust settled, over fifty people had been killed. The following spring, the city experienced a general strike involving one hundred thousand workers in the manufacturing industries. The action went on for eight weeks before an alliance of manufacturers and police successfully broke the strike.[6]

However high ethnic and class tensions ran at the outset of the 1870s, things grew even worse when the United States entered a severe economic depression in 1873. Many of the city's major financial firms collapsed, and one-quarter of workers lost their jobs. With no social safety net and private charity unable and unwilling to meet the need, workers publicly protested. A group of seven thousand took up residence in Tompkins Square Park.[7]

Thus, in New York, Gladden had a firsthand view to a range of social phenomena that would increasingly define life in the United States: an upper class that was increasingly ostentatious in its display of wealth with little concern for appearances, a working class caught in a downward spiral, and a vanishing middle class. Conflict among these groups was coming to define life in much of the nation.

But for all its troubles, New York was also the capital of American journalism. The position at the *Independent* afforded Gladden even greater stature. As his friends noted, working as the paper's religious editor brought him influence unheard of working as the pastor of a church or even as a contributor to periodicals. He now had the ability to guide the entire religious message of a widely read newspaper.

Gladden's hiring was part of the arrival of a "new regime" at the twenty-three-year-old weekly newspaper. The *Independent* had been run by Theodore Tilton, a close associate of famed Brooklyn minister Henry Ward Beecher (in fact, a few years later Beecher would be accused of having an affair with Tilton's wife, and the resulting trial drew widespread attention). But Tilton had grown "erratic and vagarious" during the late 1860s, and his "wild notions had somewhat discredited" the veritable journal, much to the chagrin of publisher Henry Bowen. By 1871, Bowen was ready for a fresh start, and initially it brought great success. The paper boasted that the early months of 1871, which also saw the beginning of Gladden's tenure as religious editor, were highly successful financially. Bowen was optimistic that "the American public will sustain" a paper that blended general-interest and religious news.[8]

This new start provided an opportunity to clarify the mission of the *Independent*. Bowen observed that in editorial matters, "We believe in the three Rs—Right, Radical, and Religious." The pairing of "radical" and "religious" echoed the description of Gladden's "rare combination of conservative liberality." Readers likewise recognized the journal's "strong conservative power and at the same time its freedom and catholicity."[9]

In practical terms, Gladden's day-to-day task was to oversee all religious coverage in the newspaper. "I was expected to write up the important news, to discuss editorially religious events and problems, and to review the religious books," he recalled. In a society where religious institutions exerted considerable influence, and where religious publishing was a vibrant industry, this was not an insignificant task. He also imbued his work with religious purpose for himself. His role, he related, was "to interpret and guide, as best I could, the movements which were bringing to earth the kingdom of heaven." This was the latest vehicle for enacting ideas Gladden had embraced since his youth: putting faith commitments into action in everyday life.[10]

Gladden appreciated the friendships he developed at the *Independent*. He enjoyed working with two other editors, William Hayes Ward and Edward Eggleston, both of whom came highly recommended by Moses Tyler as "downright good fellows." He became especially friendly with Ward, who became supervising editor of the paper soon after Gladden joined the staff. Gladden later noted that his working relationship with Ward was "the most intimate intellectual companionship that I have ever known," and that the two "freely thrashed out" between them "all the great happenings in the realm of religious thought."[11]

The four years Gladden spent at the *Independent* were an important part of his career, if for no other reason than the personal contact he enjoyed with the nation's political and intellectual elite. The *Independent*'s editorial office, he observed, "became a somewhat popular resort of literary people, and of public men and women who were then more or less conspicuous." Regular visitors (and writers for the journal) included Vice President Schuyler Colfax, Senator (and eventual Vice President) Henry Wilson, and the aging abolitionist William Lloyd Garrison. Gladden's future influence and ability to travel in powerful circles derived in large measure from his time at the *Independent*.[12]

Moreover, the paper's seamless integration of religious and secular content provided a model for Gladden's efforts to articulate a message that encompassed political, economic, and religious issues. More significantly, Bowen and Ward encouraged his developing commitment to theological liberalism. In his columns, he articulated with increasing confidence the ideas that he had begun to espouse from his pulpits during the previous decade. At the same time, he emerged as an advocate for religious minorities and a critic of efforts to muster government support for Protestant churches.

As the journal's religious editor, Gladden oversaw contributions from the best-known ministers and theologians in the country. A diverse range of viewpoints appeared in the *Independent*'s pages. Gladden and his fellow editors affirmed their own faith commitments while striving to include diverse views. "Bound to the evangelical faith by the firm belief of all its editors," they wrote, "this paper will never feel itself bound to treat unjustly or ungenerously those who differ from it." Nor would it "defend or conceal the sins" of churches or their members.[13]

This commitment reflected the same awareness of diversity and disagreement within Protestant Christianity that Gladden had encountered during his first decade of ministry. The editors noted that if they "believed themselves to be infallible, they would undoubtedly refuse to have any dealings with those who differed from them." But, because there were "so many infallible people in the world who do not agree with them," the journal's approach was to accept an expansive range of viewpoints under the umbrella term of evangelical Christianity.[14]

The broad-mindedness was borne out in practice. Gladden's inspiration in liberal theology, Horace Bushnell, wrote frequently. So did the revivalist Charles Finney, whose revivalism would hardly be mistaken for liberalism. Women's voices were well represented. The prominent educator and reformer Jennie Fowler Willing wrote advice for Sunday Schools. The Congregationalist Mary Abigail Dodge, who wrote under the pseudonym Gail Hamilton, had a regular column in which she advocated a greater role for women in the public sphere—including in the nation's churches. But the paper also gave space to men like Henry Van Dyke, who denounced the "whole women's movement" as "a revolt against the original constitution of the sexes and the authority of God as revealed in his Holy Word." In short, if a topic was being discussed in American society at large, it was being debated in the pages of the *Independent*.[15]

In addition to soliciting and editing the work of these writers and others, Gladden compiled the weekly "Religious Intelligence" column, which distilled all matter of news related to religion in the United States and abroad. Some of the contents of this column were quite trivial, such as the details of new church buildings that were dedicated or the highest prices paid to rent prominent pews in the churches of the nation's most famous preachers.

Other items in Gladden's column proved more substantive. He regularly informed readers about developments in religions other than Protestant Christianity, such as Judaism and Catholicism in the United States and Europe, as well as Hinduism and Buddhism in Asia. He examined Christianity's relationship with other faiths in the global context and tried to present the information in ways that ordinary American readers would understand. The "Religious Intelligence" feature also reported on significant debates within Protestantism on matters of theology.

Despite this breadth of perspectives, some messages and ideas were clearly favored by Gladden. He helped to champion a number of positions to the paper's large audience: first, the belief that religion was in decline in American life, but that the solution to that problem would not come through more coercive involvement of the government; second, a larger embrace of theological liberalism and the new use of science and research that underlay it; third, sympathy to at least some Roman Catholics and a rejection of the most virulent forms of anti-Catholicism; fourth, the importance of cooperation among churches of different denominations; and, finally, his conviction that moral criticism of society was insufficient unless it was matched by practical action. All of these ideas, which Gladden refined at the *Independent*, became the foundation of his religious and social message for the remainder of his career.

By the time Gladden began his tenure at the *Independent* in 1871, it was clear beyond any doubt that religion—and Protestant Christianity in particular—faced grave challenges in the United States. As one article noted, there was a "loud complaint in many quarters of the growth of infidelity" to religion. Another author observed that people no longer debated nuanced points of theology. Instead, they questioned "the very basic doctrines of our faith," such as whether God existed or whether Jesus Christ was a divine being. This observation reflected the growing acceptance of atheism and agnosticism, especially among educated elites.[16]

But Gladden recognized that the decline in religion wasn't always attributable to intellectual causes. Sometimes its source was far simpler. Americans of the post–Civil War decades were a people on the move, and one of most common movements was the push westward. The disruption of moving to less-settled regions had religious consequences.

"It is quite too common for Christians who go west to fold their religion up with their church certificates," one of Gladden's columns noted, "and lay it away in the bureau drawer so carefully that they never find it again." Whatever the cause, faith appeared to be on the decline, and Protestants like Gladden searched for ways to stem the decline.[17]

Gladden adamantly insisted that enforced religious performance was not the solution to the problem of declining religiosity. This was a very real concern in the 1870s. In 1869, the board of education in Cincinnati, Ohio, had ended Bible reading in public schools to win the support of Catholic parents who opposed the use of a Protestant translation of scripture. Protestant clergy protested, seeing this abandonment of Bible reading as yet more evidence of religion's perilous decline. A contentious period followed, though ultimately the board's decision held, further confirming fears of irreligion.[18]

During the Civil War, a group of clergy had proposed what became known as the "Christian Amendment" to the US Constitution. It declared God to be "the source of all authority and power and civil government" and the will of Jesus to be "the supreme law of the land." It also explicitly announced that the nation had "a Christian government." At the time of its introduction, this amendment was intended as a means to demonstrate the nation's spiritual commitment during the war. In the decades that followed, it became a tool favored by Protestant leaders. They believed it would secure their cultural authority in a society that was growing both more religiously diverse and increasingly secular, as events in Cincinnati seemed to demonstrate. There were numerous proponents of the amendment, including William Strong, a Supreme Court justice. Strong warned that unless the nation was made "explicitly Christian," all aspects of religion would disappear from public life.[19]

In his columns, Gladden blasted these efforts to use government power to enforce religious expression in the public sphere. He used demands for public prayer and worship as an example. "Prayer is an intensely personal thing. Public prayer has meaning only when the presumed worshipers are in sympathy with it," proclaimed one of his editorials. "Public prayer becomes a farce, a mockery, and a blasphemy when conducted . . . before those who care nothing for it."[20]

The paper was equally critical of tax exemptions for church property, viewing them as an unjust government subsidy for religion. The practice of allowing religious institutions to avoid paying taxes represented nothing short of an "alliance between church and state." Such an alliance was at odds with "American principles," particularly the tenet that "religion should be left to stand on its own merits, and live exclusively by the voluntary support of its friends."[21]

Gladden was deeply troubled by the proposed Christian amendment, and he devoted editorial space to blistering attacks on it. The proposal was not only "contrary to the spirit of American institutions" but also "a palpable and direct violation of one of the cardinal principles of Christian religion." Specifically, it sought to use force to make people adopt a particular religious faith. Ratifying the amendment was akin to putting "Christianity into the Constitution at the point of the bayonet" and conceding a "lack of faith in the weapons that are not carnal." Such an approach ought to be opposed by all true Christians.[22]

Gladden argued that such efforts ultimately made religious people look desperate and pathetic. As one editorial asked, "Has Christianity so utterly lost its power that it must stoop to ask the aid of those secular powers which her founders were not afraid to withstand?" The Christian church began as a countercultural institution opposed to the government. It therefore signaled a complete failure for Christians to demand special treatment from the state. "If our Christianity is of such a flimsy texture that nothing but a constitutional amendment will save it," he declared in another column, "the sooner it is obliterated the better for the land."[23]

Gladden's unifying argument was that these efforts to enforce religiosity ultimately harmed religion. Demanding that people pray in public, for instance, "disgusts more than it will benefit." More disturbingly, by giving people an object lesson in insincere and hypocritical religious expression, it would "familiarize their minds to the desecration of holy things."[24]

The same critique applied to the proposed constitutional amendment. Inserting language into the constitution that people did not actually believe simply made Americans hypocrites. "When the nation shall possess a genuine faith in God, that faith will find expression in every act of the national life," one editorial insisted. At such time, "a special announcement" of religiosity would be unnecessary. But if Americans did not actually believe what the amendment proclaimed, the proposal reeked of insincerity. "Doubtless there is hypocrisy enough in the land,"

and it wasn't necessary to add more by writing "it into the Constitution."²⁵

As Gladden proclaimed his support for the separation of religion from politics, he likewise made the *Independent* a major voice of theological liberalism. This effort reflected his desire to respond to the perception of declining religious commitment. He believed a progressive religious message would appeal to people who were becoming alienated from Christianity in an era of expanding scientific knowledge.

The problem, as the *Independent*'s editors diagnosed it, was that Americans were living in an age of scientific and technological advancement, yet many ministers and theologians attacked scientists. It was entirely reasonable to question new scientific theories. But Christians had a tendency to attack not just science but scientists themselves, and to "speak of them as though they were bad and dangerous men, enemies of the Church, corrupters of the youth, and destroyers of souls." Such an approach was hugely detrimental to the interests of religion. "To thoughtful persons . . . such an attitude on the part of religious men . . . is a stumbling-block which it is hard to get over." This editorial concluded that many people were "encouraged in unbelief by the posture in which a large portion of the leaders of religious opinion have put themselves toward the truths of science."²⁶

Gladden insisted that Christians had nothing to fear from new knowledge, even if that knowledge was about the origin and nature of scripture. In one "Religious Intelligence" column, he praised the "candor and liberality" of a series of lectures held at the University of Michigan on the Bible and skepticism. "We covet no triumphs for the Gospel that are not possible on such a fair field as this," he wrote. He urged Christians at the university—and by implication everywhere else—to "stand up manfully for the truth as they have received it" while nevertheless being "willing to concede to those who differ from them honesty equal to their own." Just as he argued that Christianity's survival should not be guaranteed by the force of government, Gladden argued that religious faith could not be preserved by closed-mindedness. Only through fair, honest intellectual engagement could believers maintain their convictions.²⁷

In his tenure as religious editor, Gladden championed writers who advocated similar positions. In particular, they urged that Christians needed a more solid understanding of the Bible. One author observed the ignorance prevalent among Sunday School teachers. Instructors tended to quote from scripture without understanding it, a circumstance that "gives much trouble." To combat just this sort of ignorance, the *Independent* ran a regular column that updated its readers on new developments in the study of scripture in the hopes that such information would find its way into churches and Sunday Schools.[28]

Developments in science demanded critical thinking about scripture. New geological discoveries seemed to prove that the earth was far older than Christians commonly believed and that it was not created in the six days suggested in Genesis. Darwin's theory of evolution through natural selection, which gained scientific currency through the 1860s and early 1870s, likewise undermined long-standing beliefs that humans had been specially created by God apart from natural processes. The natural origin of humanity also raised questions of what would happen after death and whether traditional views of heaven and hell could be sustained.[29]

In the face of these intellectual developments, Gladden told readers that some modification of theological ideas was necessary. He criticized Christian institutions that clung to outmoded theology at odds with modern knowledge and values. His editorial pages frequently denounced theologians and ministers who continued to proclaim as essential Christian truths historical teachings—such as the creation of the earth in seven days or the condemnation to hell of unbaptized infants—that were either disputed or rejected by many Christians. "No blow so injurious or fatal has ever been dealt at religion by any unbeliever" as the harmful effects caused by professing Christians who "cling to an old lie long after its falseness has been shown."[30]

The embrace of progress in religious thought also extended to the role of women. The journal cheered a minister's decision to abandon his prohibition on women speaking in prayer meetings. Recounting the story of a male clergyman who opposed the practice of women praying in public but who changed his mind when he heard a woman pray, the editors observed that "a prejudice that dissolves in tears at the sound of a woman's voice in prayer is hardly worth cultivating."[31]

Moreover, Gladden used the *Independent* to publicize his growing conviction that people could never attain absolute certainty in religious matters. He decried popular efforts to prove the existence of spiritual phenomena like prayer through scientific investigation. "The existence of God cannot be demonstrated by science," he proclaimed in an editorial. The reality of a divine being "may be rendered probable," but "it can never be made certain." Ultimately, "after you have marshaled all your arguments, you must end by simply believing." It was acceptable—even desirable—for religious liberals to embrace scientific innovation. But that did not mean they needed to make themselves beholden to science to sustain their faith.[32]

Gladden's tenure at the *Independent* allowed him to cover a major test of religious liberalism. In 1874, David Swing, a Presbyterian minister in Chicago, was put on trial for heresy. Swing provided a prominent target for conservative Presbyterians who were growing anxious about the spread of liberal theology. He was the pastor of the Fourth Presbyterian Church of Chicago, which at the beginning of 1874 had opened a new building that could accommodate nine hundred people (before the church was completed, Swing had preached in a packed Chicago theater). Swing's popularity reflected his seeming ability to be all things to all people. One profile of him noted that "he can see at the same time intellectually in many directions, while he seems to feel the pulsations of the human heart."[33]

Swing articulated liberal religious views of the very sort that Gladden had affirmed in North Adams and had popularized in the *Independent*. The paper praised Swing for not being "one of those who goes forth with the thunders of denunciation against sin, or with the pitiless dogmatism of theologic system," as orthodox Presbyterian theologians of another generation might have done. Nor was he a revivalist in the mode of Charles Finney, the kind of minister who preached "with passionate enthusiasm that warps and supplicates and seizes men." Rather, with "simplicity and sincerity of manner," Swing explored religious subjects in a thoughtful, intellectual manner.[34]

Another profile of Swing cast the minister as someone ideally suited to reach the growing population of skeptics and doubters. Swing "yearns with deep sympathy for a class of men who stand on the verge of the Church and of Christianity." In an attempt to reach such people, "he puts himself as far as possible in the shoes of those men." But therein lay the clergyman's problem. To do so it was necessary to go beyond the "terminology and language of the theological books and schools" and to use rhetoric that, while accessible, was also "liable to assaults by heresy-hunters."[35]

Swing was certainly assaulted: twenty-nine charges of heresy were brought against the minister. One accuser claimed that Swing had admitted to being a Unitarian, while another reported that Swing denied several key tenets of the Calvinist theology that was the foundation of Presbyterianism.[36]

Gladden and his fellow editors had already established the *Independent*'s support of broad intellectual freedom for clergy. The previous year, the paper commented on a row among New York Methodists. An invited speaker at a clergy gathering argued that the punishment for sin was the destruction not only of the body but also of the soul, a position widely deemed as heretical. In response, this clergy group proposed allowing discussion only of matters deemed inside the bounds of established belief. Gladden published a column suggesting that such a strategy would turn compelling discussions into mere recitations "of the Methodist creed and discipline." Exploration of ideas that seemed out-of-bounds was precisely what made religious conversation interesting. In the view of the *Independent*, the group should allow its speakers "full liberty to speak his bottom thought. The muzzling of free discussion is a work in which the Methodists can ill afford to have part."[37]

These views guided the *Independent*'s approach to the Swing trial, and, despite its commitment to broad-minded coverage of issues, the journal's sympathies clearly lay with the accused clergyman. When the trial began in May 1874, one of the paper's writers—likely Gladden—observed that the outcome was "already pretty clear." The combination of "the flimsiness of the evidence produced by the prosecutor" and the "singular modesty and rare candor" of Swing made the Chicago Presbytery's acquittal of Swing a foregone conclusion.[38]

This acquittal would prove significant because the trial was seen as something beyond the evaluation of one minister. Observers like Gladden believed that it reflected the larger conflict within Christianity. On one side stood Swing's accusers who represented "medieval superstition" with their insistence on the "damnation of some infants" and the belief that God "fore-ordained a vast majority of the race to everlasting death." Against such beliefs stood Swing as "the defender of a rational faith." The result of the trial confirmed what Gladden hoped: that "men with liberal tendencies have a good standing within the Presbyterian Church."[39]

But not for long. While the Chicago Presbytery had acquitted Swing, his accusers had the right to appeal to the larger—and much more conservative—Illinois Synod. Such an appeal seemed to have the support of most Presbyterians in the United States, at least as judged by the opinions expressed in the denomination's journals. It appeared, the *Independent* noted, that the denomination "sends forth David Swing without regrets and distinctly gives notice to all such men that they are not wanted within its ranks." Yet such opinions were formed on so profound a misreading of Swing that those who accused him might be found guilty of the "sin of slander."[40]

Swing recognized that his chances of a second acquittal were slim, and in the summer of 1874 his church withdrew from the Chicago Presbytery. He was foresighted to do so. At the second trial, his accusers convinced the synod of Swing's guilt. They even demanded that the minister be reinstated into the Chicago Presbytery so that he might then be dismissed. Gladden blasted the Presbyterians in the *Independent*. "The religion which delights in this kind of heretical bull-baiting is a religion which will not, we trust, take strong hold of the American people." Churchgoers in the United States were, he believed, too open-minded to accept such a policy. "The Christian people of America know that the expulsion of a man from Christian fellowship" for such teachings represented a "case of bigotry, and not of heresy."[41]

David Swing's trial highlighted that the split between orthodox and liberal Protestants had grown wider and was becoming harder to ignore. Gladden had firmly taken the side of the liberals, and he had positioned the editorial pages of the *Independent* there as well. Gladden's embrace of theological liberalism was clear during his pastorate at North Adams, but any remaining doubt of his convictions vanished during his tenure at the *Independent*.

Gladden's editorial columns similarly demonstrated his evolving views on Roman Catholics. The paper reported on matters related to Catholicism with a relative lack of judgment or bigotry. This is not to say that the *Independent* entirely avoided the commonplace anti-Catholicism of the day. Reports of Catholics burning Bibles in Rome played to old stereotypes. So, too, did an article mocking a Catholic school where faculty refused to acknowledge that the city of Rome belonged to the nation of Italy rather than the Vatican ("the facts of geography are made strictly subordinate to the theological opinions of the teacher," the author claimed). Gladden's columns often rested on stereotypical notions of the backwardness of Catholicism. Even a sympathetic treatment of the difficulties American Catholics endured could not resist the gratuitous observation that Protestants had "the pure Church of Christ, the pure Word of God, and the power of God's favor," whereas Catholicism had "a corrupted church and a corrupted Bible."[42]

Despite these lingering prejudices, Gladden steered the *Independent* toward more favorable coverage of Catholicism. This reflected his belief that the Catholic Church could move in a more modern, liberal direction. There was the potential for developments that would "make way for the entrance of liberalizing ideas" into the church. Obviously, it was not exactly broad-minded to embrace Catholics only if their religion came to more closely resemble liberal Protestantism. But the belief that the Catholic Church could modernize signaled a far more charitable view of it than many American Protestants of the day had. This tension was perhaps best exemplified by the *Independent*'s characterization of the aging Pope Pius IX as a "sincere and well-meaning but feeble old man" who wished to stop "the currents of civilization." The pontiff was not a pawn of Satan who had the power to bring down the United States, as many Americans feared. He was rather the spent product of a bygone era whose institution was marching forward without him.[43]

This view of the Catholic Church led Gladden to denounce some of the most virulent expressions of anti-Catholicism, especially those that subjected Catholics to discrimination in favor of Protestants. He criticized a proposal made by the YMCA to make up for the end of Bible reading in public schools by providing a copy of the Bible to every Roman Catholic family. The *Independent* rightly pointed out that the plan of providing "the Bible without note or comment" was not the neutral policy the YMCA depicted it to be. It reflected a distinctively Protestant view that infringed on Catholics' "rights of conscience."[44]

At times the *Independent*'s religion columns proved downright sympathetic to the position of Catholics and highly critical of arguments made by Protestants. This was especially true in matters of church and state. By the standards of the day, Gladden and his fellow editors showed great concern for the plight of religious minorities. When Catholics demanded public funding for parochial schools because public schools taught Protestant religious ideas, the *Independent* took the position that Catholics were justified in their complaints.

Though Gladden adamantly opposed using government funds for Catholic schools (a position advocated by some Catholic leaders), he accepted that elements of Protestantism should be removed from public schools. Because "the state tolerates and protects all religions," one of his editorials declared, "Protestants have no right to insist that their peculiar religious ideas and customs shall prevail in the schools." Moreover, like the Christian amendment to the constitution, efforts to teach religion in public schools were at odds with the nation's fundamental principles. "The permission of religious teaching in our schools . . . has been distinctly contrary to our national ideas. It is time that this anomaly were abandoned," he and his fellow editors concluded.[45]

What explains the *Independent*'s inconsistency toward Catholics—its intolerance of the institutional church and Vatican policy alongside its sympathy toward the needs of Catholics in the United States—was the recognition of its editors that all Catholics were not the same. In their view, attacks on public schools from the "pulpits and presses of the Roman Catholics" represented "an outcry of the hierarchy, in which the majority of the people do not join." Though obvious from the perspective of history, this was a significant realization at the time.[46]

If anything, Gladden and his fellow editors exaggerated the separation between the views of ordinary Catholics and church officials. This caused them to be surprised when the outcry they expected among American Catholics against the hierarchy failed to materialize (it also caused them to underestimate how much support existed among Catholics for parochial schools). Nevertheless, in contrast to the popular stereotype of Catholics as a collective mass that walked in lockstep with the Vatican, the *Independent* offered forceful and frequent reminders that all Catholics were not the same.

As Gladden sought to diminish the boundary separating Catholic and Protestant Americans, he also used his editorial influence to encourage members of various Protestant denominations to grow closer to one another. In the mid-nineteenth century, denominational boundaries tended to be quite strong, with each particular tradition believing it possessed the purest form of Christian truth. Yet Gladden praised a pulpit exchange between a Congregationalist minister and his Universalist counterpart, noting that both churches benefited from the experience. He also railed against exclusivism when it came to the distribution of communion. When Congregationalists in Boston suggested that communion should only be distributed to members of particular Protestant churches, he protested. Communion was meant to be shared by all Christians, not restricted to people belonging to specific denominations.[47]

One common proposal, which Gladden repeatedly championed in the *Independent*, reflected his views on recreational activities that he first espoused in North Adams. He urged cities to establish coffee houses that provided spaces for conversation, as well as games like checkers and chess, for people of limited means. Not only would such enterprises combat the abuse of alcohol by offering an alternative to saloons, they would also provide a basis for cooperation not only among Protestants but among Americans of all religious faiths. When a proposal was put forward to establish such a place in Brooklyn, Gladden cheered one minister's proposal that the endeavor "should be placed on the broadest basis" and that "Jew and Gentile, Roman Catholic and Protestant, Unitarian and Orthodox ought to have part in the enterprise." Such an establishment that encompassed many religious groups represented "one of the best applications of common sense to benevolence that has yet been made, and it ought to be introduced in all our cities."[48]

This emphasis on the practical also reflected Gladden's growing focus on the social, structural nature of society's ills. In one of the few articles that he published under his name during his tenure at the *Independent*, he urged ministers against publicly censuring particular individuals from the pulpit. A public rebuke "which is understood by the congregation as applying to certain individuals or a certain class" would do little to fix problems, save stirring up the resentments of those targeted. The minister should instead draw attention to that "sin which prevails in the community."[49] Such advice reflected Gladden's emerging conviction that problems in society could not be fixed by targeting individuals, but rather by addressing social issues in their fullness.

To critics who suggested that if God wanted to improve the world, the divine being would take the initiative and fix things directly, Gladden argued that they missed the point. Part of humanity's purpose was "to help in making the world in which we live a better world, and the men with whom we live better men."[50]

With its affirmation of liberal theology, its more charitable view of Catholics, and its emphasis on practical cooperation and the social message of Christianity, the *Independent* served as a vehicle for popularizing Gladden's increasingly progressive religious views to readers throughout the United States. The prediction of friends that the newspaper would offer him a powerful platform had proved correct.

Despite the attention that it paid to religious issues, the *Independent* was not exclusively a religious journal. Rather, it embodied a growing trend in nineteenth-century American journalism. As the *Independent*'s editors noted, religious periodicals increasingly contained a greater mix of secular material, while secular newspapers and magazines devoted more space to religious topics. "The tastes of the people are so diverse and multiform that nothing short of a large variety will meet their demand, and give to journalism any hope of general success," they wrote. The *Independent* sought to do just that.[51]

Although Gladden's principal role was guiding the journal's religious coverage, the collegiality of the *Independent*'s small offices encouraged overlapping domains. Gladden took part in discussions about the paper's coverage of broader issues, including political news. Moreover, in the absence of William Hayes Ward, Gladden occasionally oversaw the entire editorial operation of the paper. In August 1871, Ward had taken a month's vacation, and Gladden ran the *Independent* as the Tweed enterprise, which controlled New York's municipal government, collapsed in the wake of scandal. The ability to oversee coverage of such a watershed event stayed with Gladden. He considered it "one of the times of my life when I have come across something that needed to be hit and have had a chance to strike hard. Such opportunities make life worth living."[52]

National politics was central in the pages of the *Independent*. In its political message, the periodical, like Gladden, embodied the New England Republican tradition of the 1860s. As the 1870s progressed, though, it became more difficult for the journal to sustain this idealism, which in turn put Gladden at odds with his colleagues.

The *Independent* adamantly supported the Republican Party, and during the early 1870s, President Ulysses S. Grant. But the editors insisted that their support for the GOP did not reflect blind partisanship. Rather, it resulted from their understanding of the limits of the two-party system. This commitment was put to the test in 1872. Horace Greeley, the former editor of the *New York Tribune*, occasional contributor to the *Independent*, and long-standing hero to many Americans for his principled opposition to slavery before the Civil War, bolted from the GOP. He declared himself a "liberal Republican" and became the nominee of Democrats.[53]

The *Independent* urged its readers to recognize that, for better or worse, in the US political system, they had two choices. However much Americans might personally admire Greeley, "voting for him as the candidate of a third party is simply throwing away votes," while "voting for him as the accepted candidate of the [Democrats] is practically casting a Democratic vote." Quoting fears expressed by Southern blacks, the *Independent* noted that the reality of American politics dictated that "all roads out of the Republican party lead into the Democratic camp."[54]

Gladden never became fully comfortable with the paper's political reporting. He considered the political editor "neither an inspired nor an inspiring" figure, and "the narrowness of his partisanship was oftentimes intolerable." In particular, Gladden had a less favorable view of Grant than many of his colleagues did. He later expressed his assessment that the general-turned-president had an "incapacity for civil leadership" that stemmed largely from "his admiration for rich men" and his tendency to use "his prerogative unblushingly in behalf of his relatives." He found his paper too favorably disposed to Grant and unfair in its coverage of Greeley.[55]

Despite this criticism, Gladden's actual views were quite similar to those put forward in the paper. The bleak assessment of Greeley proved accurate. Although the journalist had once been a towering figure in US life, by the 1870s he seemed completely out of touch with the reality of modern politics. The only coherent thread in his campaign seemed to be a desire to go back to the antebellum world. He opposed the young labor movement. As the *Independent*'s editors observed, Greeley also opposed Reconstruction. Gladden was more sympathetic to the goals of liberal Republicans than his coworkers were, but he shared the view that Greeley "reduced the movement to an absurdity" because he did not actually share the liberals' goals and was "of too emotional a habit to be a safe leader of the nation."[56]

The invocation of African Americans as reason to reject Greeley reflected a larger commitment of the *Independent*. The underlying fear of the Democrats returning to power was the conviction on the part of its editors—which was quite prescient—that the ideological conflict of the Civil War "was not yet fought out" six years after the military conflict had ended. If the Democratic Party returned to power, "the whole work of reconstruction would be undone." African American men would lose their newly won right to vote. And, ultimately, "under some form or other slavery or its equivalent would be restored."[57]

This concern about slavery reflected the fact that the *Independent* was, at least judged by the standards of its day, quite progressive on matters of race. Several prominent staff members had been influential figures in the antebellum antislavery movement. They had no second thoughts before denouncing a US Senator who espoused racist views, noting that he "talks like a fool" and that his views had "no other foundation except that of a perverse education, stereotyping a false and unphilosophical sentiment upon the human heart."[58]

The editors were adamant that African Americans possessed "just as many rights as white men, and hold them by a derivation and sanction equally divine and sacred." But despite this outlook, Gladden and his colleagues failed to recognize the extent to which slavery had built racial inequality into the very structure of American society. They were optimistic that racism might soon be eliminated while older adults taught white children to be "despisers and haters of black people," the editors believed that bigotry would disappear if this cycle could be broken. But this belief that racism could easily be ended provided an excuse for walking away from efforts to build genuine equality. Once the two races enjoyed equal rights and privileges under law, they argued, whatever happened was fair. "Justice does not demand an equality of *condition* and attainment where there is an inequality of powers," the *Independent* declared, thus setting the stage to abandon efforts to undo the lasting effects of bondage.[59]

That is not to say, however, that the newspaper entirely abandoned recently freed African Americans. The paper was at the forefront of calling attention to the growing threat of the Ku Klux Klan and violence to African Americans in the South. During the early 1870s, as self-identified liberals took power in the Republican Party, they undercut efforts to respond forcefully to the Klan. For these officials, the specter of a powerful federal government was of greater concern than the rising number of lynchings.[60]

The *Independent* decried these "organized bands of robbers and murderers" who were "bound together by secret oaths" in a "guerilla warfare against society" with the goal "to crush the negro, defeat the normal results of the reconstruction measures, and restore to the Democracy its lost power." The newspaper's editors sharply criticized the federal government for failing to meaningfully safeguard the newfound liberties of former slaves. "The mistaken leniency with which treason has been treated by the Government is now yielding some of it earliest fruits."[61] While the *Independent* advocated stronger government intervention to punish white Southerners, its support for Southern African Americans was notably weaker.

Political corruption was another frequent target of the journal. Gladden boasted of his coverage of the Tweed ring, which embodied malfeasance in government. In the years that William M. Tweed oversaw Tammany Hall, the city's Democratic machine was, in the words of one historian, "a vast corrupt bargain." Tweed rewarded his supporters with jobs and government contracts, while government costs spiraled upward. What happened in New York seemed likely to happen elsewhere. The *Independent* emphasized the danger to the nation, suggesting that corruption risked "a grave crisis in the history of the country." This was a belief that Gladden would keep with him.[62]

For the rest of his career, Gladden fervently advocated the same political positions that occupied a central place on the *Independent*'s pages. He remained a staunch supporter of the Republican Party, championed government reform in the nation's cities, and remained committed to promoting opportunity for African Americans, though without fully acknowledging or critiquing the systematic racial inequality embedded in national life.

But Gladden's tenure at the high-profile periodical was not to last. As his friends had predicted when he took the job, conflict with Henry Bowen proved inevitable. The paper's coverage of the 1872 election was the first source of annoyance. Gladden felt the criticism of Horace Greeley went beyond well-meaning debate and amounted to mudslinging. "It appeared to me especially discreditable for a journal which sought to maintain a religious character to descend to misrepresentation and abuse of a political opponent," he noted. The protest fell on deaf ears, which made Gladden doubt "the value of my editorial opportunity."[63]

A bigger issue was an advertising strategy initiated by Bowen. In a practice that anticipated the twenty-first-century phenomenon of sponsored content, Bowen began selling space in news and editorial columns to advertisers. What appeared to unsuspecting readers to be content provided by the *Independent*'s writers and editors was in fact material provided by advertisers to induce the paper's audience to purchase particular products. Gladden was irate. This practice was not unique to the *Independent*, as he himself noted, but he found it especially troubling in a religious journal.

Gladden first broached the issue in 1873, and his criticism combined principle with concern for his own reputation. "I confess that I feel humiliated and disgraced whenever such an issue of the paper appears" that contained dubious advertising practices. "It looks as though I belonged to a set of men who, instead of seeking first the kingdom of God were seeking first advertisements, and cared very little for anything else." He added that his reputation "is all I have and I can't afford to lose it." He was certain he would lose it if he continued to be on the "staff of a religious newspaper which was in the habit of inserting paid puffs in its editorial columns."[64]

Bowen and Gladden soothed over their disagreement for a time, but tension between the two over advertisements arose again in the autumn of 1874. This time Gladden felt he had no choice but to resign. He expressed concern not just for his own reputation but for that of the *Independent* as well. "The religious newspaper whose editor is known to have contracted to sell for a sum of money the 'exclusive interest and influence of his money and editorial columns' to the venders of any commodity," he wrote, "is a religious newspaper whose opinions on moral questions cannot have much weight with the Christian or the unchristian public."[65]

Bowen responded forcefully. He accused Gladden of being a "fair-weather friend" and suggested Gladden had no right to be disgruntled by practices employed at numerous other publications. Gladden had none of it. While he conceded the commonality of the practices, he nevertheless blamed the *Independent* for being "first among religious newspapers to introduce these methods" and for pushing them "a good deal more vigorously than the others have done." He went beyond mere criticism of the advertising practice and slammed Bowen's leadership. "The *Independent* has . . . lost the confidence of a great portion of the community," Gladden wrote. "I do not think that it will ever regain what it has lost without a radical change of management."[66]

Acquaintances lamented Gladden's decision to quit. "I miss you already," wrote one, noting that Gladden possessed the ideal "knowledge, talent, breadth of vision" for religious journalism. His abandonment of it was a "waste of power." His old friend from Massachusetts, *Springfield Republican* editor Sam Bowles, reiterated that "it has always been a source of wonder to me how you could work with Bowen," and understood why Gladden had to leave. Still, he added, "I hope you will not leave journalism. The harvest is large, and the labours are few. It is bigger than the pulpit; I won't be so conceited as to say that it is better."[67]

Gladden seemed to agree. The United States was mired in an economic depression, however, and he had just burned his bridge with one of the most prominent publishers in the nation. "So you see I am adrift," he wrote to a friend. "Of course I shall go back into the pulpit. Nothing else is left me."[68]

Nearly every biography of Gladden includes that quote—and with good reason. It packed a punch and captured the sentiments of someone who, on principle, had just quit a dream job. But the sentiments also conveyed a fair amount of Gladden's characteristic melodrama. His departure from the *Independent* did not signal the end of his forays into journalism. He contributed to numerous publications in the years ahead, including to the *Independent*. In all of his subsequent writing, he continued to wed his commitment to theological liberalism with his belief in progressive politics, largely maintaining the spirit that defined the *Independent* of the early 1870s.

Nor did his resignation end his friendship with William Hayes Ward. The two collaborated for decades after, primarily in efforts to encourage cooperation among Protestant churches and to bring about the merger of closely related denominations. The issue that drove Gladden's resignation—editors and publishers allowing advertisements to masquerade as journalism—remained a cause of concern for him for the rest of his career. In the years ahead, he denounced the growing practice by which "certain great corporations pay large sums of money for influencing . . . public opinion" on the pages of periodicals. The result was that "when the innocent reader supposes himself to be instructed by some independent student of public affairs, he is reading matter which is furnished by some interested party." For Gladden, this was intolerable, and it was a phenomenon that only got worse.[69]

In the immediate term, Gladden was right in acknowledging that he needed to go back to the pulpit. Fortunately, a new pastorate awaited him in Springfield, Massachusetts. And it was the pulpit that would provide the launching pad to greater professional success during the second half of his life.

5

PASTOR

Despite his misgivings about leaving New York and giving up full-time work as a journalist, Gladden welcomed the move to Springfield. He had always liked the town and was delighted to be back in New England. Moreover, his new pastorate, the North Congregational Church, suited his evolving outlook. It was a place of "progressive temper," he noted, and its previous ministers had been "men of light and leading." He noted, perhaps with some hyperbole, that there was only one man in the entire church who "found fault with my teaching."[1]

Despite his fears, leaving the *Independent* did not end Gladden's forays into journalism. His connection with Samuel Bowles at the *Springfield Republican* remained strong, and he once again contributed material to the paper. Gladden also edited *Sunday Afternoon*, a new periodical he helped to launch in 1878. The magazine was religious in a general sense but sought to be inclusive. Though of "a distinctively Christian character," it avoided "the hindrances of dogmatic dispute and theological grievance." It combined morally uplifting fiction with analysis of political and social issues. It did so in a distinctly modern way, as Gladden avoided "commonplace and out-worn lingo" in its pages. Its "stories, poems, essays and everything else" emphasized "living thoughts and issues." The magazine strived for "the utterance of free Christian thought, especially as directed in the way of social science."[2]

In other words, *Sunday Afternoon* was a smaller-scale version of the *Independent*. It offered the same messages that Gladden had espoused at the New York paper, especially in its insistence that Christians should not wrangle with each over specific doctrines and should embrace modern knowledge. But, like at the *Independent*, Gladden struggled with his colleagues. He did not get along with *Sunday Afternoon*'s publisher and found his role circumscribed, leading him to quit his post just before the periodical collapsed entirely in 1881.[3]

Thus, at Springfield, Gladden focused on the work of being a pastor. As at North Adams, he viewed the entire community as an extension of his congregation, and he was concerned for it. When he arrived, he found the small city of approximately thirty thousand people suffering from the economic depression that began in 1873. By 1876, the city was haphazardly providing charity to 1,600 residents at an annual cost that ran as high as $25,000. City officials established a Union Relief Association, which sought to coordinate the charitable efforts of churches and businesses. Gladden wrote a report on the needs of Springfield's poor, and he "took a leading part in the enterprise" of establishing the new charity organization.[4]

While work to combat poverty occupied a large amount of Gladden's time, he supported other projects in Springfield as well. He served on a committee of Congregationalist ministers who wanted to establish regular church services for deaf community members.[5]

Even as community efforts marked a continuation of long-standing aspects of his ministry, Gladden moved in a new direction in Springfield, as he began writing more systematically about theological questions. He anchored the religious liberalism he had espoused since college more firmly in the burgeoning field of biblical studies, and he began to champion progressive Christianity more forcefully. Building on his reputation from the *Independent*, Gladden emerged as a leading advocate for this outlook. His stature would only grow in the years that followed.

Many of Gladden's arguments built on ideas he had long held, but he now articulated them with greater intellectual force and to larger audiences. As always, the cornerstone of his theological outlook was that religious ideas should progress and change as humanity developed and grew in knowledge.

Under this general principle, Gladden advocated a number of specific ideas that together formed the core of his theology for the remainder of his life. First, he rejected doctrine, along with ritual and emotion, as the basis of Christianity, instead emphasizing simple belief in Jesus. Second, Gladden increased his criticism of revivals and grew especially intolerant of revivalists' claims that a Christian life necessitated spiritual angst and suffering. Third, in one of his most significant innovations, Gladden suggested that periods of doubt and uncertainty were normal and should be embraced. He urged churchgoers not to sit in judgment of others. Finally, he offered an optimistic view of humanity and insisted that God's kingdom could be brought to earth.

Gladden's arrival in Springfield occurred amid increasingly virulent theological debates in Protestant denominations. The change was sudden. When he arrived in New York in 1871, "scarcely a ripple had appeared upon the placid surface of American orthodoxy." He had belonged to a clergy group that frequently discussed issues in theology, and none of these contentious issues arose there. "I cannot recall that any of the questions respecting the Bible," he wrote, ever coming "before the club." Within a few years, however, "the question respecting the inerrancy of the Bible began to trouble the mind of the churches."[6]

For several decades, German scholars had studied the Bible with newfound rigor. They paid close attention to linguistic clues in the text, compared different fragments of scripture to one another, and considered biblical passages alongside other ancient sources. The main goal of this project of historical criticism was to interpret the Bible in light of the political and cultural context in which its books were written. Such study cast doubt on whether a "plain sense" reading of scripture, long a core value of Protestantism, accurately revealed the intended message of the Bible.[7]

Biblical scholarship raised a host of issues. Nuances of language revealed that many of the Bible's books were not written when and by whom they purported to be. This realization posed a particular problem in the case of Jesus. One of the common arguments that Protestants had historically used to defend Jesus's divinity was his prediction in the Gospel of Matthew of the destruction of the Jerusalem Temple, which would occur nearly four decades after his death. But scholarship revealed that the passage in Matthew dated from *after* the Romans destroyed the Temple. What had seemed evidence of a divine being predicting the future instead turned out to be an event written into the

Gospel after it happened. This realization called all sorts of other aspects of the Gospels into question.[8]

Initially much of this scholarship only interested educated elites, but it affected ordinary churchgoers when it merged with an effort to revise the English translation of the Bible. This project, which began in England in the 1870s, raised a "disturbing suggestion" in the minds of American churchgoers. "Revision implied change," Gladden observed, "and change, whether of word or phrase, in the language of the Bible, could be nothing less than sacrilege." Such change forced Christians to accept that biblical interpretation might require periodic updating. If this was true of the Bible, it might also be true of other tenets of faith.[9]

Faced with these developments, Protestant Americans split into two camps. Some deferred to the plain reading of scripture and continued to defend historical beliefs, suggesting that science and biblical scholarship remained imperfectly developed. In the early twentieth century, leaders of this group would publish *The Fundamentals*, a multivolume series defending traditional Protestant Christianity (and giving birth to the term Fundamentalism).[10]

The second group wished to reconcile Christian belief with modern knowledge. The movement they pioneered became known as the New Theology. Theologians and ministers like Theodore Munger, who had succeeded Gladden in North Adams, put forth a vision of a faith that embraced the intellectual and scientific developments of the nineteenth century. These religious leaders accepted the theory of evolution, affirmed the findings of biblical scholarship, and, most broadly, insisted that Christianity and human knowledge could never be at odds.[11]

Given his decades-old embrace of innovative religious ideas, expressed in declarations that the "thirst for knowledge" was "one of the noblest principles of the human nature," it wasn't surprising that Gladden's sympathies lay with this latter group. He publicly heralded Munger's book *The Freedom of Faith*, which was the most systematic synthesis of the New Theology. "I am about as happy over it as if I had written it myself," Gladden told Munger, "and I have had no book, for five years, that I would rather have written."[12]

Not everyone was happy with the New Theology, though. The late 1870s and 1880s were a tumultuous time in American Protestantism, as liberals and conservatives jockeyed to assert dominance over the nation's churches. David Swing's trial, which Gladden covered just before leaving the *Independent*, was one battle among many. Another contentious fight occurred at the Andover Seminary in Massachusetts. Originally founded as a bastion of Christian orthodoxy when Unitarians took over Harvard in the early 1800s, Andover found its own faculty becoming increasingly liberal by the 1880s. The perceived loss of a key institution bolstered conservatives' urgent determination to stop the spread of liberalism.[13]

When he wrote the chapter in his memoir that covered these years, Gladden titled it "Hunting for Heresy." The title reflected the extent to which theological debates defined the religious culture of this period. These hunts often hit close to home. In 1877, Gladden found himself at odds with colleagues over the question of whether to grant ministerial standing to a new clergyman in the area. This minister rejected the belief that punishment in hell lasted for an eternity. Instead, he embraced a view of hell as a time-limited penalty. This belief had long existed on the margins of American theology but had begun to grow more popular.[14]

A majority of Gladden's colleagues felt that holding this view of hell was incompatible with being a Congregationalist minister. Gladden claimed they had no grounds to object because Congregationalists had no denominational creed. The nature of a tradition that prized the autonomy of individual congregations meant ministers could not police the doctrinal positions of their counterparts as Presbyterians had done with Swing. Gladden's colleagues, however, insisted that the issues raised were too significant to ignore. At the heart of the debate was a question: "Is belief in everlasting punishment essential to ordination in our ministry," or, more simply, Did a Christian minister need to believe that God sent sinners to hell for eternity? But this debate opened larger issues. Many Springfield clergymen recognized the debate over hell as indicative of a worrying "tendency to liberalism in the churches."[15]

Gladden lost this fight and found himself on the outs with colleagues. The situation confirmed his cynicism about denominational organizations, which seemed designed to allow popular, senior clergy to perpetuate outmoded thinking. Gladden increasingly likened church hierarchy to the corrupt political establishment he had battled in New York. "There is always a denominational 'machine,' more or less political in its methods, by which ecclesiastical affairs are managed, and those who incur the displeasure of this machine are apt to find their paths to promotion obstructed, and their opportunities of service limited," he wrote. For all of Protestantism's emphasis on individual conscience, established thinking often ruled the day. Religious innovators suffered at the hands of this machinery.[16]

Gladden resolved to break the established opinions and personal interests that impeded movement in religious thought. Such an effort was in keeping with his conception of Congregationalism. His denomination believed that "there always has been so there will be progress in doctrine." Though he urged caution and restraint in reevaluating belief, he was certain that progress would prove beneficial. "While we ought to make no rash innovation," he told Munger, "we ought to be willing to welcome all the light that breaks full from God's holy word." He encouraged efforts to arrange conferences and meetings of clergy to undertake "discussion of current questions in theology and biblical criticism."[17]

Indeed, even despite his disagreement with them, Gladden still met regularly with his fellow clergy. Their monthly gatherings offered an opportunity to discuss theology and the relationship between religion and political issues. Topics included "the relation of Christianity to the present Communistic movement," "what is the nature and design of punishment in God's moral government," and "what are the practical duties demanded by the times, of ministers and the educated classes generally."[18]

His continued attendance reflected Gladden's determination to reform his denomination from within. While he had supported David Swing, he objected to Swing's decision to leave the Presbyterian church rather than face appeal. "The duty of liberal men to stay in the church to which they belong—if they can be tolerated there—and, by kindness and patience and fidelity to the truth as they see it, to do what they can to enlighten and broaden the fellowship of those churches, has always appeared to me very plain," he noted. That is what he did in Springfield.[19]

Taking part in ongoing discussions soon prompted a new realization for Gladden. The conversations among the clergy inspired innovation and suggested ways in which the church might better engage with the modern world. But ministers were scared to take these conclusions back to their churches. Gladden noted that at one meeting, a "score of intelligent Congregational clergymen" all argued against telling their congregants about new research that suggested a verse in the epistle of John had been added later. "Not one of the twenty agreed with me in thinking that the fact could be safely stated" to the people in the pews. "They all admitted that the verse was spurious, but feared the effect of letting he people know a truth so disturbing."[20]

Decisions like those of his colleagues put churches in a downward spiral. When ministers did not explain new religious ideas to their congregants, churchgoers were left baffled as to why so many ministers around the country were rejecting what seemed to be long-established beliefs. This then caused uneducated church members to turn on clergy in theological disputes. In a letter to Munger, Gladden complained of how often "a minister's relation and obligations were determined and concluded by the vote of a flock of geese." Echoing a point raised in the *Independent*, he lamented that while clergy imbibed new knowledge about the age of the earth and human origins, Sunday School teachers carried on teaching children that God created the earth in seven days in 4004 BC.[21]

Gladden used the reputation he had built to bridge this divide between educated clergy and the congregations they assumed to be ignorant. His first attempt to do so came with a book, *Being a Christian: What It Means and How to Begin*, which he published in 1876. It was his first thorough exploration of liberal theology. The book marked a repudiation of revival-centric evangelical Protestantism and urged a more inclusive, understanding Christianity.

The response to *Being a Christian* persuaded Gladden that he had struck a chord with his message. One reader praised both its content and its "style so fresh," and observed that Gladden offered a needed message. "The sympathies of its author with the perplexities of inquiring souls" were "so strong and helpful, that the book cannot fail to be of great assistance to all for whom . . . it was written." Another reader cheered Gladden's message that complex theological doctrines were not essential to Christianity: "Men are finding out that God did not need Calvin to piece out his word." A third lauded Gladden's decision to avoid the complexities that marked most debates about liberal theology, writing, "It is an excellent service you have thus rendered in divesting the questions of much unnecessary obscurity and consequent difficulties." A fourth was even more direct. One of the strengths of the book was that it was "untheological."[22]

Nor was it just the already converted who appreciated Gladden's insights. A pastor lent a copy of *Being a Christian* to a man he was trying to bring into the church. The man found that Gladden's idea of conversion removed his barrier to joining. He reported especially liking "the idea that 'becoming a Christian was simply beginning to be a Christian,'" and "felt as if the book had been written expressly for him." By the end of his career, *Being a Christian* was Gladden's second most-read book. This delighted him, because it was one of his most personal as well, responding as it did not only to his congregants' questions but to his own. "I have been comforted in knowing that out of the perplexities of my boyhood, help has come to many who were seeking the way of life," he wrote.[23]

Being a Christian was just a part of Gladden's advocacy for religious liberalism. Unlike his colleagues in Springfield, Gladden fearlessly brought new ideas and perspectives to his pulpit. His sermons emphasized the same themes as *Being a Christian*. Indeed, his pulpit at North Church provided an even more systematic introduction to his liberal theology than his books did.

Key to Gladden's theology was the premise that religious ideas and institutions needed to change and progress with the times. Embracing the central tenet of the New Theology, Gladden asserted that as human knowledge grew, Christianity could not remain static. "The consensus of belief among us now is not what it once was; it is vastly different from what it once was," he wrote. "There has been progress in theology—a great deal of progress—during the last two hundred years."[24]

Given this evolving nature of religion, Christians should not base their faith in religious ideas that might change with time. The biggest mistake people made, Gladden argued, was equating religion with particular doctrines. "The devils are dogmatists," he declared. For one thing, statements of doctrine were inherently incomplete. But Christians were rarely willing to acknowledge the flaws in their favored creed or faith statement. Moreover, doctrines fell in and out of popularity. He noted that Protestants of his day rejected many ideas that had once been commonplace, including "the damnation of all the heathen, without exception" and "the damnation of some infants." Christians needed to accept that religious ideas changed, and that this was for the better.[25]

Beyond trapping religious people in outdated ways of thinking, an emphasis on doctrine needlessly separated Christians from one another. One particular problem with doctrines was the way in which they encouraged the existence of individual denominations. Each denomination became convinced that it had a monopoly on the truth. As Gladden saw happening around him, they then all sought to perpetuate themselves as the purest form of Christianity by dictating what individuals were to believe. This, Gladden insisted, got things backward. "The grace of God, the life of God, the truth of God are given always to individuals, never to organizations," he preached. Echoing his earlier emphasis on the role of prophets, he concluded that "all the progress that religion has made, has been through light that has been given to individuals, not to ecclesiastical bodies."[26]

The fundamental problem of denominations—beyond the fact that excessive commitment to them warped the message of Christianity—was that they contributed to the separation and division in society that Gladden decried. "Instead of seeking first the Kingdom of God," he complained, "the great majority of citizens . . . are seeking first either self promotion for themselves—or the success of the parties with which they have identified themselves." Those parties might be political organizations or denominational ones; either way, it diminished the common social bonds that needed reinforcement.[27]

Doctrines were a major problem, but they were not the only one. Religious rituals also changed over time and were an equally poor basis of faith. Gladden criticized those who emphasized rituals like baptism. They were focused on "the form of Christianity" rather than "its substance." In a dig at the emotion-driven revivals of his youth, he also said that "feelings . . . are uncertain and even delusive guides" and did not make someone a Christian.[28]

Gladden offered a far simpler standard for becoming a Christian: accepting Jesus. But even in this, he differed from many of his contemporaries. For him, the essence of Christianity was believing not *in* Jesus as a historical figure but *on* Jesus as "an ever-present Helper and Saviour." This formulation avoided turning Jesus into a mortal being with exemplary ethics but it also dodged the thorny debate of Christ's divinity.[29]

As his quip about emotion suggested, Gladden sharpened his attack against revivals. "Their method on the whole is a bad one," he declared of revivalists soon after Dwight Moody held a series of services in nearby Northfield, Massachusetts. Gladden forcefully rebuked the argument made by many revivalists that becoming a Christian required an intense, palpable transformation that followed emotional distress and suffering. Gladden found this view outrageous. "No delusion could be worse than this," he wrote. "You become a Christian by choosing the Christian life."[30]

Biblical followers of Jesus had simply followed after him, Gladden explained. "There is no account of their refusing to stir until some powerful impulse seized them," and the same should be true for contemporary Christians. A few people proved "so headstrong" that they could not become Christians "without a painful strife," Gladden conceded. But that did not mean "that anybody ought to imitate" their example. The idea popularized by revivalists "that suffering is a good thing in itself, that God is pleased to see us torture ourselves awhile before he consents to forgive us" caused immense harm.[31]

One consequence of this view, and a crucial innovation in his thought, was Gladden's insistence that people need not feel certain in their beliefs in order to become a Christian. Echoing Nancie Priest, who two decades earlier confessed that she wasn't sure she belonged in church, he noted the existence of "a multitude of sincere souls" who felt uncertainty about their state with God. Gladden urged people not to give in to doubt. "If you honestly think that you have done what you could to become a Christian, you have no right to doubt that you are a Christian."[32]

Gladden emphasized that doubt did not prevent someone from being a Christian. Indeed, well-meaning inquiry was "more pleasing to God than the blind and bigoted credulousness" of many churchgoers. Even the apostle Paul, Gladden noted, never achieved "perfect knowledge of religious truth." Religion by its nature dealt with the infinite. "If there is such a thing as a contradiction in terms you have it in a definition of the infinite." And if people could not come up with a permanent, definite description of religious belief, it followed that doubts and uncertainties would remain. "Theological questions," Gladden wrote, did not lead to conclusive "positive and final treatment."[33]

Gladden linked his consideration of doubt to his objection to defining Christianity by doctrine. In his view, many people's uncertainty stemmed not from doubt about Christianity itself but rather from skepticism of particular doctrines. He urged that how one lived one's life mattered more than the specifics of their beliefs. "This religion of Christ," he declared, "has one supreme concern and only one—and that is righteousness. The one thing that it wants of you is that you shall cease to do evil, and learn to do well." He added, "The result is the main thing after all." This was a pragmatic, results-focused definition of religion.[34]

The acceptance of doubt necessitated a crucial change in the behavior of most churchgoers—they needed to stop judging whether other people were sufficiently Christian. One of the hallmarks of nineteenth-century religious culture was the belief that every churchgoer was responsible for ensuring that their friends and neighbors lived good Christian lives. Gladden rejected this moral policing. "Every one of us must give account for himself unto God, and every one of us must find out for himself whether God's word is true," Gladden wrote. Religion was personal; no one could judge another individual's religious experience. "It is impossible for us to reach and tabulate the facts of other men's lives, because it is impossible for us to know what the mental experiences of other men are," he observed. Christians should not try.[35]

As Gladden privileged the religious life over religious doctrine, his theology became increasingly focused on society. This newfound emphasis was developing slowly, and it was imperfectly achieved in Springfield. Gladden still conceived of sin in fairly individual terms rather than as the systemic, social phenomenon he would eventually describe. Sin manifested itself in bad personal traits, such as the long-held deadly sins of anger, envy, and greed. The primary purpose of Jesus's mission, Gladden argued, was to help people overcome their sins.[36]

Still, even in this somewhat conventional discussion of sin, there were hints of new directions in Gladden's thought. For one, his suggestion that Christians minimize their judgment was echoed in his assertion that ministers spent too much time warning people about the possibility of future punishment for their sins. He had begun to question "the usefulness of a constant iteration of threatening." Urging people to love God and each other was good. Scaring them with the prospect of future punishment was not. (Pushing ministers to avoid the subject of future punishment had the added pragmatic benefit of keeping them from getting into arguments with colleagues about hell, thereby avoiding the strife that plagued Springfield-area churches.)[37]

Even more indicative of his future thought, when Gladden provided examples of poor moral behavior in *Being a Christian*, they all centered on economic issues: one was about a person who defrauded a bank, another about a dishonest contractor who built a shoddy house, the third about a purveyor of adulterated food. In years to come, the need to combat economic injustice would become for Gladden a central requirement of Christianity.[38]

Crucially, despite his discussion of sin and corruption, Gladden's liberal theology emphasized his positive view of human nature and optimism about humanity's potential. He had long praised "the curiosity with which the human race is endowed so amply" as the "spur of action and the motive of much high investigation." This high view of human nature received its strongest confirmation in his emphatic belief that humanity could bring the kingdom of heaven to earth. He dismissed a long-standing dispute about the word "Zion" and whether it meant heaven or "the Kingdom of God established on the earth." For Gladden, they need not be different. The kingdom of God existed in both places. It was up to Christians to eliminate the differences between the two.[39]

A final concern that emerged in Gladden's preaching at Springfield, and one that he would revisit through the remainder of his career, was the lack of reverence found in churches. This was not precisely a theological point, but it was a central part of his message about the needed qualities of modern religion. Some of his complaints seem trivial. He lamented, for example, that "the songs of the Sunday school" were all of the "'Rig-a-jig-jig and-away-we-go' variety." Nor did adult singers escape his focus. He admitted to being "greatly pained" by members of the church choir, who failed to demonstrate reverence with their "unseemly behavior." In a memo to church leaders, he remarked on "a great deal of whispering and writing notes and communication of various sorts." Moreover, "when the heads of the congregation are bowed in prayer and every part of the house is still as death," the choir annoyed him "with whispering and rustling overhead."[40]

Beneath this grousing lay a serious point. In the modern world, with less time given to concern for the supernatural and religious matters, people had lost their sense of awe and with it their ability to be reverent. Reverence in churches might produce a greater sense of the sacred in everyday life, which seemed to be missing in the ever-busier United States.

Gladden's tenure at Springfield proved successful, though not entirely satisfying to him. As he had done for years, he reflected on his professional successes and failures in a letter to his friend "dear Mose" Tyler. "The church has been steadily gaining," Gladden reported in 1881, his seventh year in New England. The "congregations and income" were both "larger this year than ever before" and his "local influence is increasing wholesomely." During the late 1870s and early 1880s, he also saw liberal theology take stronger root in New England. A "larger liberty" of religious thought existed, marking a far cry from the intolerance he encountered when he arrived in North Adams a decade-and-a-half earlier.[41]

Yet all was not well. Money still weighed heavily on Gladden's mind. His daughter Alice was attending Smith College, while his son Fred was soon to begin study at Amherst, and Helen and George were not far behind. The church had considerable outstanding debt, and payments on it consumed his salary. "I am obliged to scratch with my pen continually to keep the wolf from the door," he wrote. Though financial obligation might have driven some of the pen-scratching, Gladden clearly enjoyed the ever-growing fame that it brought him. He was increasingly recognized not only as a prominent supporter of liberal theology, but more particularly as someone able to "take a comprehensive view of the whole field" and offer a broad synthesis and explanation of progressive religion.[42]

This recognition brought Gladden to the attention of the First Congregational Church of Columbus, Ohio. Late in 1882, that church invited him to become its pastor, its members motivated by "the fact that most of us have known you through your writings for many years." They had found his work "sound, practical, cordial, healthful and helpful." Gladden accepted the offer and traded the rolling hills of the Connecticut River Valley for the flat plains of central Ohio. His decision hit his Springfield congregants hard. They noted that their church was "called to pass through a very severe trial" with Gladden's departure.[43]

In making this move, Gladden was part of a larger trend. In the closing decades of the nineteenth century, the Midwest supplanted the northeast as the center of much of American life. Ohio loomed particularly large in politics. The winners of the 1868, 1872, 1876, 1880, 1896, and 1900 presidential elections all hailed from the state. The potential for Gladden's influence in such a place was not lost on his friends. Cornell University president Andrew Dickson White observed, "You are most happily placed in the center of such an active state as Ohio which . . . is destined to affect the thinking and practice of this country probably more than any of its sister states for many years to come."[44]

Gladden had a decidedly mixed reaction to his new church and city. On the positive side, he observed that "the people are as cordial as they can be." They provided such a welcome that "a more generous and enthusiastic greeting I could not have wished for." The church also was a pleasant departure from his previous pastorates, which were marked by "a slow and laborious start." In Columbus, the congregation was "very large" at the outset and he felt "sure of a strong body of faithful men and women."[45]

On the other hand, the new city presented difficulties beyond missing "the old faces and the old voices and the old friends" of New England. "We did not expect paradise and we haven't found it," he declared bluntly. The use of soft coal made for an unpleasant natural environment. Other issues reflected Columbus's relatively recent development in comparison to the towns of New England. "Few of its streets were paved, its lighting was primitive," and its architecture "was not a delight to the eyes." In short, he told Theodore Munger, "There is work enough to do. I am only beginning to get some dim and partial notions of the work to be done." But there was also opportunity. Though the city never went through an explosive boom in population, it did grow rapidly, from just over fifty thousand people at the time of Gladden's arrival in 1883 to around two hundred thousand in 1900.[46]

In this new environment, Gladden pushed himself to cultivate new skills as a preacher. He experimented with preaching extemporaneously at his evening services rather than using a prepared text for the sermon. "That is work," he wrote to Munger, "but I am beginning to enjoy it." Gladden's happiness in Columbus led him to remain there, despite occasional bouts of wanderlust that led him to consider other pastorates.[47]

Gladden recognized that his first task was to attract more people to church. While overall attendance at services was strong, one notable segment of society was not well represented: young people, and, more specifically, young men of the professional classes. Gladden sent a circular letter to congregants asking them to inquire of "non-church-going acquaintances" their reasons for keeping away. The results were telling. Some had simply "grown tired of it" and enjoyed doing other things on Sunday, while others complained of the church being too cold and worship being too sedentary. Another found "the benefits to be derived from . . . a church organization were not apparent," and others noted that "in respect to practical every-day righteousness . . . attending church had nothing to do with . . . goodness or happiness."[48]

These responses echoed a commonplace phenomenon. During the second half of the nineteenth century, Protestant churches more and more came to be seen as the domain of women. Men found a social outlet elsewhere, particularly in the increasingly popular fraternal lodges.[49]

This reality prompted Gladden to publish *Young Men and the Churches* a few years after arriving in Columbus. The book was significant in acknowledging frankly that organized religion was not popular with "society people." Gladden had relatively little sympathy for some of the complaints about church, including its lack of excitement, but he recognized some substantive criticisms offered by people who refused to attend.[50]

Most notably, Gladden once again acknowledged his frustration with the expectations fostered by a revival culture. Far too often, people were told that going to church would result in a sudden personal transformation. He believed that those young people who stopped attending church because they'd grown tired of hearing people get emotional and "profess changes of sentiment and character which in the nature of things could not take place" had a point. This understanding of churchgoing was, in Gladden's mind, "one of the saddest features of current religious history." He urged that anyone who had "imbibed the idea that religion consists of pleasurable emotions and magical changes" ought to find "a more rational and practical" conception of it.[51]

Gladden also reiterated that joining a church did not mean conforming to every belief held by members of that congregation. He repeated his long-standing support for intellectual freedom in the church. "There are many truths of religion," he insisted, "and many subjects in which the church is interested, upon which one can freely express himself, without any violation of his natural reticence respecting his own spiritual state."[52]

This advice seemed especially relevant in matters of doctrine, and Gladden again urged readers not to obsess about specific points of theology. "Be careful," he counseled, "lest you identify Christianity with what is no longer part of Christianity, and reject it because of outworn garments of philosophy which it once wore, but has now cast off." There was enormous risk in people mistaking old doctrines for the core of Christianity. Such things were superficial and mattered little for church membership. Nor should disagreements with church members about still commonly held doctrines matter. He suggested that most people would still find more grounds for agreement than disagreement, and he urged the benefit of "ignoring your differences and walking with them as far as you are agreed."[53]

While Gladden could dismiss doctrines that people found objectionable as either outdated or nonessential to Christian faith, there was still the problem of biblical scholarship. With each passing year, additional information about the Bible became known that seemed to call into question commonly held beliefs about scripture, and with it, Christianity. In response, he published *Who Wrote the Bible?* in 1891. It ultimately became his best-selling book.[54]

With this book, Gladden hoped "to put into compact and popular form, for the benefit of intelligent readers, the principal facts which scholars are now generally agreed concerning the literary history of the Bible." Like his earlier works, this book reflected a concern that the clergy had a new view of scripture that they were scared to share with congregants. "Many facts about the Bible are now known by intelligent ministers which their congregations do not hear," he wrote. This stemmed from an "anxious and not unnatural feeling" that "the faith of the people in the Bible would be shaken if the facts were known." Washington Gladden remained steadfast in his belief that while contemporary scholarship on the Bible might bring a "shock of surprise," it ultimately would not shake peoples' faith if they properly understood the Bible. On the contrary, he believed that knowledge would make faith stronger.[55]

Who Wrote the Bible? proceeded through the Old and New Testaments, presenting a methodical study of the author and key themes of each book. The approach was the same sort he took in all his discussions of sensitive topics. Gladden explained the "natural history" that led to the modern Bible coming together through vagaries and accidents of historical process. Much "has been lost by this heedless world," he observed, while "quite a number of books have at one time or another been regarded as sacred and numbered among the Holy Scriptures." This evolving canon, Gladden insisted, was the result of human decision. "No supernatural methods have been employed" to determine what books went in and what went out.[56]

Gladden rejected claims in scripture that challenged common sense. In particular, he had little patience with people who held to various texts' claims of authorship—that Moses wrote the first five books of the Bible in their entirety, for example, despite the fact that they chronicled his death and its aftermath. He saw such people as akin to "those who maintain the sun still revolves around the earth." Nor did Gladden spare the New Testament from his critique. "There is no promise of infallibility" from its authors, he observed, and "there is no hint anywhere that any special illumination would be given to them when they took the pen into their hand."[57]

More serious than authorship was the actual content of the Bible. God had not protected the text from errors creeping in, Gladden insisted, and scripture contained "mistakes of a very serious nature." Some of the most serious errors were those related to ethics, which he called on readers to dismiss. It was the "human element" that wrote the Bible that was responsible for tales such as the one of God killing seventy thousand people just to punish King David. "When we find in these old writings statements which represent God as perfidious and unjust, we are not to try to 'harmonize' them with other statements," he wrote. "We are simply to set them aside as the views of a dark age."[58]

Indeed, it was the Christian traditionalists who tried to justify these seemingly immoral messages whom Gladden found most detrimental to the cause of religion. By twisting themselves into knots to explain unethical parts of the text as messages from God, such traditionalists "generally increase the incredibility of the narrative." In so doing, these "ultra-conservative critics" played right into "the hands of the anti-Christian critics." What Gladden found especially galling was the fact that people who viewed the Bible this way approached the text with their own agenda. They "made up their theories of the Bible out of their ideas about God, and have then gone to fit the facts of the Bible to their preconceived theories." In Gladden's view, it was imperative that Christians make no effort to defend such bad theology. "When we are asked to believe doctrines which imply that God is unjust," he wrote, "we ought with indignation to reject them."[59]

There was an even larger point that Gladden wanted to emphasize. People sympathetic to liberal theology had erred, he argued, in allowing themselves to be baited into debates about the literal meaning of scripture. The best example of this was the book of Jonah. The orthodox had made the story about God's decision to have the fish swallow Jonah, and liberals had responded by debating the plausibility of the account. In other words, religious conservatives had set the terms of debate and progressives had gone along with it. "In their dispute over the question whether Jonah did really compose that psalm in the belly of the fish, with his head festooned with seaweed," he complained, "they have almost wholly overlooked the great lessons of fidelity to duty, of the universal divine fatherhood, and the universal brotherhood, which the story so beautifully enforces." That loss of the ethical message was the greatest cost when liberals allowed themselves to be goaded into debates about the meaning of scripture.[60]

Who Wrote the Bible? epitomized the middle path that Gladden steered in his liberalism between conservative traditionalism and free thought. For all his concerns about elements of scripture, he refused to dismiss the entire Bible as myth as agnostics did. The text still had considerable value. Biblical writers, for all their faults, "possessed a degree of inspiration" that far exceeded the inspiration given "to any other religious leaders who have lived on earth." Readers appreciated Gladden's approach. One husband and wife expressed gratitude to Gladden for helping them be "set free from the traditional view in which we were brought up" while nevertheless sustaining their faith.[61]

Hidden in Gladden's analysis of scripture was a theme that had come to occupy an increasingly central part of his thought: economic issues. In discussions of the prophetic books of the Bible, he emphasized that the books were not concerned with predicting the future. Rather, they were focused on the present, and specifically the economic reality of the present. "When kings become profligate and faithless, when priests grow formal and greedy, when the rich waxed extortionate and tyrannical, these men of God arose to denounce the transgressors and threaten them with divine vengeance."[62]

The role of the prophets, in Gladden's mind, was not just to warn societies against uncontrolled wealth and corruption, but to direct that warning to religious institutions. "The tendency of religion, to become merely ritual, to divorce itself from righteousness, is inveterate," he wrote. "The religious 'machine' is always in the same danger of becoming corrupt and mischievous as is the political 'machine'; the man with the sledge-hammer who will smash it and fling it to the junk-pile has a work to do in every generation." The man with the sledgehammer was the biblical prophet.[63]

As he settled into his sixties, Gladden did so with the knowledge that he had become one of the leading proponents of the theological liberalism that had become increasingly popular in American Protestantism. More importantly, people responded favorably. A visitor to his church praised Gladden's sermon as providing "more food for thought" than any he had heard in recent memory. A minister wrote to report that he had all Gladden's books. "Your name and words are often on my lips in public address," this clergyman noted.[64]

Three decades after he had harbored anxieties whether he would earn a good reputation as an intellectual leader, Gladden had emerged as an undisputed figure through his popularization of progressive religious values. In 1899, he published *How Much Is Left of the Old Doctrines?*, which subjected traditional Christian beliefs to the analysis that *Who Wrote the Bible?* gave to scripture. It offered his most forceful assertion that "as the generations pass, and men learn more about themselves and the world in which they live . . . their point of view changes, and their doctrines are modified by their growing knowledge."[65]

Despite his stature, Gladden's anxiety did still emerge from time to time. "I am not without disturbing questions as to whether it all amounts to anything—whether what I do is at all worthwhile," he confided to Munger. But, unlike in earlier years, "such doubts do not greatly trouble me, for I know all is going well."[66]

Part of what convinced Gladden of his success was that he increasingly identified himself with the biblical prophet and acted accordingly.

In the final decades of his career, Gladden decided that he, too, would become the religious man with the sledgehammer.

6

REFORMER

In 1900, at the age of sixty-four, Washington Gladden did something new: he ran for public office. Despite his long-standing involvement in civic life, he had never sought an elected position. That changed when he entered the race for a seat on Columbus's city council.

Gladden had learned of a questionable deal between current city council members, including the one who represented his own ward, and the companies that provided city services. The public officials intended to demand bribes from these companies in exchange for a renewal of their contracts with the municipality. Gladden was angered by the apparent corruption. He announced his candidacy in a letter sent to all the city's newspapers. He did not campaign. He did not canvass. In fact, he reported—apparently with some exaggeration—"I scarcely mentioned the matter in conversation to anyone." Despite this low-key approach, he won the race on the strength of his reputation. In contrast to his predecessor, he did not view this position as a chance to augment his income. For the duration of his term, he returned his salary to the city each month.[1]

For someone like Gladden who spent much of his time thinking lofty thoughts about weighty subjects, the work of the city council proved quite mundane. Among his major accomplishments was a campaign to improve the city's water supply. Anxieties about the safety of Columbus's water predated Gladden's move from Springfield. Residents feared that the rudimentary filtration system of "gravel and sand" would do nothing to prevent "Cholera yellow fever and like diseases." Largely through his efforts, the city developed a filtration system, thanks to which typhoid all but disappeared from the region.[2]

Much of the council's other work involved renegotiating the city's contracts with companies providing municipal services: streetcars, natural gas, and water. In these negotiations, Gladden advocated for city residents against what he perceived as corporate greed. Despite the streetcar company's claim that it could not lower its rates, Gladden and the council pushed the fare cost down by a cent and a half.[3]

The principal lesson Gladden learned on the council was that seemingly trivial government decisions had a huge effect on the lives and finances of ordinary people. A reduction in transit fare might appear "a small matter to contend for." In reality, however, "it is such small matters that make a difference, with people of small incomes, between health and feeble-ness, between hope and despondency." A company "carrying fifty million passengers in a year adds to its gains half a million dollars by adding one cent to its fares," he added. But what seemed an insignificant change in fare caused "the comfort and welfare of the laboring classes" to be "greatly reduced."[4]

And such things multiplied, producing the staggering income inequality that had troubled Gladden ever since he first witnessed it in New York in the early 1870s. "When a few cents a day are added to the cost of living by very slight unnecessary additions to the price of carfare, or gas, or electricity, or oil, or water . . . the burdens of the poor are aggravated that the revenues of the rich may be enlarged," he wrote. This was ultimately the source of "our worst inequalities of conditions." Government at all levels needed to combat this inequality, and churches needed to help.[5]

Gladden's election to the city council marked the culmination of years of increased involvement in politics. Since arriving in Columbus, he had spoken and written on political and social issues. His theology of engagement with the world led him to direct, personal action. Gladden became an outspoken advocate of labor rights and a vocal critic of large corporations. He urged temperance reform in order to curb the abuse of alcohol in the interest of preventing disruption of family life. He also supported anticorruption efforts designed to improve municipal government.

Concern about social issues occupied an ever-increasing place in Gladden's thought. He became an ardent follower of Brooklyn's reform-oriented mayor, Seth Low, whom Gladden described as "one of the brightest, soundest and sharpest young men in the country." In the mid-1880s, Low embodied the ideals of urban reform circulating through the nation, and he supported policies like expanded public education and the elimination of patronage in government jobs. Gladden was so taken with Low's work to centralize Brooklyn's government in the office of mayor that he invited Low to Columbus to speak at First Church, and the two corresponded thereafter.[6]

Gladden's interest in social issues further deepened in the summer of 1888 when he and Jennie traveled to Europe. They made a brief stop in Scotland and explored the continent for a few weeks, but spent the bulk of their time in and around London. There, they enjoyed the culture available to them in the city's libraries and museums. "One wanders for hours and days through rooms filled with books, pictures, antiquities," he observed happily. But it was also a work trip. Gladden noted his wish to use the trip "to study the social problem," especially the way that England cared for its poor and working class. He was particularly impressed by how the cultural institutions he visited offered opportunities for them. "The provision that England . . . makes for the education and amusement of the people (for all these . . . institutions are free) is most magnificent," Gladden wrote. While he felt the US education system was better than England's in some respects, free access to museums and libraries showed that "there is another and higher sort of education in which she far outstrips us."[7]

As a result of his intensive study, Gladden emerged as one of the nation's leading authorities on social issues during the final decades of his career. He joined with other ministers and lay sociologists who made it their mission to improve the lives of Americans. It was through his efforts to give a religious justification to efforts to structurally reform society that Gladden became recognized as one of the pioneers of the Social Gospel movement.

To this day, Gladden remains best known for his advocacy on behalf of the working class. His own background undoubtedly inspired his sympathy for workers. His mother remained on the edge of poverty for the remainder of her life, and from time to time had to ask her grown son to "spare a little to help me" when emergencies arose. In the years before George was killed at Cold Harbor, Gladden watched his younger brother struggle enormously with work and money. In 1860, George incurred debts that would take the better part of a year to clear. "Imagine yourself in my situation a little while—no education—no money—in debt, with no means of paying, and nary prospect—health failing, hope long since departed and then after having failed, not once or twice, but a score of times, to extricate yourself and not only failed, failed, but sunk deeper every time," George wrote, attempting to make his older brother understand his circumstances.[8]

Awareness of others' financial hardship did not initially prompt much sympathy from Gladden, however. Early in his career, he espoused the popular view that people got what they deserved based on the effort they put in. "Those who do not work have no right to play," he wrote in one of his early books. In another, he proclaimed that "idleness is . . . immoral," and "a lazy man is not a moral man." Poverty, in Gladden's early view, was not the result of systemic or structural forces but rather personal failing. In his younger years, this view led him to support charity for the poor only if it was accompanied by a strict work requirement.[9]

During the second half of Gladden's life, circumstances forced him to reconsider this perspective. For one thing, the very nature of work changed around him as the United States underwent large-scale industrialization. The number of factories in the nation doubled during the 1860s alone and continued to grow for the remainder of the century. This, in turn, changed how people worked. Wage labor—that is, working for an employer who established the rate of pay and controlled workers' schedules—became a permanent way of life. Whereas it once represented a temporary stage that men passed through on the way to self-employment, more and more it became the only possible employment. By 1870, there were more wage workers than self-employed individuals in the United States for the first time in the nation's history. Ordinary Americans no longer controlled their work as they once did.[10]

The upheaval caused by a changing economy was made worse by the quarter-century of economic disorder that began in 1873. Following the depression that Gladden lived through in New York and Springfield, the economy went through two decades of boom-and-bust cycles. These years witnessed deflation, downward pressure on wages, and diminished returns for capital investment. In some parts of the country, as many as one-third of workers endured some period of unemployment during bad years.[11]

The concept of unemployment was itself new. When most workers were self-employed there might be more or less productive times, but they still had their jobs. But being dismissed by an employer for lack of work represented a new experience brought about by the new reality of wage labor.[12]

The good years of the boom-bust cycle did not undo the pain of the hard ones. Despite a small recovery in the late 1870s, American workers were worse off in 1880 than they had been in 1860. Things got worse over the next decade. "Every one of these industrial depressions pushes a multitude of families into the abyss of pauperism," Gladden worriedly observed in the wake of yet another depression that began in 1893. The number of Americans needing financial assistance was "becoming ominously large."[13]

This volatility laid bare the nation's rampant economic inequality. If all Americans faced hardship equally, upheaval might have been avoided. But as large segments of the population sank further into despair, the nation's wealthiest grew even richer. "There has been an enormous increase of wealth; but the *proportion* of that wealth that has fallen to the laboring-classes is very small, and it is constantly growing smaller," Gladden wrote. What had happened in New York in the 1860s and 1870s was now happening everywhere: the middle class was being driven downward. "The opportunity of the small capitalist or the small manufacturer lessens year by year," to the point that the working class seemed on the verge of becoming a class without any property. Such a consequence, he warned, posed a grave threat to democracy.[14]

It was in this context that Gladden began to consider economic and labor issues seriously. What started as a series of lectures in Springfield was soon published as *Working People and Their Employers*. The book, as even Gladden later conceded, dealt largely in stereotypes and showed his poor grasp of the modern economy. He glibly dismissed workers' anxieties about technology's role in displacing them or reducing them to unskilled labor. He also idealized older, rural patterns of life, suggesting that many of the nation's ills could be healed if only young people stayed on the farm. Echoing his long-standing concern about idleness, he repeatedly suggested patronizingly that many financial woes could be solved if working people would attend fewer circuses and minstrel shows.[15]

At this point in his career, Gladden placed blame equally on workers and employers. If management was unfair, laborers were unreasonable. His solutions were just as glib. Emphasizing that Christian teachings "are not . . . very radical" compared to other solutions, he urged the Golden Rule as the basis for better relationships. He suggested things might improve if people only "love your neighbors as yourselves" and "put yourselves in their places now and then." This bred skepticism of unions, which were gaining favor among workers as a way to even the playing field with employers. "I have no doubt that such combinations of laborers are often unprofitable" and "result in more loss than gain," he wrote, though he notably conceded they were not "morally wrong." In practice, however, he found most union members to be "ignorant men." They had, in his view, "fanatical and absurd views" and "want to win by revolution, or not at all."[16]

Unsurprisingly, Gladden's assessment proved more popular with employers than employees. Business owners and managers cheered the minister, hailing him as "a public benefactor" and urging that "the book should have the largest possible circulation." But even Gladden came to see the flaws in how his book treated workers. He later regretted that "the treatment of the unions is critical rather than cordial; the evils which they harbor are magnified; the higher purposes they serve are imperfectly recognized." Still, despite its flaws, Gladden's initial attempt to address economic and labor issues highlighted several themes that would remain central in his thinking.[17]

The first was quite straightforward: Christians had a moral obligation to combat economic inequality and to ease the plight of struggling workers. Gladden urged "the importance of bringing the New Testament to bear directly upon the matters now in dispute" between employers and employees. The economic questions of the day were "moral questions" that "touch the very marrow of that religion of good-will of which Christ was the founder." Because "the questions of social science" and "political economy" raised "moral questions" as well, "the pulpit must have something constructive to say about them."[18]

Gladden's second crucial recognition was that churches and ministers had the power—and the obligation—to challenge the increasing separation and impersonal interaction in modern business. The period between 1860 and 1900 witnessed the rise of the modern corporation, in which the business was controlled by stockholders and owners who rarely, if ever, interacted with their workers. "This tendency to separate the capitalist and the laborer, either through the intervention of corporations, or through the building up of immense industrial concerns by individuals or firms, is one of the things to be deplored and resisted by all employers that mean to govern themselves by the Christian law," Gladden wrote. It was time for both sides to recognize that "justice and equity, in the New Testament sense, are not collective or impersonal virtues."[19]

A third realization pointed to Gladden's future sympathies with the working class. For all of his paternalism and judgment toward workers, Gladden recognized that the existing system favored employers more often than not. The wage system was based on "the law of nature," which seemed to be "the survival of the strongest." Until that changed, workers would suffer.[20]

Gladden had ample reason to revisit his views in the years after his move to Columbus. As inequality worsened and the economy continued its roller-coaster trajectory, strikes grew more common and more violent. In 1886, one of the most tumultuous years for labor upheaval, six hundred thousand Americans participated in at least one of 1,400 different strikes. In Chicago that summer, a rally to support strikers collapsed into violence when someone threw a bomb into the crowd. At least a dozen people were killed, with many more injured.[21]

Gladden came into closer personal contact with strikes as well. The Hocking Valley coal strike of 1884 happened just outside of Columbus, and two executives of the company involved were also members of his church. Poverty also grew more difficult for Gladden to ignore. He noted in early 1892 that "persons supported in whole or in part by the state increased in Ohio 145 per cent in 8 years" and fully one-eighth of the residents of Columbus had required assistance in the previous year.[22]

Drawing from research from the professionalizing fields of social science, Gladden came to recognize poverty and related social issues as consequences of systemic, structural problems. "Enormous inequalities of condition and possessions," he wrote, had bred decidedly un-Christian "tempers and sentiments." The biggest problem remained the growing gap between the wealthy and everyone else. "The spectacle of wealth and want steadily increasing side by side, wealth growing more insolent and want more hopeless" fostered feelings of "discontent and bitterness."[23] Gone, too, was the prospect of upward mobility for most workers. "The working man of former times," Gladden wrote, "might easily be his own employer," but now workers had "no working capital" and were entirely at the whim of bosses.[24]

As he recognized this new reality, Gladden grew more sympathetic to workers and supportive of the unions they formed to improve their conditions. "I think that the trades unions are not so great sinners," he wrote to a churchgoer. This correspondent, a prominent Columbus citizen, had offered many of the critiques of unions that Gladden himself had previously made. He lamented their insistence on a set wage for all employees and their threats to strike when even an incompetent employee was dismissed. Gladden conceded there might be "a degree of injustice" in the union's method. But that was excusable. "Some measure of unfairness is always connected with war," he wrote, "and the wage system, based on competition alone, is war."[25]

Gladden expanded on this bleak view of labor relations and his growing sympathy for organized labor in several series of sermons and lectures during the 1880s and 1890s. One, a Sunday evening sermon series in Columbus, was subsequently published in the *Century* magazine and in the book *Applied Christianity*. Others, in New Haven and Chicago, formed the basis for his books *Tools and the Man* and *Social Facts and Forces*. Within the span of a few years, he had become a national leader on labor issues.

These speeches and articles all reflected Gladden's newfound conviction that Christians must better understand and address economic reality. He had clearly seen the error of his former view that the old, rural, free labor order might be restored. Factories and corporations were here to stay. How churches dealt with the new reality would prove critical in determining their future influence in society. Workers "would have their attitude towards the church determined by the way in which it dealt" with their rights. And so far, he noted in an observation that echoed critiques from workers themselves, the church's record was not good.[26]

Gladden reaffirmed his earlier argument about economic issues being moral ones. But he employed ever more urgent language to do so.

Issues of work and money were central in people's lives. If churches were to have any moral authority, they needed to speak about economics or else become irrelevant. "Economic relations are found underlying and conditioning almost everything we do," he wrote. "If industry and business are beyond Christ's jurisdiction, really not much is left to him."[27]

Indeed, he suggested that it was Christians' refusal to live by their principles that created the messy situation in which the country found itself. It was because people assumed that "loving our neighbors was only for Sundays and missionary contributions and charitable situations" and not for everyday life that national life had so deteriorated. "The want of a Christian temper has brought us into this trouble," he mused. Only "the cultivation of a Christian temper" would "bring us out of it."[28]

Though his former paternalism occasionally crept to the surface, by the 1890s Gladden's loyalties emphatically lay with workers. "I am strongly inclined to take the workingman's view," he wrote. He noted that his "close observation of the conditions of life among the working classes" convinced him that things were getting worse for them. "All men who hate oppression," he proclaimed, "are on their side."[29]

No one had a greater opportunity to ease labor tensions than members of the clergy, who occupied a social position that would let them act as mediators. But for that to happen, clergy needed to follow in Gladden's steps. They not only needed to study the issue but become acquainted with people on both sides of it as well. The minister must "know something about the labor question," Gladden wrote, but more than that "he needs to know the men who are wrestling with this question." The "human beings" were as important as the "economic theories," and "the minister needs to know what he can of both."[30]

Gladden went beyond rhetoric and urged practical remedies, all of which involved increased government oversight and greater protection for organized labor. To defend state intervention, he invoked a Christian theory by which "all property is held in trust for society," and "there is no such thing as absolute ownership." In other words, "every possessor of wealth, no matter how lawfully he may have gained it, holds it as a steward or trustee, and is bound to use it for the best interest of the society in which he lives."[31]

His conviction that corporate wealth be used for the greater good resulted from Gladden's keen recognition that public contributions made that wealth possible. He observed that for successful businesses, "the government has been cooperating with you" and "has been aiding you in your work, by furnishing you protection." Because wealth could not be claimed to be "the fruit of . . . unaided labor," the wealthy owed "the state some return."[32] By the same token, the state could justifiably intervene when the wealthy stopped using land or resources for the general good. "The soundest jurisprudence makes the right of the state superior to the right of any private proprietor," he wrote, adding, "the right of private proprietors cannot be allowed to override or obstruct the rights of the whole people."[33]

In the spirit of protecting people's rights, Gladden advocated a number of policies the government should enact. These included a ban on child labor, limits to work hours, and mandatory safety inspections of workplaces. Most significantly, he urged government take control of "all industries which are virtual monopolies," such as railroads and utilities. Public ownership would grant members of the community a stake in key businesses. This would, in turn, keep the businesses from placing "heavy burdens on the necks of the producing classes" with "shifty financiering and corrupt bargaining with politicians." Doing so would provide structural reform that would prevent the case-by-case bargaining that prompted Gladden to run for city council.[34]

Along with his advocacy of a greater role for government in economic matters, Gladden abandoned his opposition to labor unions. This was a significant step for someone who traveled in elite circles in the nineteenth century. As wage labor became more common, Americans embraced the concept of contract freedom to sustain the belief that people had control of their work. In other words, if men could no longer be self-employed, they could at least control the terms of their contract.[35]

For obvious reasons, contract freedom hardly meant freedom. Americans needed work, especially in bad economic times. Circumstances often forced the acceptance of any employment at whatever terms were offered. Nevertheless, elites maintained that contract freedom was sufficient. They attacked unions as coercive bodies that forced men to join and interfered with individuals' rights to freely enter into contracts. Elites also highlighted the violence that often accompanied strikes. Given these attitudes, it is hardly surprising that no legal protections existed for unions. In rare cases where laws giving protection to workers were enacted, courts frequently struck them down.[36]

Gladden clung to enough free labor ideology that he rejected so-called closed shops that made union membership obligatory. "Workmen who seek to prevent men from procuring employment because they do not belong to a trades-union," were, in his view, "unjust" and "tyrannical."[37]

In other ways, though, Gladden departed from many in his social circle. He recognized the important role that unions played in leveling the playing field. Workers should have "perfect equality" with employers in negotiations, and unions helped to achieve it. Moreover, he argued that occasional actions that reflected poorly on unions did not undercut their right to exist. If the standard for judging whether an organization should exist was whether or not it ever committed violence, he wryly noted, unscrupulous big businesses were sufficient reason to prevent the formation of large corporations.[38]

As Gladden grew more sympathetic toward labor unions, he became increasingly critical of large corporations. He denounced their "enormous capabilities of evil." In particular, he argued that when the "demon of avarice is let loose," the "safeguards of virtue" and "restraints on lawlessness" that kept individuals in check were "much less efficient in the case of corporations." Corporations, he wrote, had "no soul" and "no conscience." Ethical obligations that individuals would feel if they acted on their own no longer troubled businessmen who "hide themselves behind the corporation."[39]

Gladden experienced the disparity in ethics between individuals and corporations when serving on the Columbus city council. The company that supplied the city's natural gas insisted that it needed to raise rates or else it would be unable to supply the city. "The men who gave me positive assurance" on the subject "were men on whose word I could have relied explicitly in any transaction between man and man," he recalled. But it turned out they were lying in the context of a business transaction involving their corporation. Despite the men's assurances to the contrary, the company was able to continue providing service at the same rate. "As representatives of a corporation dealing with a city a different rule of morality" applied. The lesson for Gladden was that a corporation "need not be expected to tell the truth," despite the character of those who led it.[40]

In Gladden's view, this aggrandizement of corporate power reflected nothing short of the failure of American ideals. The nation had set aside its democratic principles in "permitting the strong to oppress the weak." He suggested that modern businesses represented "the most stupendous aggregations of power known to history." Not only did these massive corporations have the power to "despoil the people," but they also had the ability "by corrupt means to pervert the government." In so doing, they could essentially take control of the one institution that had the power to protect working Americans and their families.[41]

While he viewed organized labor as a much-needed counterbalance to corporations, Gladden worried about the longer-term effect of an economy defined by competition and conflict between workers and employers. A focus on the well-being of just oneself, or one's family, or one's union could not work in an interconnected world.

Ultimately, he believed the solution lay in emphasizing the "solidarity of human interests," and this was where churches could play a critical role. "Every man's interests are bound up with the interests of every other man," Gladden wrote. Consequently, religious leaders must help people "learn to guide our conduct by social aims" with a focus on "how it will affect the general welfare." Doing so might substantively change the economy rather than providing piecemeal solutions.[42]

For his part, Gladden offered cooperative enterprise as the solution. Economics driven by competition were an "enormous waste of the common resources" and destructive of "the good will and mutual trust in which all human welfare is grounded." He argued that cooperation is the heart of Christianity, and that the "corner-stone of Christian ethics" is belief in "the absolute unity of human interests." If people were guided by Christian principles, it would be an "impossibility that any social class should rise by depressing another social class."[43]

The mission of Christians needed to be a new economic model built on these principles. "The logic of Christianity must lead on to a higher and more equitable" relationship "than that which is established by the wage system," Gladden wrote. He anticipated that such a model would solve the problem of income inequality. A society built on this kind of mutual understanding would not tolerate "such enormous accumulations in the hands of individuals" as had marked the "social disease" of the previous few decades.[44]

In practice, this would mean that in addition to their wages, workers would become "partners" and "associates" with a stake in their company. In addition to their wages, each worker would receive a dividend of the profits "proportioned to the amount of his earnings." Such a prospect would acknowledge that "the workingman has an interest in the business" and would overcome the "unsympathetic if not unfriendly relations" on both sides.[45]

Gladden's evolving sympathy for workers pushed him to soften his views of socialism. During the late nineteenth century, socialists drew the disdain of respectable, middle-class Americans who associated their ideas with a destruction of property. This was Gladden's view as well in the 1870s, when he dismissed the philosophy as "simply pillage." He always remained skeptical of socialism, believing that it deprived people of initiative and tended to breed stagnation. Nevertheless, he conceded that "the philosophers of Socialism are men of deep insight and strong logic" and admitted finding Socialism appealing in the face of rampant inequality and unchecked corporate power. "Because of the social wreckage which, under the present system of industry seems to be increasing," he wrote, "many of us are strongly inclined to listen to the Socialists." If forced to choose between the Social Darwinist's highly individualistic capitalism of the day and socialism, he acknowledged, "I should take my stand with the Socialists."[46]

Gladden's writing established him not only as an authority on labor issues but also as someone who could help resolve them, both in particular circumstances and in their more general sense. In 1886, he traveled north to Cleveland where a prominent civic leader had invited him to speak. He was pleased that despite their initial "doubts about parsons" and their expectation that he would "side with their employers," the workers came to recognize him, unlike many clergy, as "one who was able to get their point of view." In the years ahead, the Ohio State Association of Congregationalists made Gladden chair of a committee that investigated labor conditions in the state. He also led several conferences that brought together workers and business leaders in the interest of solving the nation's labor trouble.[47]

While Gladden received the greatest attention for his advocacy on economic and labor issues, other social matters concerned him as well. He also became an outspoken advocate of the temperance movement and of efforts to curtail alcohol consumption.

This commitment might seem odd in light of Gladden's progressive politics. From our vantage point on the other side of prohibition, it is easy to view temperance advocates as overzealous moralists who foisted their values on the entire nation. In Gladden's case, it's important to recognize that while he endorsed temperance, he opposed efforts at prohibition (as did most Americans; enthusiasm for an outright ban on alcohol did not develop meaningfully until after 1900).[48]

More importantly, in the context of the nineteenth century, there were valid reasons for his concern about alcohol. When temperance advocates claimed that liquor harmed families, they were not employing empty rhetoric. The legal principle of coverture, by which women surrendered their legal rights to their husbands at the time of marriage, remained common in the United States. When husbands squandered money in saloons, it was not just their own funds they lost but funds of their wives as well. And women had few legal options available to leave spouses who drank heavily and were often abusive.[49]

Gladden had seen the harmful effects of alcohol in his own family. Asa Williams, his mother's second husband, was a heavy drinker. While Gladden was at college, his brother reported that their stepfather had been sent to jail for nearly a month after "pushing her over the stove" and being generally belligerent while drunk. While Asa swore off alcohol, it did not seem he would "keep sober a great while." For George, watching his mother remain in an abusive relationship with someone who drank made his own financial woes all the worse. Amanda remained with Asa out of financial necessity, and George found himself wishing for money "to place her in comfortable circumstances" rather than being left to "hope for the best."[50]

What happened in Gladden's family explained the minister's disdain for alcohol. Unlike ardent prohibitionists who were gaining popularity, Gladden did not view alcohol as inherently evil in every circumstance. He did consider its benefits to be few and far between, however. When one correspondent tried to use the minister's nuanced views about the "legitimate use of wine" to suggest that occasionally social drinking might be acceptable, Gladden replied that the consumption of wine "as a beverage by persons in health" was no different than recreational "opium eating."[51]

Gladden's primary concern was that alcohol was inextricably linked to other social ills that needed to be resolved. Money spent on liquor was money not saved, thus perpetuating a cycle of poverty. He also believed alcohol was to blame for crime. He claimed that "men who, when sober, are not disposed to harm anybody, are roused by strong drink to a homicidal fury," and further asserted that "nine-tenths . . . of the assaults and homicides that take place in our land, are the effect of intoxicating liquor."[52]

While Gladden was very much a product of his time in laying blame for all social ills on alcohol, his reason for doing so reflected his conviction that all religious people had a responsibility for the well-being of society. While he cared about the well-being of those who consumed alcohol and their families, his greater concern was about the societal implications. Even "those who are not themselves addicted to the use of strong drink must suffer in their pecuniary interests," he wrote. Because "rum builds and fills our prisons and our almshouses," its consumption "greatly increases the burden of our taxation." While Gladden's focus on alcohol reflected particular (and perhaps peculiar) concerns of the late nineteenth century, his recognition of the overlapping nature of various social issues was at the heart of his work as a reformer.[53]

Gladden championed many of the popular policy solutions to address the liquor problem. This was especially true after his move to Columbus, a city he found to be plagued by "intemperance and Sunday-[saloon] keeping." He urged restrictions on the operating hours of saloons, and especially closing them entirely on Sunday. He also advocated efforts to encourage people to open more "temperance coffee houses." Building on his long-standing encouragement to churches to stop complaining and assume an active role in improving their communities, he encouraged them to be a "promoter and patron" of such establishments. The liquor problem would not be solved in the political realm alone. The "purely moral influences" of religious institutions needed to be brought in as well to foster alternative sites of community.[54]

Indeed, Gladden grew increasingly frustrated by those who thought that policy changes alone would curb the abuse of alcohol, and this set him apart from ardent prohibitionists. He complained of the "growing determination of the American people to trust in force rather than in truth and love." This bred the "tendency to promote moral reforms by political methods." He acknowledged that there was a place for policy changes, but adjusting the law did nothing to alter underlying behavior. Thus, Gladden found himself at odds with those Christians who sought the full prohibition of alcohol. Such a policy could "forbid a man to sell or to buy liquor," but it could never "convince him that liquor is not good for him, and that he is better off without it." He assailed those churches that were "so obsessed by the notion of curing the evils of the world by law that they have largely forgotten how to use the moral forces with which they have been intrusted."[55]

Gladden's emphasis on local government in his discussions of temperance spoke to the third major area of his social advocacy: the city. This is unsurprising, given that Gladden's later career coincided with the rapid growth of the nation's urban areas. He recognized the possibilities that accompanied such growth, noting that "the greatness of opportunity" in city government could "hardly be exaggerated." The range of problems addressed by municipal administrations was "far more comprehensive than that of the government of the State or of the nation."[56]

The problem was that governments had not kept up with this growth. "The municipal machinery which answered well in a semi-rural community of four or five thousand people became utterly inadequate for the management of a population of fifty or one hundred thousand," he noted. Gladden's activism in municipal life centered on the overlapping concerns of public health and safety, good governance, and efforts to ease poverty.[57]

Gladden imbued public safety and welfare with a moral purpose. Rapidly growing cities produced slums, and "the disease and the pestilence which these conditions breed are moral as well as physical." This demanded a response. "Men and women cannot live upright, self-respecting, decent lives in such places," he wrote. Government officials had a responsibility to eliminate such housing and religious institutions needed to exert pressure on them to do so. "The existence of such plague spots," Gladden declared, "is proof that the municipality is fatally derelict in its duty."[58]

Public health in urban areas was an issue that hit close to home. Gladden's daughter Helen had died of typhoid as the result of impure water. He described her death in 1890 at the age of twenty-four as "the great sorrow" of his life. Nor was she alone. American cities were filled with disease. During the second half of the nineteenth century, the average life expectancy in the United States declined, as did average height. But these declines occurred only in metropolitan areas, an indication of their unhealthy environments.[59]

For Gladden, the failure of city governments to keep citizens healthy highlighted the need for better governance and an end to municipal corruption. The bulk of his career coincided with a period when corruption was endemic in American life. During the late nineteenth century, most public servants were not paid a salary but rather worked for fees paid in exchange for their work. In such a society, opportunities for bribery and other malfeasance ran rampant.[60]

Gladden had seen up close one of the worst hotbeds of corruption when he lived in New York in the early 1870s, and one of the draws for him of Springfield had been the lack of corruption there, thanks to the watchful gaze of Sam Bowles and the *Republican*. But Springfield was an unusual exception. Municipal government "in a vast number of cases," Gladden complained, "is an instrument employed not primarily for the promotion of the public welfare, but for plundering citizens and enriching officials."[61]

Such was the case in Columbus. "There is much that is raw and undeveloped in the municipal administration," he observed on his arrival. As with temperance, he did not object to corruption solely for its own sake. Rather, he believed it negatively affected both the physical and the moral climate of the entire city.[62]

The physical side was simple enough: Corrupt officials were more concerned with enriching themselves than with ensuring clean, safe cities. The environment was sacrificed to greed. "The public health is sacrificed through defective drainage, and uncleansed streets, and impure water," Gladden wrote, highlighting particular issues facing Columbus. The problem ran deeper than environmental issues. Poor governance also caused Americans to lose faith in all government. "So long as the kind of men are in control of our city government" who currently were, "the fewer functions we commit to them the better."[63]

The most significant problem, though, was the potential moral influence. The power that the city government had to "undermine morality, to debauch the consciences of citizens, to lower the standards of business integrity and to pervert the judgments of the youth is insidious and deadly." In other words, because Americans drew their impressions of government from their neighborhoods and communities, the actions of their local authorities had enormous power to shape their perception of values. Few influences in public life, Gladden wrote, "are more subversive of honor and character than that of a bad city government."[64]

But even when government was not overtly corrupt, there was another problem: In the interest of making public office accessible, citizens had shown little concern for the qualifications of their leaders. Reflecting on his own time in city government, Gladden noted his "deepened sense of the seriousness of the business" as well as his "vivid realization of the lack of knowledge and skill on the part of those who are handling it." He was especially troubled by the refusal of certain council members to heed the advice of professionals. He recalled that for some "the idea of employing experts to tell us what we should do" about the city's water supply was "quite preposterous," and "the word 'expert' was flung around the council chamber with much contempt."[65]

This state of affairs demanded active citizenship, and Gladden chastised religious Americans for being too self-absorbed and not concerned with community well-being—the very thing that needed to take priority. "You and I have been too busy with our mills and our mines and our merchandise, with our selfish schemes and our trivial enjoyments and our narrow professionalisms," and in the process, everyone had lost sight of the important role of cities. The result was that "the people who want the political offices are not fit to hold them, and the people who have the requisite qualifications cannot be persuaded to take them." This was social Christianity at its essence. Individuals needed to move beyond their immediate concerns and focus on the good of the whole community.[66]

To encourage this attitude, Gladden fostered direct connections between the church and the city. He proposed making municipal reform a regular activity of religious youth organizations. Doing so, he believed, would build "a large body of intelligent young men and women" who would shape the next generation of city life. Gladden also argued that churches might fill a role of providing social services. By building gyms and community centers, they might meet a demand for recreational spaces. He forcefully rejected accusations that these were "secular" things. It was the church's responsibility to save every "soul from death," and if that was accomplished "by means of a gymnasium or a bowling alley" rather than a sermon in the church itself, it did not matter.[67]

On this point, Gladden found that his ideas struck a nerve. An article urging the creation of pleasant activities for working-class people with limited incomes inspired "scores of towns" to take on the task of "furnishing wholesome and cheap entertainments" for their people. Recognizing that Americans had a right to enjoy inexpensive recreation activities, and that churches needed to play a leading role in meeting those needs, was a natural consequence of Gladden's acceptance of amusements that dated back to his time in North Adams and of his increasing concern for well-being of the working class.[68]

Gladden thought the greatest opportunity for the church in city life lay in alleviating poverty. "The responsibility of the church" in caring for the poor "has commonly been disclaimed or ignored," Gladden charged. This had profound consequences in other areas as well. By this "surrender of the charge given by its Master" to take care of the needy, the church had lost "its influence in civil society" and it had "become too closely identified with the more fortunate classes." The problems churches faced with the working class stemmed from their abandonment of care for the poor. He expressed hope that if churches rose to the challenge, "the greater part of this work would be done by them, in the best possible way."[69]

It was not that Gladden thought the government should not have a role in care for the poor. Rather, in his experience, badly managed municipal authorities had done a bad job managing charity. As was true in other areas of city life, "unscrupulous politicians" replaced "capable and experienced" civil servants and proceeded to distribute relief according to political loyalty. "Those most needy are apt to be least cared for," he observed of civic charity, while "those to whom the aid of the state is injurious rather than helpful get the lion's share of its dispensation." Here again, the problem was the "chronic unwillingness of American citizens of the better classes to take any part in the administration of municipal government."[70]

Gladden held that religious communities had both the moral imperative and the capacity to help the poor better than the government of the day could. Given the widespread perception of the "grievous and costly failure of the American municipality in its attempts to care for the poor," it was time for churches to "reclaim this business."[71]

What he advocated, though, was not moralizing church members going out into the city and proselytizing in exchange for relief. Rather, he thought they should start simply. They might "put themselves into relations of personal friendship" with poor members of the city, and the church building itself might be a "point of attraction"—not even necessarily for religious activities or instruction, but merely as a comfortable place. For churches wishing to cultivate more elaborate social service networks, he suggested that several could band together, and divide up a city block by block.[72]

As was the case with labor issues, Gladden's advocacy on municipal issues soon earned him national prominence. Early in the 1890s, he published a series of short stories in the *Century* on the fictional Cosmopolis City, in which leading citizens banded together to enact municipal reform. The 1890s witnessed the establishment of actual bodies of this nature in numerous cities. Several of these groups credited Gladden with the idea to form them, and he took part in setting up the City Club of New York. In 1894, he also attended a conference that led to the establishment of the National Municipal League, which continues to this day as the National Civil League. When the National Conference of Charities met in Washington, DC, in 1901, the group planned a series of sermons to coincide with their meeting on the subject of "the application of religion . . . to the social problem." Other ministers requested Gladden to address their own churches on topics like "The Church and the City." His involvement with city issues also fostered his connections to political leaders. In the 1890s, Theodore Roosevelt, then the police commissioner for New York, visited Columbus, and the two remained friendly thereafter.[73]

Ultimately, all three major concerns of Gladden's advocacy pointed to the same conclusion: In an interconnected world, individualistic thinking in religion no longer worked. Under an old way of thinking, it was possible "to think of saving men as separate souls." But now that it was "evident that we are indeed members one of another" and any "attempt to fence off religion into a department by itself" proved "manifestly absurd."[74]

The end result of Gladden's view was a new vision of the role of a minister and a religious community. It was "impossible . . . to segregate the church from the community." Therefore, he noted forcefully, "If the church wishes to save itself from extinction, then, it must send its light and its truth into the community." Gladden continued, in a clear indictment of individualistic Christianity, that it was not enough to "shut ourselves" in, "saving our own souls, and letting the great roaring world outside go on its way to destruction," and it was likewise insufficient to occasionally "pull a few of the passers-by in." Churches needed to be constantly involved in the full life of their communities.[75]

What was true for the church was true for the minister. "The minister's work, in these days, must lie, very largely, along the lines of social amelioration," he insisted. It was just as important for the minister to "understand the constitution of human society" as "the human soul." Separating the two "renders asunder what God has joined together." Ministers needed to preach on social subjects, and congregations needed to be aware of them.[76]

Gladden was quick to note that ministers should not talk only about politics or economics. "The pulpit that becomes nothing but a platform for the discussion of sociological questions" ultimately "loses its power" in just the same way a minister did who never discussed contemporary issues. Either approach missed the point. Religious people needed to fuse their religion with everything else. "It is the *religion* of politics, of economics, of sociology that we are to teach," he declared.[77]

By this, he meant that religious institutions had the power to transform character in a way that would correct fundamental defects in society. The only way there would be "any radical or permanent cure discovered for poverty, for grinding monopoly or municipal corruption, for bribery or debauchery or crime," would be "as men's minds and hearts are opened to receive the truths of the spiritual world," he wrote. The only "adequate social reform" was that which stemmed from "a genuine revival of religion." But Gladden's idea of a religious revival was vastly different from those typically proclaimed from US pulpits. "It must be a religion which is less concerned with getting men to heaven than about fitting them for their proper work on earth; which does not set itself over against the secular life in contrast, but enters into the secular life and subdues its power and rules it by law, and transfigures it by its light."[78] Religious, political, and social life could not be separated.

Gladden's forward-thinking approach to labor issues and city governance did not translate to progressive views in all areas. In particular, he was quite unsupportive of one of the other major causes of the day: women's rights, and particularly women's suffrage.

Gladden's relative lack of enthusiasm for women's rights was particularly out of character given the influential role of women like Nancie Priest and Hattie Hamilton in his early thought. Moreover, during his time at the *Independent*, Mary Abigail Dodge regularly used her columns to advocate women's suffrage, as well as for greater acceptance of public speaking and preaching by women.[79]

In some respects, Gladden was ahead of his time in his view that women should lead productive, fulfilling lives. He championed women's education and noted his own view that he preferred "strong-minded women" to "weak-minded ones." He also attacked the domestic ideal that encouraged women to refrain from substantive labor. "Vigorous physical exercise every woman ought to have, and if it can be taken in the way of work, so much the better," he declared. Gladden challenged the popular view that it represented a "disgrace" for women "to be found working with your hands." Nor did he simply mean manual labor. He criticized "the foolish customs of society" that had kept women out of professions like medicine, and he cheerfully predicted that "fifty years hence the world will wonder how people could have lived so long without female physicians."[80]

But while Gladden was forward-thinking on women's education and professional opportunities, he proved lackluster in his support of women's suffrage. He claimed not to oppose voting rights for women; he just didn't think that women themselves desired them. "Women ought to have the ballot when they want it," he observed, "but I doubt the wisdom of thrusting it upon them before they are ready to take it." Gladden invoked anecdotal evidence from Massachusetts, where he believed fewer than one in twenty women voted when given the opportunity. He concluded that "it looks rather doubtful to me whether such a movement is, at present, of any practical value."[81]

Such claims ignored the reality that many women, including those with whom Gladden was well acquainted, eagerly desired the right to vote. But he seemingly viewed these women as anomalous and not reflective of general sentiments. While he did not oppose women's suffrage, the cause never joined municipal reform and temperance as an issue of significant concern to him. His lack of enthusiasm is all the more surprising given the strong links that existed between the temperance and suffrage movements. Temperance advocates like Frances Willard believed that giving women the right to vote would improve the moral fabric of communities.[82]

There might have been an additional reason for Gladden's reticence on suffrage. When the issue was debated, it proved to be a contentious one. In the later years of Gladden's career, he increasingly sought to devote his efforts to causes that brought people together. His willingness to take on another contentious debate paled in comparison to the prospect of devoting his time and effort to bringing people together across socioeconomic, denominational, and political divides.

7

UNIFIER

As Gladden emphasized political and social issues in his preaching and writing, he came to recognize an underlying problem that connected these issues. American society had become fragmented. Animosity between workers and employers, economic inequality, and the lack of social empathy that underlay poor governance all had a common cause. People in the United States had grown isolated in their immediate socioeconomic, religious, and political groups. They had lost the broader sense of community and common purpose. Gladden increasingly saw his task not merely as responding to particular social ills. Rather, he found a larger purpose in fostering a renewed sense of unity in a divided, polarized nation.

Gladden's commitment to being a unifying force came as his prominence rose to even greater heights. His demand as a lecturer and preacher grew as he approached his seventieth birthday in 1906. Soon after, he received an offer for newspaper syndication of his sermons which would "treat of timely, or live, topics." In anticipation of that birthday, he composed an address of "Recollections of a Life Time," and he delivered it "a great many times, all over the country, from Maine to California." With what was now a characteristic lack of humility, he boasted that this address was "the most popular and successful thing that I have ever done," and that "everywhere there has been inquiry when it was going into print."[1]

But Gladden did not merely use his newfound stature for personal aggrandizement. Rather, he used it to emphasize the need for

Americans to come together across class, religious, and partisan lines. Most crucially, he urged the church to take a central role in breaking down boundaries and easing social division.

The sense that Americans were growing divided in all ways became impossible to ignore as Gladden's life went on. At the most basic level, people increasingly lived and worked around others of the same socioeconomic status. When Gladden entered adulthood, most people resided in villages and small cities where the wealthy and those of more modest means lived in close proximity to one another. With the growth of large cities and the expanding gulf between the very rich and the very poor, the opportunity for direct encounters across class lines diminished.[2]

Not only were Americans more stratified socially, but people were now more likely to be stuck in their circumstances. In the early years of Gladden's career, many American workers could reasonably expect to enjoy some upward mobility. Men who began as wage laborers in the employment of others could look forward to eventually owning their own business. By the final decades of the nineteenth century that was no longer true. As Gladden acknowledged, "Thirty years ago the wage-worker might hope, if he saved a few hundred dollars, to set up business for himself . . . that chance is steadily diminishing." Employees and owners increasingly represented different segments of the population with few shared experiences. For the first time, class consciousness became widespread among working Americans. More and more, people felt connected to those who shared their socioeconomic status and at odds with those who did not.[3]

Faced with this new reality, Gladden's first concern was to restore the fraying bonds of community. As the United States urbanized and metropolitan areas grew larger, a sense of alienation increasingly resulted. "Our modern life, in our cities and large towns, is so intense that the opportunities are few for the cultivation of friendships beyond a very natural circle," he lamented. The social stratification that characterized cities was mirrored in churches. Gladden complained of the "notorious and discreditable fact" that church members did not even know each other. People "who for years have worshiped in the same sanctuary" would "pass each other daily in the street without recognition."[4]

But if churches suffered from the same problem as the rest of society, they were also well situated to solve it. Gladden believed the church provided an ideal institution for helping people overcome the loneliness of modern city life. But some changes needed to be made first.

First, Gladden argued that churches had become too large to effectively foster community. The competitive impulses that had led pastors and congregations to prioritize church growth above all else had not served the interests of their members. He urged ministers to keep their congregations to such a size "that some good measure of acquaintance and friendship may be maintained among its members, and between its members and their ministers." Moreover, in planning their activities, churches should specifically address alienation in the city. Gladden suggested that every church should host a weekly social event, not for any explicitly religious purpose, and especially not for people to spend an hour "in conversation with their every-day friends and cronies." Rather, this would be a time for "becoming acquainted with strangers." One of the hallmarks of this, Gladden urged, was that it would allow people to get to know one another without all the elaborate conventions of the day. There would be no need for a formal introduction. Rather, the church would simply be a place where people could initiate conversation and friendship.[5]

While Gladden appreciated any social bonds that formed, he particularly wanted churches to foster community across class lines. In his view, it was urgent that churches do so for the sake of their continued relevance and, indeed, for their very survival. "The Christian church is on trial before this generation upon this very issue," he warned. Society at large was trying to determine "whether there exists within it a genuine brotherhood by which the barriers of social caste can be broken down." Class conflict was the fear of the day, and if it got worse it threatened "the disruption of existing society." In this culture, "the Christian church" seemed to be the one institution that could act in such a way that "this separation can be averted."[6]

Unfortunately, as many of Gladden's contemporaries noted, the church's record of breaking down class barriers was abysmal. "The church is already under suspicion on the part of many people," wrote one correspondent. "The laboring men suspect our motives and many honest students of the time criticize us. It is high time to take a stand."

An editor at the *Century* confirmed this assessment, observing, the churches are not breaking down the line between the 'swells' and the common people" and that most ministers were desirous of "preaching to crowded houses composed of people of the cultivated class." The problem was that this had an enormous effect on society at large, not just the churches. "If the church is to help in the general movement for the regeneration of the country by the abolition of graft and police corruption, it must get nearer to the common people," this New York editor continued. As Gladden had long argued, religious institutions that held themselves aloof from much of the population lost the moral authority to lead.[7]

Gladden's correspondents were right. Churches did a better job perpetuating social and economic distinctions than transcending them. Partly this reflected the poor record of many Protestant churches on labor issues, which Gladden worked to address. But it also reflected a simpler reality: Wealthy and middle-class churches actively sought similarly situated members and actively discouraged poorer people from attending. Indeed, members of the working class had long recognized this reality and criticized churches for it.[8]

To combat socioeconomic stratification, Gladden urged that church membership be based on neighborhood rather than social status. Residents of a particular vicinity, he wrote, "should be impartially gathered in, rich and poor, learned and unlearned, with no distinction of caste or color." He rebuked the objection that, given the geographical stratification of cities, neighborhoods would be segregated by economic status. Even accounting for this, most cities had enough proximity among people of different classes to allow diverse congregations. "There are few neighborhoods in which many poor people may not be found, and few which are not accessible to some well to do people," he observed. The issue was willingness, not geography. "Wherever the sentiment of the church heartily favors it, the rich and the poor will be worshiping together," he wrote. Churches were socially stratified not because geography demanded it but because their members chose to be.[9]

Gladden blasted a popular practice that allowed churches to claim they were transcending socioeconomic divides without actually doing so: holding separate services for poor people at another location. His awareness of this phenomenon developed in earnest during his trip to London in 1888. While there, he noted large numbers of outdoor services. These developed based on the assumption that the poor "will not come to the church." Further inquiry revealed that they would not go to regular services because "the poor are not, as a general thing, wanted in the churches . . . the average worshipper objects to their presence in the same sanctuary with himself." This realization made Gladden irate. "If this is true of the churches," he wrote, "the sooner the churches are burned down and blotted out the better. A church into which the poor are not wanted is a church into which Christ will not come."[10]

Open-air services were not as ubiquitous in the United States, but a similar impulse underlay the common practice of wealthy churches establishing "mission chapels" in less desirable neighborhoods. They encouraged poor and working-class people to go to these satellite churches. In Gladden's view, this arrangement was no better. It similarly divided people along class lines and conveyed the message that certain people were unwelcome in churches. Even when members of the main church visited these chapels, it was as "an act of condescension" rather than a desire for genuine community. The defense commonly offered of these chapels—that poorer people would prefer to attend modest chapels in their own neighborhoods—struck Gladden as a view "largely imputed" on the poor. It was really the opinion of better-off congregants "who in their hearts would rather them not come" to their church.[11]

The need for churches to encompass a cross-section of American society represented the fundamental lesson American Christians needed to learn. Recognizing this was "a thousand times more important than all that is involved in our disputes about polities and liturgies and doctrines," Gladden wrote. Ignoring this teaching of Christianity was a "damnable heresy," he proclaimed, and it was an "intolerable schism" that "Christ's poor are practically cut off from the fellowship of their more prosperous neighbors." It was also a schism that threatened the future viability of churches.[12]

As he worked to transcend class division, Gladden also worked to alleviate the divisions of Protestantism that stemmed from debates about belief and practice. The roots of this commitment similarly lay in the growth of cities and the changes they brought to American life. As metropolitan areas boomed, churches discovered there were "large regions" of them "lying unevangelized." The problem was that each denomination wanted a presence in these areas. Churches of different denominations would essentially fight for territory. This was, Gladden believed, to their detriment. "In almost every city in the land the collusions and confusions arising from this source are shameful, and the waste of resources thus entailed is little less than criminal," he wrote.[13]

It was not just "the waste of the Lord's money" that irked Gladden. Rather, it was the impression this denominational rivalry gave about churches. "The pushing rivalry, so patent to all observers," left a sense of "the egoism of the whole proceeding." Protestants seemed more concerned with building individual churches than with doing what benefited Christianity as a whole. While this problem was felt most acutely in cities, it plagued smaller towns too. In communities that might reasonably only support one or two churches, five or six competed for members and money that simply did not exist.[14]

Too many Protestant churches competing with one another for too few resources was a long-standing problem in American life and one that had grown during Gladden's life. He recognized the issue when he covered religion for the *Independent* in the 1870s. By the late nineteenth century, it was undeniable that there were too many churches—or, more accurately, there was insufficient money and members to sustain all these churches.[15]

Gladden had offered one solution in the *Independent*: every county would establish "a Christian convention, to which all the churches of the country should belong." It would meet a couple of times each year to discuss the state of religion in the region. Its main purpose would be "to prevent the multiplication of churches for sectarian reasons and to encourage the union of feeble societies where the circumstances seemed to warrant it."[16]

Gladden was convinced that cooperation among churches was possible, even among those that disagreed about doctrine. The crucial foundation for this was his liberal theological outlook that downplayed doctrine. Just as people could become Christian without accepting every doctrine a church taught, he believed that churches could work together and even worship together without agreeing on everything. As long as they accepted "the lordship and leadership of Jesus Christ," other "philosophical distinctions which they are in the habit of making" did not matter. Debates over doctrine had no bearing on cooperation for "the better prosecution of the Christian work."[17]

Gladden thought that unity in one aspect of religious life would foster unity in others. Closer ties among churches would help break down class barriers within congregations and allow more effective outreach to the poor, thereby easing social division. He urged cooperation among churches of all denominations to determine who did not attend church in their neighborhood, village, or even city. Gladden suggested that they systematically canvass the vicinity together. But "instead of seeking to gather into its fold all those in the territory who have no church home," they would instead find out what church those people preferred.[18]

Gladden often emphasized an end to denominational rivalry in his sermons, but in the early 1880s he took that message to a larger audience. Through the winter of 1882–1883, he published a series of short stories in the *Century* magazine on the fictional "Christian League of Connecticut." The story's protagonist sounded a lot like Gladden: a full-bearded Congregationalist pastor who was likely to be mistaken for a journalist or artist. The fictional clergyman set out to establish an association of churches in his imaginary town of New Albion for purposes of discussing "the interests of morality and religion in this community."[19]

The members of this association quickly reached an assessment that, unsurprisingly, sounded like Gladden's. "The Christian work of this town is imperfectly done, because what is everybody's business is nobody's. The churchless classes are not reached; the poor are neglected; pauperism thrives upon careless and indiscriminate charity," one character lamented. The lack of cooperation among churches had a tangible, negative effect on community life.[20]

The fictional league presented a model for bringing churches together for the community without contentious arguments about doctrine or practice. Gladden brought a wide range of denominations together as its participants. Baptists, Methodists, and Episcopalians were included. But so too were Adventists and Universalists, denominations that many of Gladden's fellow Congregationalists considered outside the mainstream of Protestantism.

The group's mission ensured that theological questions did not matter. Its work reflected Gladden's long-standing commitments: reaching out to those who did not attend church, providing "wholesome diversion" with places to read or enjoy conversation, and working to end poverty and crime. On the other hand, its members "shall never be required to assent to any creed or confession of faith, nor shall doctrinal or theological discussions of any kind ever be allowed in its meetings."[21]

League members conducted a canvass of the town to link residents with churches, helped workers establish a multidenominational church in a nearby industrial community, and worked to help a local congregation retire their debt. By the end of the story, not only had other towns created their own groups but a statewide organization modeled on the Christian League had also been established.[22]

The central theme of the Christian League stories, which Gladden made through his protagonist, was a critique of denominationalism. "Believing in these denominational peculiarities does no man any good whatever," the story's Congregationalist minister observed. Making them the center of one's belief "saves no man's soul." All that was accomplished "by exalting these small distinctions" was that towns had "three churches when there is barely room for one."[23]

The Christian League club stories proved to be one of Gladden's most influential works. In accepting the series, the *Century*'s editors heralded it as "full of admirable criticism, common sense, and suggestion," adding "all the details seem (either through your ability as a narrator or through the innate excellence of the scheme) perfectly practicable." They correctly anticipated that the stories would connect with readers. Gladden continued to receive praise for the "Christian League" decades later, including from the noted muckraking journalist Ray Stannard Baker, who recalled that it "stirred me in a way I have never forgotten."[24]

More significantly, the stories inspired real-world organizations designed to bring churches closer together. Cooperative bodies emerged in countless cities throughout the United States. Statewide organizations soon followed in places such as Maine, New York, Ohio, and Wisconsin. The most ambitious of these projects was a national body, the Federal Council of the Churches of Christ in America, which was founded in 1908. Gladden attended the planning conference for the Federal Council. One of the organization's founders traced its roots to the Christian League stories. The Federal Council of Churches represented the cornerstone of the twentieth-century ecumenical movement, which sought to forge closer ties among Christian churches across the globe. Gladden's stories were a critical intellectual foundation of that movement.[25]

There were limits to Gladden's success at uniting Protestants, however. In the early twentieth century, he led efforts to merge the Congregationalists with two smaller denominations: the United Brethren and the Methodist Protestants. Opposition to the merger ran high, driven by fears that it would require each tradition to surrender defining aspects of its identity. Congregationalists worried that any union would mean the end of the autonomy of individual churches. One minister blasted Gladden, promising to "do my utmost, little though it be, to repudiate any union that robs Congregationalism of its glorious name and the great principles that gave it birth." The attempted merger collapsed, and the lesson was clear. It was easy to persuade churches to cooperate with one another. It was another thing entirely to ask churchgoers to give up their denominational identity—in the case of Congregationalists, the very thing that set them apart.[26]

The criticism Gladden drew in his effort to unite three Protestant denominations paled in comparison to attacks he received for his outspoken defense of Roman Catholics and his efforts to bridge the long-standing divide between Catholics and Protestants in the United States. Gladden's first decade in Columbus coincided with what he described as a "most discouraging outbreak of religious rancor." Numerous secretive organizations emerged, all preaching intolerance "directed solely against Roman Catholics." While central Ohio was a hotbed of such activity, anti-Catholic sentiments ran high throughout Midwestern states.[27]

No organization more fully embodied this anti-Catholic spirit than the American Protective Association (APA). The group emerged in the 1880s, drawing membership in large part from recent immigrants from Britain who harbored hostility to Irish Catholics. More generally, its members expressed anxieties about the transformation of the US economy, and the loss of personal control over work amid mass industrialization. Though Catholic immigrants bore no responsibility for structural changes to the economy, they presented an easy target, especially in financially hard times.[28]

These anti-Catholic organizations worked to elect their members to office and to win the support of public officials. In the area around Columbus, nearly every Republican candidate for local office was reputed to be a member of one nativist group or another. Gladden believed that Ohio Governor William McKinley owed "a large slice" of his own support "to the A.P.A. vote" and that half the members of the state legislature belonged to the organization.[29]

Many Protestant churches directly supported nativist groups. Some held special events at which guest speakers—billed as experts—espoused anti-Catholic rhetoric. Even Gladden's own church was not immune to the phenomenon. The man he hired to oversee one of First Church's satellite mission chapels turned out to be a member (much as Gladden objected to these chapels in principle, he nevertheless had one in Columbus). "I found him circulating those devilish documents, and getting the ignorant people into the order," Gladden lamented, noting that he promptly fired the man.[30]

Anti-Catholic groups used propaganda to stoke fears, especially of Catholic immigrants. One fraudulent document, purportedly written by well-known bishops in the United States, claimed that "many thousands of the faithful" were "coming daily to swell the ranks of our catholic army." The document reinforced stereotypes of Catholic opposition to public education, implying that the church's power depended on ignorant members. The same bishops supposedly declared that they "view with alarm the rapid spread of educated intelligence" and "are opposed to any system of schools that teaches the youth more than Roman catechism." Another forgery was even more over the top. Claiming to be written by the pope, it declared that Americans had lost the right to their country. The Catholic Church would take control. It would then "be the duty of the faithful to exterminate all heretics found within the jurisdiction of the United States." Still another widely circulated story held that a cabal of Jesuit priests had plotted the assassination of Abraham Lincoln.[31]

Despite his initial surprise that anyone took these documents seriously—the second one "reads like the fabrication of a very clumsy humorist," he observed—Gladden recognized the dangerous effects of these secret societies. When political movements developed unchecked in the echo chambers of exclusive meetings, "the most preposterous lies can be started . . . for there is no one there to challenge them." At that point, the lies passed for truth. Before anyone could stop them, "they can pass from mouth to mouth until they have filled the whole community with their malarious influence." Even more troubling was the ease with which so many people accepted the claims of nativists. Gladden was disheartened to discover "a class of persons who are ready to believe the most preposterous statements" and "the bigger the lie, the more greedily swallow it." Nor was this a small segment of the population. "It is amazing—it is simply appalling—to see how large this class is, in all our communities."[32]

That is precisely what happened. Despite investigations that disproved any allegation that Catholics were amassing weapons to use against their neighbors, rumors spread like wildfire through the early 1890s. Thanks to these rumors, "communities have been filled with terror," Gladden observed. Quoting a source, he noted the belief that "Catholics are about making a wholesale attack upon Protestants, killing and plundering, and destroying our churches."[33]

Fears of infiltration ran rampant, with people falsely claiming that Catholics had taken over municipal government and police forces in anticipation of planned attacks against their fellow citizens. "You are met on the street by excited persons who ask what you think about these Catholics drilling in all their churches, and getting ready for war," Gladden wrote. In Ohio towns, members of anti-Catholic groups arranged networks of sympathizers to spy on their Catholic neighbors. One Columbus minister, Gladden reported, had announced at a meeting of clergy that "he had purchased a Winchester rifle to defend himself against the Romanists."[34]

Gladden, whose late adolescence had coincided with the virulent anti-immigrant nativism of the 1850s and who had witnessed the tragic results when religious hostility erupted into violence in New York in 1871, recognized the enormous harm that this toxic mix of bigotry and paranoia could bring. He admitted to the *Century*'s Richard Gilder that he was incapable of examining the topic from an objective position and saw no reason to do so. "I should not like to have one think that I could look with a stolid mind on such a spectacle," he noted. Indeed, the APA's actions left him little sympathy for its members. "There is no depth of inanity or perfidy into which they will not plunge," he observed. "Their religious rancor makes them perfectly insane and irresponsible."[35]

Gladden was determined not to allow them to use their public platform to obscure just how insidious the group's guiding principles were. While the APA spoke in lofty terms of "preserving constitutional liberty and maintaining the government of the United States," he noted that in their secret oath members promised never to favor or "aid the nomination, election, or appointment of a Roman Catholic" to any political office. Such an oath was an unconstitutional religious test. As such, Gladden observed, it flew in the face of the APA's public claim to support the US Constitution.[36]

Beyond throwing the force of his reputation against nativist organizations, Gladden sought to prevent the APA from claiming to represent Protestantism. This was not entirely easy given that the organization drew some of its support from evangelical Christians like the followers of revivalist Dwight L. Moody. "Protestants must speak out," Gladden declared. "We must make it plain to Catholics that the intelligence and respectability of the Protestant churches are not in this movement, and are in deadly enmity to it." It was imperative that Protestants make clear that the forces of bigotry did not speak for them.[37]

Gladden's campaign culminated in an article in the *Century*, which was one of the most long-planned contributions he made to the magazine. He spent the better part of 1893 researching and writing it and refused to substantially edit it. "For the sake of the truth we are upholding," he wrote to his editor, "it must not be crippled or emasculated."[38]

Gladden intentionally timed the article's completion for the spring municipal elections in 1894. That represented "the critical time." Nativists hoped to use those contests to increase their grasp on political power. Gladden had high hopes for his effort. "I think that this blow between the eyes just then, will stun them a little." He got his wish. The article ran in March 1894.[39]

There were some ironies to Gladden's attack on the APA. Given his general sympathy for the poor and working class, his critiques of the group's members occasionally came perilously close to stereotype-driven, class-based attacks, as revealed by his reference to the "intelligence and respectability" of Protestants who opposed the APA. He likewise ridiculed the group's membership as consisting of "only the lowest stratum of Protestants," particularly the "ignorant working people" who were "roped in" by opportunistic "small politicians and shyster lawyers." These questionable figures saw an opportunity to get ahead by playing on bigotry. It relieved Gladden to discover "none of the best business houses" were present on the APA's list of companies that supported its goals, "and the lawyers and doctors are a scrawny lot for the most part." Gladden employed similar arguments to reassure the *Century*'s editors that his article would not offend their readers. He noted of the APA that "the class of which it is mainly composed do not read the *Century*."[40]

This slight indulgence in class stereotyping did not mean that Gladden excused the better classes. On the contrary, the refusal of his social equals to denounce the APA was one of the most worrying elements of the whole situation. "The amazing thing is that half-way decent men will stand by and see these methods in lively operation, and never lift a finger in protest," he wrote. His own urge to act stemmed in large part from the realization that bigotry could spread rapidly through a community—and indeed through the state or nation—in large part because the majority of well-meaning people would do and say nothing to stop it. "The absolutely frightful thing is that an organization employing such methods, working on such levels of ignorance, can get such a hold of the country as this one has gotten now," he lamented. The inaction of influential Americans was a major part of the reason why.[41]

The controversy died down rapidly. Respectable Republicans, including those like William McKinley of Ohio who had previously drawn support from the group, openly denounced the APA, believing greater political fortune could be found by trying to assemble a coalition that included Catholics. Within a couple of years, the group had become so insignificant that it was not worthwhile "to dignify it with a reference." Still, the experience stuck with Gladden. "What a melancholy revelation it was of human credulity and of the rancors that spring from religious controversy," he observed a few years later.[42]

Gladden's efforts to combat nativism reflected two larger commitments. The first was the commitment to religious freedom he had espoused since his days at the *Independent* in the 1870s. "The theory is that this is a land of religious liberty," he wrote. This entailed a promise to everyone "that if they become citizens of this land they will find equal footing for their faith, no matter what it may be, with every other faith."[43]

For Gladden, religious liberty was a vehicle for equality. It wasn't a means to force one's own beliefs on another. When Roman Catholics objected to Bible reading in school on the grounds that the translation commonly used was the Protestant one, Gladden adopted a position largely unheard of for a Protestant clergyman: he accepted Catholic calls to end Bible reading in public schools. When new citizens "find themselves taxed to support public schools in which the reading of a version of the Bible which they have been taught to regard as spurious is required by law," they could reasonably claim that an advantage had been given "to one form of religion over another." This, Gladden suggested, was "the very thing we have promised not to do."[44]

In making this argument, Gladden was staking out a different position from the Protestant supporters of groups like the APA. Their idea followed the lines of several decades of efforts to grant Protestantism special legal status. It was the same mind-set that had prompted the conflict over the Bible in Cincinnati and the push for the Christian amendment to the Constitution.

To be clear, Gladden did not dispute that the United States was a "Christian land." He was neither a secularist nor a relativist who saw all religions as equally valid. But he did not believe, as many of his co-religionists did, that it was inherently a Protestant land. He reiterated that Protestant Christianity should not maintain its dominance by "legal enactment" or through force. If Protestant churches could not maintain their influence through positive measures, they did not deserve a place of privilege. The way to "fill the land with Christian influences" was through "the teaching of the Christian forces, the Christian home, the Christian church, and the Sunday school." Laws, constitutional amendments, and anti-Catholic propaganda campaigns simply made Protestants look pathetic. If "Protestant Christianity, with the start of two centuries and a half, cannot maintain itself on an equal footing with other forms of faith, then its work is done and it must pass," he wrote.[45]

Beyond his desire to combat nativism and defend religious liberty, Gladden had a loftier goal of uniting Protestants and Catholics in cooperative endeavors. He expressed to his congregation the hope that "the Protestant Christians in this city could learn to think of the Roman Catholics as their Christian brethren," and that "the feeling could be reciprocated." Doing so would put an end to "the notion that these two great divisions of the Christian church are natural enemies."[46]

Though he had not included Catholics in the Christian League stories, he urged their involvement in cooperative projects as he would any Protestant denomination. He championed a model proposed in Buffalo, where Protestant and Catholic churches combined to divide the city block by block. Each church took responsibility for a section of the city. Their tasks included connecting nonaffiliated individuals with the church of their choice and ensuring that social needs were met, particularly as related to alleviating poverty.[47]

Akin to his fictional Christian League of Connecticut, Gladden saw cooperation as a means to bring Catholics and Protestants together without wading into contentious doctrinal issues. "If, by a plan like this, in which surely no theological questions are raised, these two great divisions of Christians could be brought together in friendly labor for the poor, the gain to the kingdom of God would be of unspeakable value," he wrote. While overcoming "the animosities of Protestant and Catholic" would "be a great and beautiful achievement," it would come with the added benefit of providing tangible good for the poor.[48]

Gladden's crucial innovation was that he did not merely advocate closer ties with Catholics, but he also worked to make such ties possible by helping his fellow Protestants better understand Catholicism. Rather than invoking the common view of the Catholic Church as a bastardization of Christian teaching, he instead explained why Catholics believed their church to be the true manifestation of Christianity. For them, he noted, "the church must be an organized body." It was not an amorphous concept as it was for Protestants. God did not seek to bring chaos. Therefore his church would be only "an ecclesiastical organization," and that organization would continue through history.[49]

"If you admit all this, you will find it hard to deny that the Roman Catholic Church is the church—the organized ecclesiasticism by which God is represented in the world," Gladden noted in a sermon. "There is no other ecclesiastical organization which, in my judgment, can make out so strong a claim to the character of continuity and universality as the Roman Catholic Church can make." Gladden was quick to acknowledge that this was not his own view of the church or of Christian teaching. But that was beside the point. Given his desire to combat religious bigotry, Gladden recognized the importance of helping Protestants understand the basis of Catholic belief.[50]

Ordinary Protestants came to see Gladden as a resource for learning more about their Catholic neighbors, especially since not all clergy were as charitable as he was. One man who described his "sincere desire to learn more of the inside of the Roman Catholic Church and Catholicism" wrote to Gladden. Acknowledging the "difficulty of obtaining an unbiased treatment" of the subject, he noted he selected Gladden as someone to whom he could "appeal for advice" and "whose record shows him above that common danger" of many materials characterized by "prejudice, narrow-mindedness, and uninformed opinion without judgment."[51]

Gladden repeatedly showed an ability to empathize with the position of Catholics, even on issues on which he disagreed with them. He rejected the demand of many Catholics for public support of parochial schools and urged that church leaders who advocated for such "bear watching." But he found he could be sympathetic to their position in light of groups like the APA. "If I were a Roman Catholic I would certainly not permit my children to attend a school under the management" of a nativist group that had fired Catholic teachers, he wrote. The true threat to American education came from nativists, not from Catholics. "The opposition of some Roman Catholic priests to our school system is an insignificant point when compared to such organized deviltry" as the APA.[52]

Moreover, in another departure from many of his contemporaries, including other liberal Protestants, Gladden was willing to credit Catholics with superiority when he felt they deserved it. He observed that Catholics did a better job welcoming the poor to their churches. Whereas Protestant churches found no shortage of ways to make the poor feel unwelcome, "if these were Roman Catholic churches the poor would be found in them," he wrote. Likewise, he credited Catholics with providing a higher quality religious education to children than many Protestant Sunday Schools did.[53]

Gladden was not naïve. He recognized that many Catholics had very different opinions from him on a range of political questions, including public education. But he believed that forceful rejection of the APA was a critical first step in developing the goodwill needed to overcome such disagreements. He hoped that his record would allow him to speak to Catholics on behalf of Protestants at times of disagreement: "You know that we are your friends . . . let us reason together and try to come to some wise conclusion on the questions that divide us." This reflected his larger belief that "it is well for those who differ to understand each other; thus they may be able to respect one another, even if they do not agree."[54]

By his defense of them against the forces of nativism and his atypical goodwill toward their tradition, Gladden earned the lasting esteem of his Catholic neighbors. Gladden welcomed their goodwill. A feature about him in the *Congregationalist* noted that his honorary degree from Notre Dame, given "in recognition of his catholicity of spirit and refusal to participate in the A.P.A. movement," hung in his study and he "cherishes it among his choicest possessions."[55]

Individual Catholics proved no less effusive in their praise of Gladden. During a visit to Minnesota, local Catholics tried to arrange a dinner honoring him. One man "spoke of the kindly feeling that many Catholics have for you because of the spirit of fair play that you have always shown in your attitude toward the Catholic Church." Another wrote to acknowledge Gladden's "Christian attitude in respect to your Catholic fellow-countrymen" and to thank him for the "public service which you rendered our country" in dealing "a blow which sent the A.P.A. movement reeling." And, at the age of eighty, he traveled to western Pennsylvania to speak at an event organized by the Knights of Columbus. They extended the invitation to Gladden because "there is no non-catholic in the country who has done more to get fair play for the catholics than yourself."[56]

Gladden's outspokenness met a much more mixed response from his fellow Protestants. Some, like the mayor of Denver who had reluctantly joined the APA after feeling pressured to do so, expressed gratitude that "the Ministers of the Gospel . . . are doing what they can to expose this infamous, unamerican order."[57]

But many others attacked him. Gladden recognized before he published his article on the APA that it would bring "personal discomfort" for him. Indeed, he had already experienced some discomfort. At the height of the APA's power, he had been a serious candidate for the presidency of the Ohio State University. Through some maneuvering, nativist members of the legislature succeeded in sabotaging Gladden's candidacy. His desire for unity had a cost.[58]

Gladden also worked to bring unity to a nation bitterly divided by politics. This was not an easy task in the post–Civil War United States. The nation's political climate was deeply polarized, and the two parties had numerically equivalent bases of support, which made for contentious elections. The polarization was exacerbated by the fact that Americans' party affiliation was determined less by their views on policy and more by their identity. Both the Democrats and the Republicans encompassed a wide range of policy positions. Democrats were white Southerners and immigrants in cities like New York. Republicans drew their support from African Americans and from white Northerners. Party affiliation became a key signifier of identity. One could identify as a Republican even while disagreeing with positions held by many of the party's prominent politicians. Though this would begin to change in Gladden's later years, up through the 1880s elections were not fought primarily on policy differences. Rather, as one historian has noted, campaigns were about "stimulating party, ethnic, sectional, and religious loyalties and ensuring turnout." Gladden perceived this noting that "the supreme duty of every member of either party" had become simply "the duty to support his party" regardless of issues or principles.[59]

Since his adolescence when as a young Whig he worked on a Democratic newspaper, Gladden had not allowed his own political commitments to become all-consuming. In Springfield, he and his friend and mentor Sam Bowles had been on opposite sides of the highly contentious 1876 election. Gladden supported the Republican candidate Rutherford Hayes (who lost the popular vote but was ultimately granted victory in the Electoral College), and Bowles favored Democrat Samuel Tilden. Their friendship was not impeded by the debate, however, and the two men buried their disagreements after the election was resolved.[60]

Moving to Ohio, which then—as now—was a "pivotal state" in elections, changed Gladden's outlook on party politics. This was especially true in the state capital. "The intensity of the partisanship was noteworthy" in Columbus, Gladden wrote, and "it was difficult for many worthy people to have any respect for a man who was not on one side or the other."[61]

Despite his long-standing affiliation with the Republican Party, Gladden found himself in conflict with the Ohio GOP. When he arrived, there were two election days in Ohio: one in October for state races and another in November for federal offices. Gladden objected, believing that the separate elections needlessly prolonged campaigns and the acrimony that accompanied them. He started a petition to move state elections to November. "The Republican machine was determined to kill it," he observed, because the two elections brought additional resources into the state. But, Gladden gleefully reported, "They were not strong enough." His proposal became law, though his commitment to principle over party left him on the outs with state Republicans.⁶²

In his own decisions, Gladden attempted to allow principle to guide his voting rather than party. In 1884, he refused to vote for the party's nominee, James Blaine, who he linked to the most corrupt corners of the party and who ran a nativist campaign. He held up the Democrat who won that year, Grover Cleveland, as "one of our bravest and most conscientious chief magistrates." Gladden's break from the GOP proved permanent, though he did support particular Republican candidates. When he ran for city council in 1900, he did so as an independent.⁶³

In his later years, Gladden infused his critique of partisanship with religious language. Specifically, he blamed Americans' tendency to be "virulent partisans" on the lack of "any sense of the presence of God in human affairs." He linked a belief in God with the recognition of human equality. "Belief in God as the father of all men is the belief that all men are brothers," he wrote. When such things were absent, people were more concerned with preventing their opponents from gaining power or keeping them from achieving success rather than finding common ground. Americans had become "bent on putting the worst possible construction upon the actions of their opponents." Even worse, when it came to the other political party, people were "determined to prevent them from doing right," lest their adversaries "get credit for it."⁶⁴

Gladden's anxiety about this status quo stemmed from his fear of the consequences: partisan hostility was inimical to democratic values. He issued a dire warning: "I do not believe that our democracy can continue to exist unless this great truth of the brotherhood of man is restored and lifted up and emphasized as the great constructive idea of all our civil life." The nation's future hung in the balance.⁶⁵

But he was not merely complaining. He believed it possible for Americans to overcome divisive partisanship, and he lived in hope of the day "when the strife of party and faction shall give place to a joyful cooperation of the men of good will." Policy needed to be in service to a larger ideal, not mere expediency. He urged leaders to consider reform as "devotion to a moral ideal, as supreme above all momentary choices." Truly effective policy making would show a "willingness to sacrifice present gains for future well being."⁶⁶

Respect for all citizens as equal, consideration of broad ideals, and recognition of future goals would, Gladden believed, break the partisan rancor that defined US politics throughout his adult life. It was certainly an idealistic vision, and one less grounded in specific proposals than other proposals he advocated. But it reflected his own life experience that well-meaning people could transcend partisan rancor.

Much as women's rights proved to be a blind spot for Gladden in his advocacy of political reform, immigrants did not fully reap the benefit of his efforts to bring Americans together. To be clear, he was not virulently anti-immigrant. His efforts to combat anti-Catholic nativism demonstrate that much. But he never fully rejected the popular prejudices of the day, and these attitudes found their way into much of his writing.

This was not an insignificant failing on Gladden's part, as immigration was a very real issue during the later decades of his life. By 1890, approximately one in every seven Americans was foreign born. Moreover, the nation's population had increased by more than 25 percent in the decade between 1880 and 1890 alone, and a third of that increase had come from immigration. Simply put, immigration became impossible to ignore in much of the country.[67]

Gladden had a very low view of many of the immigrants. "That the great majority of these immigrants are deplorably ignorant is not to be questioned," he proclaimed. Whereas earlier generations of migrants had represented the better classes of the countries of origin, that was no longer true. The newer arrivals came from the "lower grades of the peasantry and the refuse of the trades," he lamented.[68]

When it came to immigrants, Gladden did not object to their presence so much as he objected to their being granted the right to vote. "We have admitted to the highest privilege of citizenship men by the millions, born in other lands, who know little or nothing about the Constitution of this country or its laws," he insisted. The result was an "infusion of all this ignorance" into the pool of voters, which in turn "greatly lowers the average of intelligence." In dire warnings that were uncomfortably similar to the nativist critiques of Catholics he denounced, Gladden predicted "a breaking strain upon our political system will come within half a century." In explaining his reasoning for such prognostications, he linked the partisanship he so disliked to the rise in uneducated, foreign-born voters. "The intelligent man makes up his own mind with reference to political action," whereas, "the ignorant man goes with his race, or his sect, or his party." With the growth of this second group, he asserted, government would be "swamped by its overload of ignorance and barbarism."[69]

Gladden's solution to the problem of seemingly ignorant people voting was to advocate restrictions on voting rights. In making this argument, he echoed a common proposal of elite Americans in the late nineteenth century who thought suffrage had been too generously extended. In a similar vein, Gladden expressed concerns about native-born citizens voting if they showed signs of "ignorance," though he did attempt to find solutions to these problems. He urged that instead of complaining that immigrants did not understand American government, church members organize programs to educate newcomers in civics. Still, it is impossible to overlook the anti-immigrant sentiments that he conveyed, especially as his solution to the problems he described involved curtailing citizenship opportunities. He urged the adoption of tougher naturalization policies, including a fuller demonstration of civic knowledge before immigrants could vote.[70]

Gladden's failure to critically interrogate his assumptions about immigrants prevented him from championing a spirit of unity among native- and foreign-born people in the United States. Instead, he echoed divisive rhetoric that advanced the perception that most immigrants were beneath the standards of American civic life. This represented a particular failure in an era when such a voice challenging anti-immigrant sentiments was especially needed. It also marked an inability on Gladden's part to transfer his outspoken efforts to break down socioeconomic, religious, and political divisions into the realm of culture and ethnicity.

This notable failure should not obscure the extent to which Gladden's critiques of social-economic stratification, anti-Catholicism, and extreme partisanship challenged common cultural assumptions. In the later years of his life, Gladden would embrace the role of critic with even greater commitment. The attacks he drew in his defense of Catholics would prove to be an apt preview of what was to come.

8

CRITIC

In the final years of his life, Washington Gladden remained outspoken on a range of issues. But as society changed around him, his role shifted from that of respected reformer and advocate of unity to that of a critic speaking on the margins. He attacked the use of ill-gained corporate money by religious organizations, raising the ire of those who were all too happy to take the funds. He lamented the rise of Jim Crow and the way it enshrined racial inequality in national life at a time when many white Americans accepted it or looked the other way. Most notably, he grew more outspoken in his critique of war. In the last two years of his life, as many of his fellow clergymen rushed to cheer American entry into World War I, Gladden remained skeptical of the conflict's purpose.

His greater criticism brought a change in Gladden's relationship with long-standing friends and colleagues. Whereas many of the people in his social and intellectual spheres had generally adopted his views on matters like municipal reform, union rights, and the like, when it came to issues of corporate money and war, he remained a lonely voice. At the same time, on other issues, such as developing US imperialism and race relations, he failed to carry his social criticism to its logical conclusion. Instead, he offered lukewarm critique that pleased no one.

All of this coincided with Gladden's gradual retirement. He had continued to work even after Jennie died in 1908. By 1913, though, after several years of sharing the pastoral responsibility of First Church with Carl S. Patton, he accepted the position of Pastor Emeritus. Retirement did not bring an end to activity. The following year, Gladden embarked on a multi-week trip to California, with stops in Los Angeles and Berkeley. Though plagued at times by health difficulties, he reported he was having "a beautiful time here—working very hard . . . , but enjoying it all immensely."[1]

But there was a slight but notable shift in how Gladden was perceived in the nation at large. He found himself working harder to achieve the publicity he had once attained easily. He lamented that the editors of major periodicals showed little interest in publishing excerpts of his *Recollections*. Despite the fact that the *Century* had been his "main outlet" for publications, he struggled to interest its editors in his memoir. In almost desperate tones, he pointed out that the magazine and its staff "have a considerable place" in the book. "It would be a great favor to me," he added, "if somehow the *Century* could take notice of it." He added with characteristic pomposity that "it is quite the best thing I have done, I am sure."[2]

The struggle for the publicity that earlier he would have received reflected two realities. Gladden was now an old man and a new generation of leaders stood at the forefront of American political and religious life. Moreover, in his retirement, he advocated for less popular positions, but he did so by trying to claim a middle ground that often did not exist. In this way, his final years highlighted a problem that would plague progressive religious leaders through the twentieth century. It was difficult to remain comfortably ensconced in respectable denominations while simultaneously articulating a countercultural message.

For much of his career, Gladden had been an outspoken critic of corporate greed and malfeasance. After 1900, he grew more vocally critical of American Christianity's tendency to tolerate such practices so long as it reaped some of the rewards. But he soon discovered that taking this position separated him from many of his long-standing allies. In many quarters Gladden's critique was unwelcome, and the aging minister himself was beginning to be perceived as something of a relic.

The defining moment of this critique came in early 1905, soon after Gladden became moderator of the National Council of the Congregational Churches. The American Board of Foreign Missions, the missionary organization connected to Congregationalist churches, received a donation of $100,000 from John D. Rockefeller, the president of Standard Oil. What followed was a heated debate about the ethics of money and the relationship between corporate America and the nation's churches.³

The first decade of the twentieth century was a high point of suspicion about big business. Few companies drew more scorn than Standard Oil. Of particular concern was the way the corporation used its power to shape other industries. Using subsidiary companies, Rockefeller surreptitiously took control of crucial railroad lines. These rail companies then offered discounts for the shipment of oil—both to Standard and to its competitors. In the end, the might of Standard and its rail subsidiaries pushed competing railroad companies out of business. These practices alarmed officials in Washington, including President Theodore Roosevelt. But Rockefeller's careful obscuring of connections between Standard Oil and the rail lines made it difficult to prove the magnate guilty of nefarious practices.⁴

Given the dubious nature of Rockefeller's business practices, a number of prominent Congregationalists called on the mission board to return the money. Because of Gladden's prominence, as well as the particular significance that came with his position as moderator of the National Council, he emerged as the cause's primary spokesperson when he expressed support for declining the funds. But while his position brought moral authority, it had little real power. Because Congregationalism lacked a central governing body, the American Board of Foreign Missions operated as an independent entity.

No one disputed that Standard Oil engaged in ethically suspect practices. The question was whether that had any bearing on Rockefeller's gift to the mission board. Board members initially claimed they had not solicited the money, and as Gladden summarized their position, when the funds "were freely offered, they could not be rationally refused." But then the story changed. A member of the board had solicited the money. Even more curiously, perhaps anticipating the controversy the donation would cause, the board spent all the money before it publicly announced the gift.⁵

The Rockefeller "tainted money" debate, as it became known (using a phrase that Gladden helped to popularize), exploded beyond Congregationalism. It became a subject of national discussion in mainstream periodicals as well. The Rockefeller family contributed to numerous charitable organizations, including the foreign mission boards of several other Protestant denominations. Thus the issues raised quickly became relevant to a considerable number of Americans.

Everyone agreed that the ethical questions at stake transcended a one-time charitable gift. As the editors of the *Congregationalist* noted, in a society where extremely wealthy individuals routinely contributed to charities, Rockefeller's donation raised questions that "must be answered sooner or later by those who administer any kind of benevolent enterprises." The same moral dilemma facing the mission board would face churches, as well as religiously affiliated charities and educational institutions that benefited from the largesse of corporate magnates.[6]

Having lost their claim that Rockefeller's money was an unsolicited gift, board members and their allies floated a few other justifications for accepting the money. To the question raised by the *Century* of "whether there is such a thing as tainted money," many people said no. Graham Taylor, a theologian and reformer from Chicago, insisted money was a morally neutral social product. It should "be considered as separable from the person of its acquirer and possessor." As soon as the $100,000 came into the hands of the mission board, where it had come from ceased to be relevant.[7]

Moreover, Rockefeller's legal claim to the money was sufficient for many of Gladden's opponents. A subcommittee of the mission board that had investigated the donation concluded, "Before gifts are received the responsibility is not ours." Other observers agreed. As long as the money legally belonged to Rockefeller when he gave it, the board should not concern itself. Indeed, members believed they could not "properly decline to receive money from its legal owner."[8]

Critics charged that by subjecting Rockefeller to such scrutiny, Gladden was demanding the mission board take on responsibilities for which it was ill-suited. This also risked alienating other contributors. The demand that the board return the gift was, according to the liberal periodical the *Outlook*, "a notice to every intended donor that his donation may subject him to a public criticism and a private investigation of his whole life and character."[9]

The defense of taking the money boiled down to this claim that charities should not judge their donors. Representatives of the board believed they would have been in the wrong if "we had tried to stop the money of any man who wished to give it." The editors of the *Outlook* insisted it wasn't "the business of a church, charitable organization, or missionary society to sit in judgment on the character of the contributions to its work." In this case, the accusations against Rockefeller were legal, not religious, in nature. "He who is accused of violating the laws of the land should be tried by the tribunals of the land" and not "before the missionary body" of Congregationalism, that journal's editors further observed. Therefore, they concluded, it was wrong "for Dr. Gladden to sit in judgment on Mr. Rockefeller." Others shared these sentiments privately. The editor of the *Congregationalist* declared it erroneous "to brand Mr. Rockefeller as unfit to give any of his money to the Kingdom of God" and insisted moreover that the mission board "was not organized to pronounce formal and official adverse judgment upon Mr. Rockefeller or any other man."[10]

Gladden had none of it, and he demanded that religious organizations hold corporate America to a high ethical standard. Claims that the company had the legal right to the money did not account for how that money had been acquired. Things "within the letter of the law" were still ethically wrong. The company's "high-handed methods of finance, the unscrupulous and brutal way in which it always pushes its interests, with utter disregard to the ordinary principles of business morality, are too flagrant to be ignored," he wrote. Morally speaking, wealth acquired as Rockefeller had done "differs but little . . . from stolen money," Gladden wrote. There was no doubt that Standard Oil's executives were among those "who have obtained great wealth by predatory methods, by evasions and defiance of law," and whose actions "corrupt the character and destroy the foundations of the social order."[11]

In giving money to the church, morally questionable corporations threatened to corrupt it as well, and Gladden wondered if that process had already begun. In his view, the willingness of prominent religious leaders to defend the Standard Oil gift "exhibited, in a startling manner, the extent to which the moral perceptions even of leaders in the church have been blunted and confused by the worship of money." The plain fact was that it had "become quite too easy to subordinate many of the higher considerations for the sake of getting money."[12]

For Gladden, moral leadership meant acknowledging that there were things of greater importance than money. A "clear calling" for churches, he wrote, "is to make detestable, in the sight of the youth, the conduct of men who are amassing wealth by methods which tend to the overthrow of free government and the destruction of the social order."

But religious institutions could not sustain this moral authority if they eagerly took large sums of cash from such people. Doing so inevitably corrupted them. "No amount of money that such givers can contribute can compensate for the lowering of ideals and the blurring of consciences which this kind of partnership involves," he warned. And even if consciences managed to remain clear, they hardly appeared so. He predicted that Congregational churches would be "crippled or hampered in their work" and "suffer the discredit" that followed the Rockefeller contribution.[13]

Gladden soon found his position to be a relatively lonely one. He drew support from the *Century*'s editors, which was unsurprising given his long-standing relationship with the journal. They complained about bad people buying the favor of good people "by the simple means of appropriating some of their excess wealth to education, philanthropy, or religion." But the editorial pages of other popular periodicals, including the *Congregationalist* and the *Outlook*, remained adamant in their support of the mission board to accept the donation.[14]

For their part, the board's members proved immovable. When the question of returning the money was put to a vote of the full board, only 25 of the 189 members who voted sided with Gladden. The emerging consensus was that Gladden's principled stand ultimately caused grave harm to causes he cared about. Because the "finances of the Board have been seriously injured," one observer wrote, "the cause of Christ" was also "injured by the course Dr. Gladden has pursued." Another disputed Gladden's claim that donated funds were inseparably linked to their contributor. If it were true, this standard would "require the investigation and judgment" of every contribution. A third person boldly announced he was "not afraid of 'tainted money'" and "rejoice in its being used for the building up of the kingdom of God." He posed an oft-repeated question: If Gladden did not want Rockefeller's money, what would he have the industrialist do with it? Giving funds to religious work seemed far better than most other things that could be done with $100,000.[15]

Though harder to find, Gladden did have some support, especially from people who shared his suspicion of corporations. "You are a trump kick him again," read one telegram, applauding Gladden's attack on Rockefeller. Another correspondent praised his "just contempt of the millionaires who rob the people and wreck the business of those who dare enter into competition against them." Such "robbers . . . should be in jail." A reader of the *Outlook* chastised the editors for their position, echoing Gladden in her pronouncement that "if a half-hearted Christianity approves the methods which Mr. Rockefeller represents, by all means let it accept the one hundred thousand dollars." But, she added, "the world will laugh it to scorn."[16]

Other supporters drew connections between Gladden's refusal of Rockefeller's money and his other efforts to transcend divisions in society. One minister linked the issue to the larger class problem plaguing the major Protestant denominations, observing that accepting the money would only exacerbate it. "The church is already under suspicion on the part of many people. The laboring people suspect our motives and many honest students of the times criticize us," he wrote. Another correspondent saw the Rockefeller money decision as another instance of Gladden advocating an unpopular position, drawing parallels between the "tainted-money battle" and the "righteous warfare you waged against the A.P.A. movement" during the previous decade.[17]

Receiving some support, Gladden pressed on. He traveled from Columbus to Seattle to attend the annual meeting of the mission board. There, he called on the board to adopt a policy to neither "invite nor solicit donations to its funds from persons whose gains have been made by methods morally reprehensible or socially injurious."[18]

After countering arguments made against him—most notably by suggesting that scrutiny of large gifts like Rockefeller's that resulted in public recognition of the giver did not necessitate scrutiny of all gifts—Gladden made an impassioned plea to the board. The speech reflected both his commitment to the cause and his bitter frustration that few people acknowledged the weight of his critique. "Don't tell me I am making too much of a small matter. I know what I am talking about. I have been on the firing line in this warfare for a good many years," he pleaded. The problem was everyone else. "The appalling thing about it all is that so many of those who ought to be our leaders know so little and seem to care so little," he told the mission board. He concluded by linking the Standard Oil money with his long-standing concern that the church was perceived as a haven for the wealthy. "I implore you," he declared, "that you will not, by your action here today, put any more obstacles in the way of those who seek to make the Congregational Church the church of the common people."[19]

Gladden's passion did little to change the situation. In practical terms, not much could be done with the Rockefeller gift since the money had already been spent. Nor were any symbolic steps taken to signal regret for accepting it. The board reelected all its officers and, even more notably, all members of the Prudential Committee, which had been responsible for the Rockefeller gift. This made it evident, in the view of the *Congregationalist*, "that only a very small minority of the Board support Dr. Gladden."[20]

The periodical's report of the response to the speech highlighted Gladden's shifting stature during his later years. On the one hand he remained beloved. The report noted the "kindly and even reverent expressions" made about the minister, even "from those who are opposed to his positions and regard them as impracticable." The goodwill that Gladden had earned would allow him to persist in this cause, "and still continue in the esteem and affection of his brethren." But that esteem had a clear limit in practical terms.[21]

In the end, Gladden's position did better than his critics suggested. Some of his allies proved equally unwilling to let the matter drop. Though the board did not adopt his policy, several months later its members agreed informally not to accept money from donors like Rockefeller who were widely seen as harming society. While the decision pleased Gladden, it came too late. Public interest had already waned and the perception remained that he had fought for an unpopular, impossible cause.[22]

During these same years, Gladden espoused a critique—albeit an uneven one—of the growing plight of African Americans as Jim Crow laws took hold. Ever since the end of Reconstruction in 1877, states of the former Confederacy had clawed back the rights and freedoms granted to African Americans. The right to vote all but vanished. By 1896, the US Supreme Court gave its blessing to the new status quo with its decision in *Plessy v. Ferguson* that enshrined "separate but equal" in law.

Five years after the *Plessy* decision, Gladden became president of the American Missionary Association, an affiliated organization of the Congregational Church. Established before the Civil War by Northern Congregationalists, it was instrumental in funding educational institutions for emancipated African Americans, including Fisk University and

Berea College (where Gladden also served as a trustee). This involvement forced Gladden to consider questions of race and inequality more closely than he had earlier in his career.[23]

Ultimately, Gladden's record on race was mixed. Just as conventional opinion kept him from carrying his views on women to a full endorsement of their suffrage rights and his opposition to nativism did not keep him from espousing anti-immigrant opinions, his assumptions about African Americans and his unquestioning acceptance of the Southern critique of Reconstruction led him to take a restrained approach to questions of race.

Gladden's most forward-thinking views on race came in the context of education. His leadership of the American Missionary Association coincided with debates about the proper training for Southern blacks, embodied by the conflict between Booker T. Washington and W. E. B. Du Bois. Though the difference between them has been overstated, the two men disagreed about the scope of education. Washington championed industrial education, which was the preferred position of Southern whites. It was also the popular view among Northern Protestant clergy, including many of Gladden's liberal colleagues.[24]

By contrast, Gladden became one of Du Bois's most vocal supporters among white clergy. The two met in 1903 when Gladden traveled to Atlanta to speak at Atlanta University, where Du Bois taught, and to participate in a conference on the status of African Americans in national life. Du Bois gave Gladden a copy of his recently published *The Souls of Black Folk*, which drew the minister's attention. Whereas many white liberal Protestants accused Du Bois of being too negative, Gladden was quite sympathetic to his views. He acknowledged the merit of Du Bois's conception of double consciousness, and he denounced his colleagues who criticized the book. "We who have surrounded him with a social atmosphere which is somewhat stifling are rather heartless when we exhort him to take deep breaths and not mind it," Gladden chided. He often recommended *The Souls of Black Folk* to others.[25]

In part because of Du Bois's influence, Gladden denied that industrial training could be accomplished without education in a broader range of subjects. He vehemently rejected "the notion that education can be put up in air-tight, non-communicating compartments," as well as the related claim that "the negro's heart and hands can be adequately trained without developing his brain."[26]

Gladden also differed from other, more conciliatory Northern clergy in his general attitude toward Southern states. While many of his friends and colleagues had long since given up on remaking the South, Gladden had not. Four decades after the Civil War, it was still "the duty of the people of the North" to assist white Southerners who are "overburdened by their task of providing elementary education for the vast numbers of illiterate blacks." He was part of a small but influential group of Northern reformers who remained concerned with addressing the entrenched social problems of the South.[27]

Indeed, Gladden went well beyond most white, Northern clergy in criticizing the emerging Jim Crow South. He conceded that if the goal was to keep African Americans "in ignorance and subjection," little more was needed than "hard hearts and brutal wills." Such a system might even have some permanence. But it would not last forever, and Gladden warned Southerners of the consequences of such policy. With the Civil War, the United States had already paid an enormous price for the subjugation of blacks. "If we insist on trying the same experiment over again in a slightly different form, another day of judgment will come, and will not tarry." For Gladden, Americans needed to recognize that they lived in a "moral universe" and policies like Jim Crow that ran counter to morality could not last.[28]

Yet the force of Gladden's advocacy for African Americans, and more broadly his critique of racial segregation, was undermined by other positions that he advanced. While he denounced segregation in principle, he saw little need to combat it urgently. Employing the same argument he made with immigrants, Gladden urged education and civic training for African Americans before they sought full political and social equality. Once again, the potential of his critique fell victim to his gradualism.[29]

Part of what contributed to this outlook was the fact that Gladden, like many Americans of his generation, had grown quite bitter about the legacy of Reconstruction. He denounced the project as a "sad muddle" that had caused considerable damage to society. It was strange that Gladden came to these conclusions about Reconstruction toward the end of his life, given the accuracy of his diagnosis of its problems during the 1870s. Because of their "lively faith in the efficacy of the ballot," Northerners believed that by giving the vote to Southern blacks they had "given the Southern question its final answer." In other words, voting was sufficient for the preservation of political rights. But even with the right to vote, the freedman had been "driven to the wall in Mississippi, where his race [is] in the majority; just as he will surely be in South Carolina and in Louisiana, unless Federal bayonets protect him."[30]

In this Gladden was absolutely correct. Northerners failed to anticipate the vehemence with which Southern whites opposed giving voting rights to African Americans. Violence spread through the South as Reconstruction wore on. Without the support of federal troops, black voters could not exercise their rights and increasingly faced violent attacks.[31]

But while Gladden was right in noting Reconstruction's over-reliance on the ballot, he went horribly wrong in the rest of his thinking on what had happened in the post–Civil War South. His central failure was his insistence on laying blame at the feet of Southern whites and blacks, implying that both groups bore equal responsibility. He correctly acknowledged that "blacks in some portions of the South have suffered at the hands of the whites terrible violence and outrage." Yet Gladden undermined his critique of attacks on African Americans by noting with equal disdain that "whites in the same places have suffered from the corruptions and extortions of Negro majorities and Negro office-holders." These sufferings inflicted on Southern whites were "wrongs which the people of no Northern state would quietly ignore."[32]

By framing the situation in this way, Gladden did more than suggest that both whites and blacks bore equal blame for the deteriorating situation in the South. He placed greater culpability on African Americans. The actions of whites seemed to him a justifiable response to the fact that black voters had "placed in office rascals who have robbed the state." The violence blacks experienced had a simple cause: "the wrath of the plundered recoils upon them with terrible effect." In describing Southern whites as plundered, Gladden seemingly forgot the decades of white plunder that formed the basis of slavery.[33]

Gladden insisted that violence against African Americans could never be justified. But he saw it as a natural outcome of circumstances—the same circumstances he decried in the North. Political power had been granted to people lacking the knowledge to use it. Reconstruction was "based on the disenfranchisement of the people of intelligence and character, and the enthronement of the illiterate and degraded." This, he thought, was the great mistake of granting suffrage to freedmen first. There was no motive to seek further education. "Office and political plunder were as free to the ignorant as to the educated," Gladden observed. There was little need for education "when wealth and power were easily enough obtained" without one.[34]

As his career progressed, Gladden moved further away from his pre–Civil War commitments. Like many Americans, he lost faith in efforts to change the South. He came to believe, without providing much evidence for his position, that Jim Crow could have been avoided if antebellum elites had been restored to political power. Had that occurred, "we would have been spared that hopeless separation of the races and that violent exacerbation of racial hostility which the attempt to establish negro supremacy inevitably provoked."[35]

Time and again, Gladden returned to this critique. While he usually denounced segregation, he also routinely criticized African American voting in the post–Civil War South. He blamed government corruption on the prevalence of uneducated voters, and black Southerners were high on his list. "The introduction of several millions of lately emancipated slaves into the full privilege of citizenship has let the average of intelligence down," he complained. To be sure, he did not support suffrage restrictions on racial lines. Gladden was adamant that he did not want the "ignorant white man" voting either. But it is hard to overlook his conclusion that "much mischief was done when the negroes voted" in the South.[36]

Indeed, despite his denunciation of the "hopeless separation of the races," Gladden at times seemed to tolerate the position of Southerners. Part of his defense for broad education for African Americans rested on the existence of segregation. "If, as seems to be determined, there is to be social separation between the races, that is itself a decisive reason why the black man must have access to the highest culture," he wrote. Segregation required separate professions, which meant the need for African American physicians and lawyers.[37]

At other times, however, Gladden advanced a vision of integration, suggesting that his apparent acceptance of segregation was merely an argument for broad education. Yet his vision brought the collapse of racial barriers at the expense of African Americans. This problematic aspect of this thought became apparent in the Christian League stories. One of the goals of the Christian League was the "suppression of these colored churches" in New Albion. As one protagonist declared, "We will have no color-line in the Christianity for which this club stands. I'll go as far as any other man in fraternizing with colored men; but, with colored churches, never. The sectarianism whose only basis is the color of the skin is the meanest kind of sectarianism."[38]

The idea expressed here—that racism and segregation were wrong, but that the onus was on African Americans to come into white churches and institutions that in reality did not want them—exemplified the inconsistent character of Gladden's views on race.

Gladden similarly struggled to turn his ideological commitments into logical critiques when it came to US imperialism. This became an issue in the late 1890s. The nation gained its first overseas territories following the Spanish-American War. While the annexation of Cuba and Puerto Rico prompted some discussion, it was the acquisition of the Philippines that caused heated debate. Partly, this was a result of geography: Cuba was just offshore, whereas the Philippines were on the other side of the world. Filipinos also resisted the US occupation, and that raised concerns about whether Americans should remain there. With these territorial acquisitions framed in moral terms, Protestant ministers emerged as prominent defenders of an expansionist foreign policy.[39]

Gladden shared the belief that the United States should assume control of the territories acquired from Spain. He cast his views in terms of moral responsibility. In both Puerto Rico and the Philippines "we have destroyed the existing government," he wrote. However one might have felt about the war, he believed, "we have no right to consign them to anarchy."[40]

Nor was Gladden oblivious to the precarious situation in which the United States found itself. While he invoked rhetoric popular among other American Protestants when he noted the nation's "opportunity of performing great services for humanity," he acknowledged that the situation "exposes us to the peril of melancholy failure." He also observed the reality that the United States might inflict harm in its newly acquired territories. "Greed and selfishness and cunning and cruelty" would likely follow American power abroad. In addition, there was also a possibility that "crafty and cruel men" would take power and "rob and oppress the poor and the ignorant." Equally troubling, Americans might export the "corruptions of our politics" that had troubled Gladden for several decades.[41]

In many respects, Gladden seemed tailor-made for the anti-imperialist movement. Opponents of the expanding US empire were often northeast intellectuals who harbored anxieties about the corruption of American politics. But Gladden could not escape the appeal of elevating the people of these newly acquired territories to the status of "civilization." As was the case with African Americans, Gladden, for all his rhetoric of equality and brotherhood, could not avoid the hierarchical thought of his day. "The millions thus taken under our care are," he declared, "people in a low state of civilization, almost all ignorant of letters and untrained in the arts of civil and industrial life." Lands acquired from Spain, as well as Hawaii, which had been annexed a few years earlier, were populated by "child races . . . not far removed from barbarism."[42]

Gladden forcefully rejected the argument advanced by opponents of US expansion that people of the newly acquired lands could rule themselves if granted independence. "To expect that such populations will be elevated by governing themselves is unadulterated foolishness," he wrote. Employing language that invoked some of the most racist assumptions he ever used, he denied the capacity of Filipinos to develop their country. "Child races like these do not rise by their own effort; they sink instead of rising," he wrote. "Civilization is born from above."[43]

Especially uncharacteristic—yet quite disturbing—was the way Gladden's arguments about these territories moved beyond paternalism by adopting language that spoke of Americans' right to control the land of "uncivilized" peoples for the purpose of economic development. "Vast tracts of the most productive land upon the globe are occupied and rendered worthless and pestilent by barbarism," he observed. "These regions must be rescued and made productive. The world needs their products." Equally out of character was his disparagement of those who argued for the right of self-determination. "It is simply amazing that grown men, with the pages of history before their eyes, should go on applying the maxims of the Declaration of Independence to populations like those of the Philippines."[44]

To be sure, the idea of uplift abroad drew on the same assumptions that led Gladden to question whether African Americans and working-class immigrants should have the right to vote, so in some respects these arguments aligned with other elements of his thought. Yet the repeated characterizations of Asians as near barbarians marked a departure from earlier years when Gladden challenged the racist assumptions of his neighbors in North Adams. The suggestion that industrial development should be forced on people also was inconsistent with Gladden's critique of the effects of the industrial economy in the United States. Perhaps most significantly, in making this argument, Gladden was linking uplift and reform with the power of the government and the military. This was precisely what he argued against in the domestic context.

Ultimately, these inconsistencies are explained by the fact that Gladden could not escape his era's belief in progress. Though he was more critical than many contemporaries and did not see progress as inevitably a good thing, he did make that assumption in the case of the United States' new territories. The benefit of the United States taking control was that the residents would gain access to "religious freedom, education, the ideals of American democracy," all things Gladden believed to be markers of societal progress. In the case of these territories, the promise of progress outweighed the problematic steps needed to achieve it.[45]

In some small ways, Gladden avoided the worst biases of his contemporaries. He did not share the desire of many US Protestants to convert people in the territories acquired from Spain away from Catholicism. He also urged that voting rights be extended as quickly as possible, so that native peoples could have political power "as soon as they are qualified to exercise it."[46]

At the same time, Gladden acknowledged that the record of European imperialism was not good, and that the only way for the United States to take over foreign territories in a way consistent with his religious values was to abandon the traditional model of colonies. "The strong races have often meant evil by their intervention," he wrote, but "God meant it for good." It was entirely possible for the United States to be a morally just imperial power. When it came to foreign intervention, "there is no reason why our nation should not mean by it what God means. We may discern his purpose and work with him."[47]

Still, there is no getting around Gladden's endorsement of the imperialist project. He believed it possible for the United States to assume control of land belonging to others, and to do it in a Christian way.

Though he wanted to send schoolteachers instead of soldiers, his "peaceful invasion of arts and industries" was, ultimately, an invasion.[48]

What made Gladden's acceptance of the US imperialist project all the more uncharacteristic was that it was at odds with his strong reticence about war. A critique of militarism was central to his mature religious thought. This critique became all the more relevant in the final years of his life, as World War I broke out in Europe and the United States inched closer to entering the conflict. His articulation of his opposition to war formed the basis of a series of powerful sermons he delivered after the start of the war but before the entry of the United States.

Part of Gladden's opposition to war was due to the simple fact that he had lived through the Civil War. He had lost his brother in it and had witnessed firsthand the carnage modern warfare caused. More than that, military conflicts permanently distorted the very essence of the nation. "War is hell, and it sets up continual pandemonium in any commonwealth . . . it spreads its blight through every department of life," he wrote. In Gladden's view, the greatest losses came "outside of the army and after the war." In the case of the United States, he blamed the social ills he combatted throughout his career on the legacy of the Civil War. That conflict brought many "moral losses," including "the weakening of the social bond, the unbridling of greed, the letting loose of the plunderers," and "the fomenting of suspicion and distrust." The shadow of the 1860s loomed large, and Gladden feared the damage that an even greater war might cause.[49]

In an even broader sense, Gladden's opposition to war rested on the same foundation as his other social and political thought. He believed that humanity was interconnected—all the more so in the modern world—and warfare was at odds with this connection. The primary ties were commercial. "People all round the world are laboring . . . to replenish your wardrobe, to furnish your dining room and your bedroom," he wrote. He recognized the reality of a rapidly globalizing world: "The people of all the earth are working together, working for one another" and thus it was "idiotic for them to make war on one another."[50]

The problem was political leaders. From Gladden's perspective, the average person recognized the increased global interconnectedness and benefited from the "steadily rising ethical conceptions" of humanity.

But the assumption that these facts would prevent war "gave too large credit to the intelligence and sagacity of the rulers of the world." The optimistic view underestimated both "the bigotries and stupidities" of political leaders and "the strength of and the obsession of militarism."[51]

Gladden's opposition to the war had deeper roots in his religious beliefs. Not only was the Great War at odds with modern life, it was also inimical to Christian values. The central message of Christianity was of the superiority of "spiritual weapons"—truth delivered with love was sufficient to overcome physical force and coercion. But Christianity had an abysmal record when it came to militarism and war. Gladden denounced the "shameful fact" that "organized Christianity has never in any consistent and concerted way arrayed itself against war." Rather, churches had "been either tacitly assenting to war, or making apology for it, or taking part in it." This seemed to be borne out in the present conflict, as Protestant leaders rushed to endorse American entry into the war. One clergyman lamented that "many of our ministerial brothers who started out as liberals have forgotten the conception of religion" which Gladden advocated.[52]

The reason for this was that Christians had neglected this core teaching. They had failed "to believe in the might of the moral and spiritual forces." When Christianity "entered into its fatal alliance" with the Roman Empire, it embraced militarism while it "fatally lowered its standards of piety and morality." Faith and force did not mix. The effects of this carried down into post–Reformation Protestantism just as much as they did into Catholicism. Throughout Christianity the linking of religion and military force had "introduced elements of corruption into its life from which it has never been able to free itself."[53]

Perhaps because of that corruption, churches had failed to influence international affairs. "There has been no clear, convincing, persistent testimony" from churches against the claims of European governments that "the natural relation of states is one of enmity and antagonism." The proximate cause of the Great War was the militarism of Europe's leaders. But the ultimate blame lay with Christians. "Clearer and clearer it is becoming that the churches ought to have prevented this war," Gladden declared, and "ought to have put an end to all war long before this."[54]

The roots of Christianity's support of war went deeper than its alliance with the state; they also grew out of bad theology. Thus, Gladden linked his larger theological liberalism with his opposition to militarism. He had long argued that the core message of Christianity was that God was the father of all people. Therefore, bonds of brotherhood connected all humanity.

Historical Christian theologians had lost this inclusive message with its doctrine of original sin. "The fact of fatherhood was canceled," he declared, "by their doctrine of the fall of man." The belief that God was the father of all gave way to the belief that he was the father only of Christians—and only particular Christians at that.[55]

This view of humanity made conflict inevitable. "Instead of coming to think that all men are brothers and must behave brotherly we have been instructed that all men are by nature enemies and haters of one another," Gladden proclaimed, emphasizing the fault of Christianity in fostering the view that "men are by nature antagonists." The road from this message to large-scale war was a short one. As he explained it, "Theology warrants the rulers of all states in believing that the people of all other states are their enemies." The point was powerful. Though warfare departed from the true spirit of Christianity, it nevertheless reflected the message that Christians had proclaimed for centuries.[56]

Despite his view that militarism stood at odds with Christianity, Gladden never became a complete pacifist. He accepted military action when "it promises to take away oppression, to break fetters, to release captives, to banish ignorance and darkness and misery." In other words, there were such evils that were "worse than the evils of war," and war was allowable to combat them. But the current war was not fought for those reasons.[57]

From the war's earliest days, Gladden predicted the Great War's calamitous effects. "There will be no gain, absolutely none," for any of the nations involved. Recalling what he witnessed during the Civil War, he noted war's inevitable effects: "waste, want, destruction, desolation, poverty, misery, sorrow, and death—death in its most frightful forms, with its most ghastly circumstances." And this was just a typical war. But modern technology had brought a "titanic enginery of destruction" and would "make all the previous records of carnage and desolation look small and pale."[58]

Even amid his skepticism about the war, Gladden offered pastoral care for soldiers. He also composed a new hymn, "America and Her Allies," which sought to imbue the conflict with a more palatable purpose. The United States and its allies had banded together "to rid the world of lies, to fill all hearts with truth and trust and willing sacrifice; to free all lands from hate and spite and fear." Yet even his support for the US effort did not keep Gladden from continuing to criticize what he found to be a troubling linking of religion with nationalism. He never developed the war fever that many of his fellow Protestants, including liberals ones, caught.[59]

The elderly Gladden blasted as "atheists or blasphemers" people who gave "their god the national name" and spoke of a "German god," "British god," or the "French god." True faith, he argued, required acknowledging a universal God and establishing that "the kingdom of good will" necessitated an "overcoming faith" that transcended national division.[60]

What set Gladden apart from his contemporaries was his refusal to exempt his own nation from this judgment. In his final article, written at the height of American involvement in the conflict, he challenged his fellow citizens. "We hold in our minds conceptions of God that are not much better than the Kaiser's," he wrote. Gladden noted Americans' wartime tendency to think of the divine being "as an American God," and to "pray to Him to damn the Kaiser." Such beliefs made US Christians no better than the enemy they despised. "They belittle the worth of our faith by belittling God and so postpone the day when true faith shall finally triumph over petty doubts," he declared. Even amid the patriotic fervor of a major war, Gladden remained committed to the hopeful view that humanity might advance morally and usher in the kingdom of God.[61]

Gladden received encouragement from like-minded thinkers. One young clergyman wrote that "in an hour when church leaders, both lay and clerical, are placing such feverish stress—to me, unchristian—on a narrow, nationalistic patriotism," it was heartening to read the words of someone who sought "to lay foundations for and establish the Kingdom of God, rather than to plead the cause of any one nation." But as this correspondent indicated, at the height of the war, this was a lonely position.[62]

Ever the optimist, Gladden held out hope that some "great gains" might emerge from the carnage of the Great War. Like many of his contemporaries, he thought the war to end all wars would, in fact, end war. The conflict would provide "a demonstration, not only of the horrors of war, but of its futility, its stupidity as the arbiter of international relationships." If anything good might come from the carnage, it would be "a mighty revulsion against war" that would bring its end. "There is gathering in the hearts of the children of men, all the world over, a wrath, deep, hot, portentous, against the whole system of war . . . an indignation that will blaze and roar in the palaces and the chancelleries and the senate houses," he predicted. This anger against war would bring its end.[63]

In practical terms, he predicted that "within ten years the Christian Church could make any general or serious war a moral impossibility." Christianity already had the numerical strength to sway public opinion in the United States and Europe. The first step was for Christians to involve themselves in negotiations to end the war. This meant direct engagement with the political process. Christians "ought to watch, vigilantly, the selection of the representatives," he urged, "and see that men are secured who believe in peace." Engaged Christians could assure the establishment of a "League of Peace," a body proposed by Gladden that closely resembled the League of Nations. Observers expressed admiration for his "plans for world organization."[64]

In the longer term, Gladden believed the growing acceptance of liberal theology signaled an end to the distorted message of Christianity that had led to so much conflict. Before long a time would come when world leaders made "the principle of brotherhood the corner-stone of a universal commonwealth." With true Christian teaching realized, worldwide unity would soon follow. In advocating this position, Gladden anticipated the trajectory of American religious thought. Within a decade, many Protestants would reject militarism and advocate international unity and cooperation.[65]

Yet, even as Gladden offered these hopeful prognostications, he saw another possibility: that this war was merely the warm-up to a longer, bloodier conflict. Were it to happen, he predicted that in the next war "the havoc will be fiercer, because the butchering tools will be deadlier." With considerable foresight, he anticipated the worst. If each leader continued to espouse "the hellish suspicion that all the other nations are enemies, all bent on their destruction," the world was about twenty-five years from another "fell harvesting" in which another "five or ten million more people" would "kill one another."⁶⁶

In the last years of his life, Gladden had emerged as a critic—albeit an imperfect one—of the emerging political and social world of the twentieth century. While he failed to take a strong stand against US imperialism, had a mixed record defending African Americans, and proved only marginally successful in attacking corporate greed, his final acts of criticism were his boldest. At a time when few Americans, especially those like Gladden who traveled in elite circles, had the moral courage to criticize the war effort, Gladden not only challenged the efficacy of war but also denounced jingoistic patriotism. It was a final act that confirmed that, despite his inability to fully be one, Gladden had the convictions of a social critic.

The carnage of the Second World War would vastly outpace his grim prediction, but Gladden did not live to see the failure of the United States—or other European countries—to embrace his vision. By the spring of 1918, Gladden's health had deteriorated. Unable to work, he struggled physically and financially and depended on the generosity of friends. "I have not lost hope of being able to do something for myself again by and by, but for five months, my resources have been greatly reduced and my expenses much increased," he confided. "If it were not for generous gifts I might be somewhat straitened. But there has been enough, all the while, to keep me comfortable and thankful."⁶⁷ He never had the chance to begin to work again as his health continued to deteriorate in the weeks and months ahead.

Finally, on July 2, 1918, Washington Gladden died at the age of eighty-two. Given his hopes for the war's conclusion, it was perhaps to his benefit that he did not live to witness its aftermath. He had noted early in the conflict that "tradition of isolation and antagonism dies hard." Gladden did not live to see how true this was, as the United States abandoned the League of Nations and withdrew from the world stage.⁶⁸

AFTERWORD

In the years following Gladden's death, his ideas appeared to flourish. The year before he died, in 1917, the pastor and theologian Walter Rauschenbusch had published *A Theology for the Social Gospel*, a widely read treatise that encapsulated the views that Gladden had popularized over the previous half-century. The Social Gospel, it seemed, was the future of mainstream Protestantism in the United States.[1]

Ultimately, though, it was not to be. Gladden's form of theological liberalism remained popular into the 1920s. By the 1930s, however, it began to lose power. This stemmed from several sources. For one thing, while this religious outlook proved popular, it never succeeded in becoming fully dominant. The culture of religious revivals remained resilient. Shortly before Gladden's death, an acquaintance lamented the continued popularity of revivalists who offered a religious message diametrically opposed to that of Gladden: "If what they call religion is religion then I am quite wrong in my whole conception of the Christian method, message, and spirit." At the same time, an intellectual backlash to theological liberalism had begun. During the final decade of Gladden's life, the series of essays laid the foundation for Christian fundamentalism.[2]

A bigger problem, though, were issues inherent within the religious left itself. Ministers in the Social Gospel tradition increasingly abandoned the sharpest elements of their critique while growing ever closer to political and cultural elites. It became possible to find a clergyman who could ostensibly claim to follow in Gladden's footsteps, while nevertheless enjoying a lavish lifestyle and supporting the efforts of wealthy Americans to curb workers' rights and cut New Deal social welfare programs. Ministers like these prompted onlookers to suggest that followers of the Social Gospel had sold out to mass culture.[3]

Meanwhile, another group of Social Gospel ministers and laity moved even further to the political left and adopted increasingly radical positions. Unlike Gladden, this group fully embraced socialism and called for structural changes to society. Adherents of this outlook also adopted a commitment to racial equality that Gladden had not. They proved enormously influential in providing the intellectual basis for the civil rights and antiwar movements of the 1950s and 1960s. But they also pushed liberalism further to the left of the culture at large.[4]

The future trajectory of the Social Gospel highlighted Gladden's uniqueness. Throughout his career, he effectively balanced the competing role of being a cultural insider and outsider. He enjoyed connections to political and intellectual elites, and he was able to exert considerable influence as a result. Yet throughout his life he remained a critic of the status quo. From his youthful opposition to slavery before it became a national cause to his late-career rejection of corporate money and critique of war, Gladden remained something of an outsider. He consistently refused to give religious cover to conventional political or social views that he viewed as antithetical to the message of Christianity.

His intellectual descendants were less successful in doing so. As the Social Gospel gained in popularity, the Protestant ministers who espoused it established closer relationships with political and cultural elites. By the end of the 1920s, the two groups overlapped entirely. The combined force of religious liberalism and political progressivism lost the potency of its force. On the far left, the Social Gospel critique still had force. But it had largely become detached from its institutional foundations. At times, such as during the civil rights movement, it could ignite public opinion and inspire significant change. With the decline of mainline Protestant churches in the late twentieth century, however, its ability to do so steadily diminished.

The triumph of Gladden's message of religious liberalism and progressive politics depended in large measure on his ability to navigate the culture at large. That ability made him unique. But it has also challenged those who have sought to follow in his footsteps and carry on the modern liberal tradition he created.

NOTES

PREFACE

1. Gladden is the focus or a significant figure in a range of works: Jacob Dorn, *Washington Gladden: Prophet of the Social Gospel* (Columbus: Ohio State University Press, 1967); Richard K. Morton, *The Systematic Thought of Washington Gladden* (New York: Humanities Press, 1968); Ronald C. White, *The Social Gospel: Religion and Reform in Changing America* (Philadelphia: Temple University Press, 1976); Susan A. Curtis, *A Consuming Faith: The Social Gospel and Modern American Culture* (Baltimore: Johns Hopkins University Press, 1991); Gary Dorrien, *The Making of American Liberal Theology I: Imagining Progressive Religion, 1805–1900* (Louisville, KY: Westminster John Knox Press, 2001); Paul Boyer, "An Ohio Leader of the Social Gospel Movement: Reassessing Washington Gladden," *Ohio History* 116 (2009): 88–100.

2. See the editor's note on Washington Gladden, "The Unescapable Law," *Independent* 88 (November 13, 1916): 279.

3. See the editor's note attached to Washington Gladden, "Do We Believe in God?" *Independent* 95 (June 20, 1918): 87.

I. OBSERVER

1. Lewis Matson to Washington Gladden, February 18, 1855, and March 17, 1855, MIC 4, reel 1, frames 11–17, Washington Gladden Papers (microfilm), Ohio History Connection (Columbus, Ohio).

2. Lewis Matson to Washington Gladden, June 17, 1855, MIC 4, reel 1, frames 30–31, Gladden Papers.

3. S. N. Daniels to Washington Gladden, February 10, 1854, MIC 4, reel 1, frame 9, Gladden Papers; Nettie L. Brister to Gladden, June 28, 1858, quoted in Dorn, *Washington Gladden*, 25.

4. Daniels to Gladden, February 10, 1854, frame 10; E. B. Parsons to Washington Gladden, November 21, 1857, MSS 900, box 1, folder 5, Gladden Papers.

5. "Daniels Family History," Daniels Folder, Owego Historical Society (Owego, NY); Washington Gladden, *Recollections* (Boston: Houghton Mifflin, 1909), 4–5, 8–9.

6. Gladden, *Recollections*, 9, 11.

7. Gladden, *Recollections*, 17.

8. "Daniels Family History."

9. Clipping from *Owego Times*, July 29, 1897, Gladden Folder, Owego Historical Society; George Truman, "River Transportation," in *Owego Sketches by Owego Authors*, L. W. Kingman, ed. (Owego, NY: Ladies' Aid Society of the Baptist Church, 1904), 18–23; "The New Hotel in Owego," *Owego Gazette* 39, no. 33 (April 8, 1852), 2; James Hijiya, "Making a Railroad: The Political Economy of Ithaca and Owego, 1828–1842," *New York History* 54 (April 1973): 149–50.

10. Gladden, *Recollections*, 33; Washington Gladden, "Reminiscences of Owego," in *Owego Sketches*, 4.

11. Gladden, *Recollections*, 40–41.

12. Daniel Walker Howe, *What Hath God Wrought: The Transformation of America, 1815–1848* (New York: Oxford University Press, 2007), 226–29.

13. Gladden, *Recollections*, 43–44; Sean Wilentz, *The Rise of American Democracy: Jefferson to Lincoln* (New York: W.W. Norton, 2005), 488–90.

14. Wilentz, *The Rise of American Democracy*, 658–66.

15. Gladden, *Recollections*, 43–44.

16. "The Death of a Beloved Daughter," *Owego Gazette* 39, no. 35 (April 22, 1852), 1.

17. "Suicide in Richford," *Owego Gazette* 39, no. 22 (January 22, 1852), 2; "A Family Poisoned," *Owego Gazette* 39, no. 23 (January 29, 1852), 2.

18. John T. Greenleaf, "Education in Owego," in *Owego Sketches*, 47; Gladden, *Recollections*, 75–79; see also the advertisements in the *Owego Gazette* 39, no. 19 (January 1, 1852), 3.

19. "Daniels Family History," Owego Historical Society; Lewis Matson to Washington Gladden, October 5, 1857, MIC 4, reel 1, frames 61–62, Gladden Papers; Dorn, *Washington Gladden*, 25.

20. Lewis Matson to Washington Gladden, September 9, 1856, MIC 4, reel 1, frame 44, Gladden Papers.

21. Hattie Hamilton to Washington Gladden, June 1, 1859, MIC 4, reel 1, frame 150, Gladden Papers.

22. Hattie Hamilton to Washington Gladden, January 19, 1858, MSS 900, box 1, folder 1, Gladden Papers; Hamilton to Gladden, August 10, 1859, MSS 900, box 1, folder 6, Gladden Papers; Hamilton to Gladden, September 19, 1859, MIC 4, reel 1, frame 173, Gladden Papers.

23. Lewis Matson to Washington Gladden, March 1856, MIC 4, reel 1, frame 40, Gladden Papers; Hattie Hamilton to Washington Gladden, November 11, 1858, MSS 900, box 1, folder 5, Gladden Papers.

24. Hattie Hamilton to Washington Gladden, October 1, 1858, MIC 4, reel 1, frame 103; May 12, 1858, MIC 4, reel 1, frame 73; September 9, 1859, MIC 4, reel 1, frame 175, Gladden Papers; Curtis, *A Consuming Faith*, 41.

25. Hattie Hamilton to Washington Gladden, June 4, 1858, MIC 4, reel 1, frame 78; Hamilton to Gladden, September 11, 1858, MIC 4, reel 1, frame 97, Gladden Papers; see the handwritten statement of March 8, 1856, MIC 4, reel 1, frames 35–36, Gladden Papers.

26. Hamilton to Gladden, August 10, 1859; Hamilton to Gladden, October 1, 1858, frame 104.

27. Hamilton to Gladden, October 1, 1858, frames 104, 107.

28. Hamilton to Gladden, May 12, 1858, frame 74.

29. Hamilton to Gladden, May 12, 1858, frame 74; Hamilton to Gladden, January 19, 1858.

30. Hamilton to Gladden, May 12, 1858, frame 74. Hamilton noted that Gladden made reference to one of Beecher's books in a letter to her; see Hamilton to Gladden, June 4, 1858, frame 79. On Beecher's religious thought, see Dorrien, *The Making of American Liberal Theology I*, 191–98.

31. Gladden, *Recollections*, 68.

32. Gladden, *Recollections*, 69–70.

33. Gladden, *Recollections*, 70.

34. John Bascom, "Led by the Spirit," *Independent* 24 (February 1, 1872): 2.

35. Gladden, *Recollections*, 71; Ray Palmer, "Dr. Mark Hopkins," *Independent* 24 (August 1, 1872): 4.

36. Mark Hopkins, *Lectures on Moral Science* (Boston: Gould and Lincoln, 1870), 159, 190, 192; on Hopkins's reputation, see Dorrien, *The Making of American Liberal Theology I*, 269, and Bruce Kuklick, *A History of Philosophy in America, 1720–2000* (Oxford: Oxford University Press, 2001), 74–76; for an interpretation of Hopkins's thought that emphasizes his conservatism, see Da-

vid Sehat, *The Myth of American Religious Freedom* (updated edition) (New York: Oxford University Press, 2016), 187–89.

37. Hopkins, *Lectures on Moral Science*, 36–37, 39.
38. Hopkins, *Lectures on Moral Science*, 38, 95, 188, 194.
39. Hopkins, *Lectures on Moral Science*, 113, 259.
40. Hopkins, *Lectures on Moral Science*, 88, 90–91.
41. S. N. Daniels to Washington Gladden, 1857, MIC 4, reel 1, frame 52; Amanda Williams to Washington Gladden, September 16, 1858, MIC 4, reel 1, frame 101, Gladden Papers.
42. Gladden, *Recollections*, 79.
43. Gladden, "My Vacation Experience," *Williams Quarterly* 6 (June 1, 1859): 362–69; Amanda Williams to Gladden, April 2, 1859, MIC 4, reel 1, frame 133, Gladden Papers; Gladden, *Recollections*, 79; Dorn, *Washington Gladden*, 21.
44. Gladden, *Recollections*, 82–83.
45. Nancie A. W. Priest to Washington Gladden, April 21, 1859, MIC 4, reel 1, frame 144, Gladden Papers; see "Nancy Priest Wakefield," in *National Repository: Devoted to General and Religious Literature, Criticism, and Art, Volume I*, Daniel Curry, ed. (Cincinnati, OH: Hitchcock and Walden, 1877), 441–44.
46. Priest to Gladden, April 21, 1859, frames 145–47, and September 9, 1859, MIC 4, reel 1, frame 162, Gladden Papers.
47. Priest to Gladden, April 21, 1859, frame 144, and Priest to Gladden, September 9, 1859, frame 162, Gladden Papers; Priest to Gladden, August 6, 1859, MSS 900, box 1, folder 6, Gladden Papers.
48. Priest to Gladden, April 21, 1859, frames 143–44.
49. Priest to Gladden, April 21, 1859, frame 145.
50. Priest to Gladden, September 9, 1859, frame 164.
51. Gladden, *Recollections*, 47.
52. Priest to Gladden, September 9, 1859, frame 162; George Gladden to Washington Gladden, April 11, 1859, MIC 4, reel 1, frame 138, Gladden Papers; Priest to Gladden, September 9, 1859, frame 164; Hamilton to Gladden, September 19, 1859, frames 171–72.
53. Letter of John L. T. Phillips, August 20, 1859, frame 160, reel 1; Nettie Brister to Washington Gladden, February 3, 1859, MIC 4, reel 1, frame 128, Gladden Papers; Gladden, *Recollections*, 85–86.
54. Fredrick Parmenter to Moses Tyler, June 6, 1862, Tyler Correspondence v. 1 (1854–1866), Moses Coit Tyler Collection, Division of Rare and Manuscript Collections, Cornell University Library (Ithaca, NY).
55. Moses Tyler Letter, March 23, 1856, Tyler Correspondence v. 1.

56. Ed Forman to Washington Gladden, February 6, 1860, MSS 900, box 1, folder 6, Gladden Papers; Gladden, *Recollections*, 88.
57. "Daniels Family History," Owego Historical Society; Gladden, *Recollections*, 89, 98.
58. Amanda Williams to Washington Gladden, October 8, 1861, MIC 4, reel 1, frame 185, Gladden Papers.

2. SURVIVOR

1. Gladden, *Recollections*, 139, 144; Drew Gilpin Faust, *This Republic of Suffering* (New York: Vintage, 2008), 4, 107–10; James McPherson, *Battle Cry of Freedom: The Civil War Era* (New York: Oxford University Press, 1988), 483.
2. Faust, *This Republic of Suffering*, 15–16.
3. Gladden to Tyler, undated, Tyler Correspondence, v. 1, Tyler Papers; Gladden, *Recollections*, 140–41.
4. See Anne C. Rose, *Victorian America and the Civil War* (New York: Cambridge University Press, 1992), 4–5.
5. "Daniels Family History," Owego Historical Society; Dorn, *Washington Gladden*, 104–5.
6. Washington Gladden to Moses Tyler, May 23, 1860, Tyler Correspondence v. 1, Tyler Papers; Gladden, *Recollections*, 116.
7. Washington Gladden, *Recollections*, 90.
8. Sven Beckert, *The Monied Metropolis: New York City and the Consolidation of the American Bourgeoisie, 1850–1896* (Cambridge: Cambridge University Press, 2001), 19–20, 24–28, 47, 51–52.
9. Gladden to Tyler, May 23, 1860; E. B. Daniels to Washington Gladden, July 22, 1860, MSS 900, box 1, folder 6, Gladden Papers.
10. Gladden to Tyler, May 23, 1860.
11. George M. Frederickson, "The Coming of the Lord: The Northern Protestant Clergy and the Civil War Crisis," in *Religion and the American Civil War*, Randall M. Miller, Harry S. Stout, and Charles Reagan Wilson, eds. (New York: Oxford University Press, 1998), 111.
12. Gladden, *Recollections*, 89; Dorrien, *The Making of American Liberal Theology* I, 194.
13. Gladden, *Recollections*, 89–90; Beckert, *The Monied Metropolis*, 59.
14. Gladden, *Recollections*, 89.
15. Gladden, *Recollections*, 114; Beckert, *The Monied Metropolis*, 18–22.
16. Gladden, *Recollections*, 114; Beckert, *The Monied Metropolis*, 135.
17. Gladden, *Recollections*, 115–16.

18. Daniels Family Record; Gladden to Moses Tyler, December 1, 1863, Tyler Correspondence, v. 1.

19. Amanda Williams to Gladden, May 11, 1863, MIC 4, reel 1, frame 195, Gladden Papers.

20. Gladden to the First Congregational Church of Morrisania, September 6, 1863, MSS 900, box 1, folder 7, Gladden Papers.

21. Gladden to Tyler, December 1, 1863.

22. Moses Tyler to Gladden, December 2, 1863, MIC 4, reel 1, frame 204, Gladden Papers; Gladden, *Recollections*; Dorn, *Washington Gladden*, 32–33.

23. Gladden to Tyler, December 1, 1863.

24. Gladden, *Recollections*, 110–11; see also McPherson, *Battle Cry of Freedom*, 247; Beckert, *The Monied Metropolis*, 78, 84–88, 95.

25. McPherson, *Battle Cry of Freedom*, 592, 602; Beckert, *The Monied Metropolis*, 132–33.

26. Gladden, *Recollections*, 131–32; Faust, *This Republic of Suffering*, 141.

27. McPherson, *Battle Cry of Freedom*, 610–11; Beckert, *The Monied Metropolis*, 137–41.

28. Gladden, *Recollections*, 131–33.

29. Frederickson, "The Coming of the Lord," 116; Dorrien, *The Making of American Liberal Theology I*, 198–201.

30. Gladden to Tyler, December 1, 1862; Kathryn Gin Lum, *Damned Nation: Hell in America from the Revolution to Reconstruction* (New York: Oxford University Press, 2014), 202.

31. Faust, *This Republic of Suffering*, 162–70.

32. Washington Gladden to Moses Coit Tyler, undated.

33. Gladden, *Recollections*, 136; McPherson, *Battle Cry of Freedom*, 719–21, 734–35.

34. Washington Gladden Letter, June 5, 1864, MIC 4, reel 1, frames 196–97, Gladden Papers.

35. Gladden to Tyler, undated.

36. Faust, *This Republic of Suffering*, 109–10, 135; Richard White, *The Republic for Which It Stands: The United States during Reconstruction and the Gilded Age, 1865–1896* (New York: Oxford University Press, 2017), 28.

37. Gladden, *Recollections*, 138, 144.

38. Gladden to Tyler, undated.

39. Gladden, *Recollections*, 94.

40. Gladden, *Recollections*, 95; on Lincoln's religion and how it was perceived at the time, see Charles Reagan Wilson, "Religion and the American Civil War in Comparative Perspective," in Miller et al., *Religion and the American Civil War*, 403.

41. Gladden, *Recollections*, 95–96.

NOTES

42. Gladden, *Recollections*, 108; Washington Gladden to Moses Coit Tyler, June 22, 1865, Tyler Correspondence, v. 1, Tyler Papers; White, *The Republic for Which It Stands*, 15–16.

43. Gladden, *Recollections*, 97.

44. Gladden, *Recollections*, 124; see also Rose, *Victorian America and the Civil War*.

45. Gladden, *Recollections*, 94, 118; Beckert, *The Monied Metropolis*, 37–38.

46. Mark Hopkins to Washington Gladden, December 26, 1865, MIC 4, reel 1, frame 212, and Moses Tyler to Washington Gladden, February 19, 1866, MIC 4, reel 1, frame 218, Gladden Papers.

47. Gladden to Tyler, December 1, 1863.

48. Gladden, "The Philosophy of Missionary Work" (June 21, 1863), MIC 4, reel 13, frames 143–44, Gladden Papers.

49. Gladden, "The First Temptation" (August 25, 1861), MIC 4, reel 12, frames 1027–28, Gladden Papers.

50. Gladden, "The First Temptation," frame 1026.

51. Gladden, "The Philosophy of Missionary Work," frame 142; "The First Temptation," frame 1033.

52. Gladden, "Bookworms and Gossips," *Independent* 22 (August 11, 1870): 2.

53. Henry B. Stanton, *Random Recollections* (New York: Harper & Brothers 1887), 41–42. Gladden, *Recollections*, 10; on the Second Great Awakening, see Lum, *Damned Nation*, especially chapter 2; on upstate New York in particular, see Paul E. Johnson, *A Shopkeeper's Millennium: Society and Revivals in Rochester, New York, 1815–1837* (1978; New York: Hill and Wang, 2004).

54. Gladden, *Recollections*, 10; Matson to Gladden, March 1856, frames 39–40; Amanda Williams to Washington Gladden, January 22, 1859, MIC 4, reel 1, frames 124–25, Gladden Papers.

55. W. H. Carring to Washington Gladden, March 7, 1859, MSS 900, box 1, folder 1, Gladden Papers; Rose, *Victorian America and the Civil War*, 20–21; Lum, *Damned Nation*, 155.

56. Gladden, "Christian Growth" (February 12, 1860), MIC 4, reel 12, frames 617–18, Gladden Papers.

57. Nancie Priest to Washington Gladden, August 6, 1859, MSS 900, box 1, folder 6, Gladden Papers; Gladden, "The First Temptation," frame 1033.

58. Gladden, *Recollections*, 88.

59. Washington Gladden to Theodore Munger, November 22, 1895, folder 49, box 1, series I, Theodore T. Munger Papers, Sterling Library (New Haven, CT); see also Dorn, *Washington Gladden*, 379–84.

60. Henry Ward Beecher to Washington Gladden, October 9, 1866, reel 1, frame 245, Gladden Papers; White, *The Republic for Which It Stands*, especially chapter 1.

61. Gladden, *Recollections*, 158–59, 163.

3. REBEL

1. "Religious Intelligence," *Springfield Republican* (March 2, 1867): 1; Gladden, *Recollections*, 163; "New England News Items," *Springfield Republican* (August 7, 1869): 8; "Daniels Family History," Owego Historical Society; Dorn, *Washington Gladden*, 105–6.

2. Gladden to Moses Tyler, April 1, 1867, MSS 900, box 1, folder 7, Gladden Papers; Ebenezer Daniels to Gladden, June 2, 1867, MIC 4, reel 1, frame 286, Gladden Papers.

3. Gladden, *Recollections*, 161–62.

4. Moses Tyler to Washington Gladden, February 19, 1866, MIC 4, reel 1, frame 218, Gladden Papers.

5. Gladden, *Recollections*, 164; "New England News Items," *Springfield Republican* (September 26, 1868): 8; untitled notice, *Springfield Republican* (September 4, 1869): 4; on the *Independent*, see John A. Thompson, *Reformers and War: Progressive Publicists and the First World War* (Cambridge: Cambridge University Press, 2009), 20–21.

6. "New England News Items," *Springfield Republican* (October 12, 1867): 8; Washington Gladden, *Plain Thoughts on the Art of Living: Designed for Young Men and Women* (Boston: Ticknor and Fields, 1868), 27; on the pervasiveness of such rhetoric, see White, *The Republic for Which It Stands*, 5.

7. Gladden, *Plain Thoughts on the Art of Living*, 76, 85, 179, 183; see Beckert, *The Monied Metropolis*, 9.

8. Gladden, *Plain Thoughts on the Art of Living*, 5, 8, 11; see also Rose, *Victorian America and the Civil War*, 55–56.

9. Gladden, *Plain Thoughts on the Art of Living*, 166; on Anthony Comstock, see R. Marie Griffith, *Moral Combat: How Sex Divided American Christians and Fractured American Politics* (New York: Basic Books, 2017), 3–4; Gary Gerstle, *Liberty and Coercion: The Paradox of American Government from the Founding to the Present* (Princeton, NJ: Princeton University Press, 2015), 102–4.

10. Gladden, *Plain Thoughts on the Art of Living*, 52.

11. Gladden, *Recollections*, 163; "New Order of Worship," *Springfield Republican* (August 24, 1867): 1.

12. Gladden to Tyler, April 1, 1867.

13. Washington Gladden, "Are Dr. Bushnell's Views Heretical?" *Independent* 19 (October 17, 1867): 1.

14. Holifield, *Theology in America: Christian Thought from the Age of the Puritans to the Civil War* (New Haven, CT: Yale University Press, 2003), 458-59

15. See Holifield, *Theology in America*, 132–33, 462.

16. Holifield, *Theology in America*, 463–64.

17. Gladden; *Recollections*, 165; Holifield, *Theology in America*, 460.

18. Horace Bushnell to Washington Gladden, 1867, MIC 4, reel 1, frame 270, Gladden Papers.

19. Gladden to Tyler, April 1, 1867.

20. Moses Tyler to Gladden, July 10, 1867, MIC 4, reel 1, frame 294, Gladden Papers; Gladden, *Recollections*, 166.

21. Gladden, *Recollections*, 167.

22. Gladden, "Are Dr. Bushnell's Views Heretical?" 1; on the theological implications of mid-nineteenth-century humanitarianism, see James Turner, *Without God, Without Creed: The Origins of Unbelief in America* (Baltimore: Johns Hopkins University Press, 1985), 142–43.

23. Gladden, "Are Dr. Bushnell's Views Heretical?" 1.

24. Washington Gladden, "Compensations of Common-Sense," *Independent* 21 (March 18, 1869): 1; *Recollections*, 163.

25. Gladden, "Are Dr. Bushnell's Views Heretical?" 1.

26. Clay McCauley to Washington Gladden, October 21, 1867, MIC 4, reel 1, frames 311–12, Gladden Papers.

27. Gladden, *Recollections*, 168–69.

28. Washington Gladden, "The Amusement Question," *Independent* 19 (February 28, 1867): 1

29. Gladden, "The Amusement Question," 1.

30. Washington Gladden, "The Heresy of the Checker-Board," *Independent* 19 (July 4, 1867): 2.

31. Gladden, "The Heresy of the Checker-Board," 2.

32. Washington Gladden, "Forbidden Amusements," *Independent* (April 4, 1867): 1. "The Heresy of the Checker-Board," 2.

33. Gladden, "The Amusement Question," 1.

34. Gladden, "Forbidden Amusements," 1.

35. Gladden, "Forbidden Amusements," 1.

36. Gladden, *Plain Thoughts on the Art of Living*, 177–78.

37. Gladden, *Plain Thoughts on the Art of Living*, 175–76.

38. "New England News Items," *Springfield Republican* (October 12, 1867): 8; Horace Bushnell to Gladden, July 7, 1867, MIC 4, reel 1, frame 292,

and George William Curtis to Gladden, February 13, 1867, MIC 4, reel 1, frame 259, Gladden Papers.

39. Gladden, "Forbidden Amusements," 1; Gladden, *Recollections*, 169; Theodore L. Cuyler, "A Christian View of Amusements," *Independent* (May 16, 1867): 1.

40. Anonymous letter to Washington Gladden, April 6, 1867, MIC 4, reel 1, frames 273–75, Gladden Papers.

41. Ebenezer Daniels to Washington Gladden, June 2, 1867, MIC 4, reel 1, frames 286–88, Gladden Papers.

42. Anonymous to Gladden, April 6, 1867, frame 273.

43. Gladden, *Recollections*, 170–71.

44. Gladden, *Recollections*, 159–61.

45. Gladden, "What Shall We Wear to Church?" *Independent* 21 (February 4, 1869): 2.

46. Gladden, "What Shall We Wear to Church?" 2.

47. Gladden, *Recollections*, 171–72.

48. "The Chinese New Years," *Springfield Republican* (February 24, 1871): 3; see also Erika Lee, *At America's Gates: Chinese Immigration during the Exclusion Era, 1882–1943* (Chapel Hill: University of North Carolina Press, 2003), 23–30.

49. Washington Gladden, "The Arrival of the Coming Chinaman," *Independent* 22 (June 30, 1870): 1.

50. Washington Gladden, "Have We Barbarians among Us?" *Independent* 22 (October 13, 1870): 1.

51. Gladden, "The Arrival of the Coming Chinaman," 1.

52. Gladden, "The Arrival of the Coming Chinaman," 1; "Have We Barbarians among Us?" 1.

53. "The Chinese New Years," 3.

54. Joshua Paddison, *American Heathens: Religion, Race, and Reconstruction in California* (Berkeley and San Marino: University of California Press and the Huntington Library, 2012).

55. Gladden, *Recollections*, 173.

56. Gladden, *Plain Thoughts on the Art of Living*, 124, 147.

57. Gladden, *Plain Thoughts on the Art of Living*, 6, 180.

58. "Rev. Washington Gladden," *Springfield Republican* (January 20, 1871): 2.

59. Henry C. Bowen to Washington Gladden, January 6, 1871, MIC 4, reel 1, frame 398, and Bowen to Gladden, January 18, 1871, MIC 4, reel 1, frame 400, Gladden Papers.

60. Moses Coit Tyler to Washington Gladden, January 20, 1871, MIC 4, reel 1, frames 409–10; E. H. Sears to Gladden, March 3, 1872, MIC 4, reel 1,

frame 420; Sam Bowles to Gladden, January 24, 1871, MIC 4, reel 1, frames 407–8, Gladden Papers.

61. "Rev. Washington Gladden," 2.

62. Gladden, *Recollections*, 182.

63. Moses Tyler to Washington Gladden, January 29, 1871, frames 410–11; Bowles to Gladden, January 24, 1871, frame 408; Gladden, *Recollections*, 182.

64. Washington Gladden to Theodore Munger, December 3, 1880, folder 49, box 1, Munger Papers.

4. JOURNALIST

1. Beckert, *The Monied Metropolis*, 147–48.

2. White, *The Republic for Which It Stands*, 194–95; Beckert, *The Monied Metropolis*, 123.

3. Gladden, *Recollections*, 193; Beckert, *The Monied Metropolis*, 151–55.

4. "The Nether Side of New York," *Independent* 24 (July 11, 1872): 6; Gladden, *Recollections*, 199.

5. Gladden, *Recollections*, 183.

6. Beckert, *The Monied Metropolis*, 182, 192–93.

7. Beckert, *The Monied Metropolis*, 209.

8. "A Word about 'The Independent,'" *Independent* 23, April 6, 1871, 6; Gladden, *Recollections*, 182–83.

9. "A Word about 'The Independent,'" 6; James Marsh to Gladden, November 6, 1874, MIC 4, reel 1, frame 444, and E. H. Sears to Gladden, March 3, 1872, MIC 4, reel 1, frame 420, Gladden Papers.

10. Washington Gladden, "Remembrance of William Hayes Ward," *Independent* 87 (September 11, 1916): 375; Gladden, *Recollections*, 184.

11. Tyler to Gladden, January 20, 1871, frame 410; Gladden, "Remembrance of Ward," 375.

12. Gladden, *Recollections*, 188–90.

13. "A Word about 'The Independent,'" 6.

14. "Where We Stand," *Independent* 24 (January 25, 1872): 4.

15. Henry J. Van Dyke, "Woman-Preaching Forbidden by Scripture," *Independent* 24 (March 7, 1872): 8.

16. "How Infidels Are Made," *Independent* 24 (June 20, 1872): 4; "Congregational Creedlessness," *Independent* 24 (February 1, 1872): 6; on this phenomenon more broadly, see Leigh Eric Schmidt, *Village Atheists: How America's Unbelievers Made Their Way in a Godly Nation* (Princeton, NJ: Princeton University Press, 2016).

17. "Religious Intelligence," *Independent* 24 (September 5, 1872): 6–7; White, *The Republic for Which It Stands*, 408–10.

18. Steven K. Green, *The Second Disestablishment: Church and State in Nineteenth-Century America* (New York: Oxford University Press, 2010), 275–87.

19. "Religious Intelligence," *Independent* 25 (February 6, 1873): 175; Frederickson, "The Coming of the Lord," 122.

20. "Official Prayer," *Independent* 23 (February 23, 1871): 4.

21. "Ecclesiastical Property and Taxation," *Independent* 24 (March 7, 1872): 6.

22. "Ritualism in Politics," *Independent* 24 (February 8, 1872): 4.

23. "The Young Men's Faithlessness," *Independent* 24 (June 20, 1872): 4; "Religious Intelligence," *Independent* 25 (February 6, 1873): 175.

24. "Official Prayer," 4.

25. "Ritualism in Politics," 4.

26. "How Infidels Are Made," 4.

27. "Religious Intelligence," *Independent* 24 (February 1, 1872), 6.

28. C. S. Robinson, "Search the Scriptures," *Independent* 24 (August 22, 1872): 1.

29. See Turner, *Without God, Without Creed*; Jon H. Roberts, *Darwinism and the Divine in America: Protestant Intellectuals and Organic Evolution, 1859–1900* (Madison: University of Wisconsin Press, 1988).

30. "How Infidels Are Made," 4.

31. Editorial, *Independent* 23 (April 20, 1871): 4; "Religious Intelligence," *Independent* 23 (April 20, 1871): 5.

32. "The Prayer-Gauge Again," *Independent* 24 (August 29, 1872): 4.

33. H. N. Powers, "Heart and Brains: Prof. David Swing," *Independent* 26 (March 26, 1874): 5; on the Swing trial, see Dorrien, *The Making of American Liberal Theology I*, 275–79; Heath Carter, *Union Made: Working People and the Rise of Social Christianity in Chicago* (New York: Oxford University Press, 2015), 54.

34. Powers, "Heart and Brains," 5.

35. Edwin L. Hurd, "Swing and Atwater," *Independent* 26 (September 3, 1874): 2.

36. "The Swing Trial," *Independent* 26 (May 14, 1874): 16–17.

37. "Religious Intelligence," *Independent* 25 (January 9, 1873): 19–20.

38. "The Swing Trial," 16–17.

39. "The Swing Trial," 16–17.

40. Editorial, *Independent* 26 (June 4, 1874): 16.

41. "Religious Intelligence," *Independent* 26 (November 5, 1874): 18.

42. See, for example, several items in "Religious Intelligence," *Independent* (May 2, 1872): 6; "Burning Bibles in Rome," *Independent* 24 (June 27, 1872): 1; "Religious Intelligence," *Independent* 24 (August 1, 1872): 6; "The Pope's Last Letter," *Independent* 24 (August 1, 1872): 6; "The Young Men's Faithlessness," 4.

43. "Religious Intelligence," *Independent* 24 (January 4, 1872): 6; "Religious Intelligence," *Independent* 25 (January 2, 1873): 17. Gladden was not alone among Catholics or Protestants in seeing this possibility; see Jay P. Dolan, *In Search of an American Catholicism: A History of Religion and Culture in Tension* (New York: Oxford University Press, 2002), especially chapter 3.

44. "The Young Men's Faithlessness," 4.

45. "The Catholics and the Schools," *Independent* 24 (January 11, 1872): 4.

46. "The Catholics and the Schools," 4.

47. "Religious Intelligence," *Independent* 24 (May 23, 1872): 4; "Religious Intelligence," *Independent* 25 (January 23, 1873): 115.

48. "Religious Intelligence," *Independent* 24 (May 30, 1872): 4; "Religious Intelligence," *Independent* 25 (January 23, 1873): 115.

49. Washington Gladden, "The Bondage of the Pulpit," *Independent* 23 (February 2, 1871): 3.

50. "The Prayer-Gauge Again," 4.

51. "Secular and Religious Journalism," *Independent* 23 (February 23, 1871): 4.

52. Gladden, *Recollections*, 204–5.

53. On the 1872 election, see Heather Cox Richardson, *To Make Men Free: A History of the Republican Party* (New York: Basic Books, 2014), 81–107.

54. "The Nomination of Mr. Greeley," *Independent* 24 (May 9, 1872): 4.

55. Gladden, *Recollections*, 187, 192, 194.

56. Gladden, *Recollections*, 210–11; White, *The Republic for Which It Stands*, 210–11.

57. "The Political Outlook," *Independent* 23 (March 23, 1871): 4.

58. "A Fit of Negrophobia," *Independent* 24 (February 8, 1872): 4; Gladden, *Recollections*, 185.

59. "A Fit of Negrophobia," 4.

60. White, *The Republic for Which It Stands*, 188–91.

61. "The Ku-Klux Outrages," *Independent* 23 (March 16, 1871): 4.

62. "The Political Outlook," 4; White, *The Republic for Which It Stands*, 196–200.

63. Gladden, *Recollections*, 212.

64. Washington Gladden to Henry C. Bowen, May 22, 1873, MSS 900, box 1, folder 8, Gladden Papers.

65. Washington Gladden to Henry C. Bowen, October 31, 1874, MSS 900, box 1, folder 8, Gladden Papers.
66. Washington Gladden to Henry C. Bowen, November 5, 1874, MIC 4, reel 1, frame 442, Gladden Papers.
67. S. M. Atwood to Washington Gladden, December 4, 1874, MIC 4, reel 1, frames 446–47; Sam Bowles to Washington Gladden, November 6, 1874, MIC 4, reel 1, frame 443, Gladden Papers.
68. Washington Gladden to Lyman Abbott, November 3, 1874, MIC 4, reel 1, frame 435, Gladden Papers.
69. William Hayes Ward to Washington Gladden, August 18, 1910, MIC 4, reel 9, frame 296, Gladden Papers; Gladden, *Recollections*, 236–37.

5. PASTOR

1. Washington Gladden to Theodore T. Munger, August 5, 1885, folder 49, box 1, series I, Munger Papers; Gladden, *Recollections*, 240.
2. "A New Springfield Magazine," *Springfield Republican* (November 10, 1877): 6.
3. Gladden, *Recollections*, 272–73; see also Dorn, *Washington Gladden*, 67–68.
4. "Washington Gladden," *Springfield Republican* (February 14, 1877): 4; George S. Merriam, *The Life and Times of Samuel Bowles*, vol. 2 (New York: Century Co., 1885), 325–26.
5. Minutes of the Hampden Association of Congregational Churches, February 11, 1879, Congregational Library and Archives (Boston, MA).
6. Gladden, *Recollections*, 215–26, 259.
7. Turner, *Without God, Without Creed*, 143–50.
8. Holifield, *Theology in America*, 188–89.
9. Gladden, *Recollections*, 259.
10. George M. Marsden, *Fundamentalism and American Culture*, 2nd ed. (New York: Oxford University Press, 2006), 21–39, 118–23.
11. Dorrien, *The Making of American Liberal Theology* I, 293–304; William R. Hutchison, *The Modernist Impulse in American Protestantism* (Durham, NC: Duke University Press, 1992), 87–110.
12. Washington Gladden, "Impertinence" (October 21, 1860), MIC 4, reel 12, frame 832, Gladden Papers; Gladden to Munger, August 5, 1883.
13. Dorrien, *The Making of American Liberal Theology* I, 290–93.
14. See Gin Lum, *Damned Nation*, 22–23.

NOTES

15. Minutes of the Hampden Association of Congregational Churches, November 13, 1877, Congregational Library and Archive (Boston, MA); Gladden, *Recollections*, 262–64.

16. Gladden, *Recollections*, 268.

17. Gladden to Theodore Munger, June 18, 1879, and December 3, 1880, folder 49, box 1, series I, Munger Papers.

18. Minutes of the Hampden Association of Congregational Churches, July 9, 1878, February 11, 1879, February 8, 1881, July 12, 1881.

19. Gladden, *Recollections*, 230.

20. Gladden, *Recollections*, 260–61.

21. Gladden to Munger, June 18, 1879; Margaret Bendroth, *The Last Puritans: Mainline Protestants and the Power of the Past* (Chapel Hill: University of North Carolina Press, 2015), 112.

22. George C. Noyes to Washington Gladden, April 26, 1876, MIC 4, reel 1, frame 471, Gladden Papers; Howard Crosby to Washington Gladden, April 18, 1876, MIC 4, reel 1, frames 469–70; C. D. Hilman to Washington Gladden, April 27, 1876, MIC 4, reel 1, frames 473–74; William W. Adams to Washington Gladden, October 13, 1876, MIC 4, reel 1, frame 478, Gladden Papers.

23. J. H. Eastman to Washington Gladden, undated, MIC 4, reel 1, frame 486, Gladden Papers; Gladden, *Recollections*, 258.

24. Washiington Gladden, "St. Louis Council" (November 21, 1880), MIC 4, reel 1, frame 517, Gladden Papers.

25. Washington Gladden, *Being a Christian: What It Means and How to Begin* (Boston: Congregational Publishing Society, 1876), 9; Gladden, "St. Louis Council," frame 517.

26. Washington Gladden, "Practical Defects in the Religion of To-Day" (February 8, 1880), MIC 4, reel 16, frames 102–3, Gladden Papers.

27. Washington Gladden, "The Foundations of the State" (May 30, 1880), MIC 4, reel 16, frame 282, Gladden Papers.

28. Gladden, *Being a Christian*, 9–10.

29. Gladden, *Being a Christian*, 15.

30. Washington Gladden, "Waiting for the Holy Spirit" (September 12, 1880), MIC 4, reel 16, frame 443, Gladden Papers; Gladden, *Being a Christian*, 61.

31. Gladden, *Being a Christian*, 65, 69, 71.

32. Gladden, *Being a Christian*, 79, 92–93.

33. Washington Gladden, "The Whimsicality of Unbelief" (May 30, 1880), MIC 4, reel 16, frame 257, Gladden Papers; "The Limitations of Religious Thought" (November 28, 1880), MIC 4, reel 16, frames 535, 538, 545, Gladden Papers.

34. Gladden, "The Whimsicality of Unbelief," frames 265–66.

35. Gladden, *Being a Christian*, 96; Gin Lum, *Damned Nation*, 60–61.

36. Gladden, *Being a Christian*, 35.

37. Washington Gladden, "Preaching the Law," *Independent* 28 (May 18, 1876): 1.

38. Gladden, *Being a Christian*, 22.

39. Washington Gladden, "Impertinence," frame 832; "Mount Sinai and Mount Zion" (September 5, 1880), MIC 4, reel 16, frame 406, Gladden Papers.

40. Gladden, "Practical Defects in the Religion of To-Day," frame 90; Transcription of Washington Gladden to the Parish Committee of North Congregational Church, December 13, 1878, MSS 900, box 1, folder 8, Gladden Papers.

41. Washington Gladden to Theodore Munger, November 2, 1885, folder 49, box 1, series I, Munger Papers.

42. Washington Gladden to Moses Coit Tyler, May 24, 1881, and George A. Jackson to Washington Gladden, August 3, 1877, MSS 900, box 1, folder 8, Gladden Papers.

43. Committee of the First Congregational Church Society of Columbus to Washington Gladden, November 2, 1882, MIC 4, reel 2, frame 111, Gladden Papers; Committee of the Church and Parish of the North Church of Springfield to Washington Gladden, November 20, 1882, MIC 4, reel 2, frame 121, Gladden Papers.

44. Andrew Dickson White to Washington Gladden, February 18, 1884, MIC 4, reel 2, frame 121, Gladden Papers; White, *The Republic for Which It Stands*, 16–17.

45. Washington Gladden to Theodore Munger, January 16, 1883, MSS 900, box 1, folder 9, Gladden Papers.

46. Gladden to Munger, January 16, 1883; Gladden, *Recollections*, 284–85.

47. Gladden to Munger, November 2, 1885.

48. Irvin Butterworth to Washington Gladden, November 4, 1884, MIC 4, reel 2, frames 278–79, Gladden Papers.

49. White, *The Republic for Which It Stands*, 169–70.

50. Washington Gladden, *Young Men and the Churches: Why Some of Them Are Outside, and Why They Ought to Come In* (Boston: Congregational Sunday School and Publishing Society, 1885), 12.

51. Gladden, *Young Men and the Churches*, 31.

52. Gladden, *Young Men and the Churches*, 32.

53. Gladden, *Young Men and the Churches*, 55–56.

54. Gladden, *Recollections*, 321.

55. Washington Gladden, *Who Wrote the Bible? A Book for the People* (Boston: Houghton Mifflin, 1891), 1, 5–6.

56. Gladden, *Who Wrote the Bible?* 15, 322.
57. Gladden, *Who Wrote the Bible?* 185, 209.
58. Gladden, *Who Wrote the Bible?* 154, 210.
59. Gladden, *Who Wrote the Bible?* 95, 134, 224, 359.
60. Gladden, *Who Wrote the Bible?* 142–43.
61. Gladden, *Who Wrote the Bible?* 212; Arthur S. Cooley to Washington Gladden, August 1, 1917, MIC 4, reel 12, frame 211, Gladden Papers.
62. Gladden, *Who Wrote the Bible?* 110.
63. Gladden, *Who Wrote the Bible?* 114.
64. Calvin Whitney to Washington Gladden, January 20, 1902, MIC 4, reel 3, frame 533, and H. N. Dascomb to Washington Gladden, February 14, 1906, MIC 4, reel 7, frame 346, Gladden Papers.
65. Washington Gladden, *How Much Is Left of the Old Doctrines? A Book for the People* (Boston: Houghton Mifflin, 1899), 2.
66. Washington Gladden to Theodore Munger, August 23, 1902, folder 49, box 1, series I, Munger Papers.

6. REFORMER

1. Gladden, *Recollections*, 336–37; William M. Knight to Washington Gladden, September 22, 1900, MIC 4, reel 3, frame 75, Gladden Papers; some evidence suggests that Gladden did discuss the decision with a few people; see Dorn, *Washington Gladden*, 320n48.
2. J. J. Janney to the *Ohio State Journal*, July 19, 1880, MSS 142, box 1, folder 9, Janney Family Papers, Ohio History Connection (Columbus, Ohio).
3. Gladden, *Recollections*, 341.
4. Gladden, *Recollections*, 341.
5. Gladden, *Recollections*, 337, 341–42.
6. Washington Gladden to Richard Gilder, May 17, 1888, Series I, Box 39, Century Company Collection, New York Public Library (New York, NY); Gladden, *Recollections*, 329; on Low, see L. E. Fredman, "Seth Low: Theorist of Municipal Reform," *Journal of American Studies* 6 (April 1972): 19–39.
7. Gladden to Richard Gilder, April 29, 1888, Series I, Box 39, Century Company Collection; Jennie Gladden to Alice and Fred Gladden, June 24, 1888, MIC 4, reel 2, frame 470, Gladden Papers; Washington Gladden to the Gladden Children, June 28, 1888, MIC 4, reel 2, frame 489, Gladden Papers; Dorn, *Washington Gladden*, 403.
8. Amanda Williams to Washington Gladden, October 8, 1867, reel 1, frame 309, Gladden Papers; George Gladden to Washington Gladden, May 9, 1860, MSS 900, box 1, folder 6, Gladden Papers.

9. Gladden, *Plain Thoughts on the Art of Living*, 181; Washington Gladden, *Working People and Their Employers* (Boston: Lockwood, Brooks, 1876), 10; on the history of such attitudes, see Brent Ruswick, *Almost Worthy: The Poor, Paupers, and the Science of Charity in America, 1877–1917* (Bloomington: Indiana University Press, 2012), 6–9.

10. White, *The Republic for Which It Stands*, 237; Daniel T. Rodgers, *The Work Ethic in Industrial America* (Chicago: University of Chicago Press, 1978), 22–24, 30–40.

11. Nell Irvin Painter, *Standing at Armageddon: The United States, 1877–1919* (New York: W.W. Norton, 1987), 4.

12. White, *The Republic for Which It Stands*, 268–69.

13. Washington Gladden, *Tools and the Man: Property and Industry under Christian Law* (Boston: Houghton Mifflin, 1893), 125; White, *The Republic for Which It Stands*, 278.

14. Gladden, *Working People and Their Employers*, 204; *Tools and the Man*, 187–88.

15. Gladden, *Working People and Their Employers*, 14–19, 65–66, 69.

16. Gladden, *Working People and Their Employers*, 23, 43, 40, 138–39.

17. J. M. Osborn to Washington Gladden, May 21, 1877, MIC 4, reel 1, frame 498, Gladden Papers; Gladden, *Recollections*, 256.

18. Gladden, *Working People and Their Employers*, 3, 36.

19. Gladden, *Working People and Their Employers*, 170–72; see also Oliver Zunz, *Making America Corporate, 1870–1920* (Chicago: University of Chicago Press, 1990).

20. Gladden, *Working People and Their Employers*, 43.

21. Painter, *Standing at Armageddon*, 47–50.

22. Gladden, *Recollections*, 291–92; Washington Gladden to Richard Gilder, January 25, 1892, Series I, Box 39, Century Company Collection.

23. Gladden, *Tools and the Man*, 26, 28.

24. Gladden, *Social Facts and Forces* (New York: G.P. Putnam, 1897), 21; on the relationship between religion and the social sciences, see Sehat, *The Myth of American Religious Freedom*, 193–98; Christopher D. Cantwell, Heath W. Carter, and Janine Giordano Drake, eds., *The Pew and the Picket Line: Christianity and the American Working Class* (Urbana: University of Illinois Press, 2016), 5–6.

25. Washington Gladden to J. J. Janney, February 1, 1892, box 1, folder 2, Janney Family Collection.

26. Gladden, *Social Facts and Forces* , 34–35; Gladden, *Recollections*, 294; Carter, *Union Made*, 3.

27. Gladden, *Tools and the Man*, 38.

28. Gladden, *Tools and the Man*, 144.

NOTES

29. Gladden, *Tools and the Man*, 124; Gladden, *Social Facts and Forces*, 66.

30. Washington Gladden, *The Christian Pastor and the Working Church* (Edinburgh: T. & T. Clark, 1898), 173.

31. Gladden, *Tools and the Man*, 10.

32. Gladden, *Tools and the Man*, 100.

33. Gladden, *Tools and the Man*, 72.

34. Gladden, *Tools and the Man*, 288–300; *Social Facts and Forces*, 40–41; *Recollections*, 342.

35. White, *The Republic for Which It Stands*, 237.

36. White, *The Republic for Which It Stands*, 241–42; Sehat, *The Myth of American Religious Freedom*, especially chapter 8.

37. Gladden, *Tools and the Man*, 161.

38. Gladden, *Tools and the Man*, 164, 167.

39. Gladden, *Social Facts and Forces*, 90–91.

40. Gladden, *Recollections*, 343–44.

41. Washington Gladden, "Religion Vital to Democracy," *Independent* 52 (December 6, 1900): 2908.

42. Gladden, *Social Facts and Forces*, 72

43. Gladden, *Recollections*, 302; *Tools and the Man*, 179.

44. Gladden, *Tools and the Man*, 182; *Recollections*, 315.

45. Gladden, *Tools and the Man*, 208–9, 213.

46. Gladden, *Working People and Their Employers*, 199; *Recollections*, 306; *Tools and the Man*, 255–56, 280.

47. Gladden, *Recollections*, 300–301, 304.

48. Jackson Lears, *Rebirth of a Nation: The Making of Modern America, 1877–1920* (New York: Harper Perennial, 2009), 160.

49. White, *The Republic for which It Stands*, 164.

50. George Gladden to Washington Gladden, December 12, 1858, MSS 900, box 1, folder 5, and February 13, 1859, MSS 900, box 1, folder 6, Gladden Papers.

51. Washington Gladden to Charles Cranmore, February 21, 1867, MIC 4, reel 1, frames 262–63, Gladden Papers.

52. Gladden, *Working People and Their Employers*, 163.

53. Gladden, *Working People and Their Employers*, 145.

54. Gladden to Theodore Munger, January 16, 1883; Washington Gladden, "Good Morals in Columbus" (March 21, 1886), MIC 4, reel 19, frame 183, Gladden Papers; Gladden, *The Christian Pastor and the Working Church*, 440–41.

55. Washington Gladden, *The Great War: Six Sermons* (Columbus, OH: McClelland, 1915), 49–50.

56. Gladden, *Social Facts and Forces*, 164.
57. Gladden, *Recollections*, 330–31.
58. Gladden, *Social Facts and Forces*, 170–71.
59. "Gladden in Council"; White, *The Republic for which It Stands*, 477–81.
60. White, *The Republic for which It Stands*, 2.
61. Gladden, *Social Facts and Forces*, 184.
62. Gladden to Munger, January 16, 1883.
63. Gladden, *Social Facts and Forces*, 185.
64. Gladden, *Social Facts and Forces*, 186.
65. Gladden, *Recollections*, 350–51.
66. Gladden, *Social Facts and Forces*, 190; Washington Gladden, *Parish Problems: Hints and Help for the People of the Churches* (New York: Century Co., 1887), 230.
67. Gladden, *The Christian Pastor and the Working Church*, 408.
68. Gladden to Richard Gilder, February 11, 1887, Century Collection.
69. Gladden, *The Christian Pastor and the Working Church*, 451; Gladden, *Social Salvation* (Boston: Houghton Mifflin, 1902), 36–37.
70. Gladden, *The Christian Pastor and the Working Church*, 451, 462, 466.
71. Gladden, *The Christian Pastor and the Working Church*, 467.
72. Gladden, *The Christian Pastor and the Working Church*, 467–68.
73. Richard D. Harlan to Washington Gladden, November 17, 1900, MIC 4, reel 3, frames 129–130; Fred H. Hines to Washington Gladden, March 9, 1901, MIC 4, reel 3, frame 231, Gladden Papers; Gladden, *Recollections*, 329–30; Dorn, *Washington Gladden*, 319.
74. Gladden, *The Christian Pastor and the Working Church*, 103.
75. Gladden, *The Christian Pastor and the Working Church*, 47–48.
76. Gladden, *Social Salvation*, 15; Gladden, *The Christian Pastor and the Working Church*, 103.
77. Gladden, *The Christian Pastor and the Working Church*, 120; Gladden, *Social Salvation*, 26.
78. Gladden, *Social Salvation*, 30.
79. See Gail Hamilton, "Man-Preaching and Woman-Preaching," *Independent* 23 (February 9, 1871): 1; and "The Good of Being Provided For," *Independent* 23 (April 13, 1871): 1.
80. Gladden, *Plain Thoughts on the Art of Living*, 19, 21, 24–25.
81. Washington Gladden to J. J. Janney, January 28, 1886, folder 1, box 1, Janney Family Papers.
82. Lears, *Rebirth of a Nation*, 160.

7. UNIFIER

1. Guy T. Viskinskki to Washington Gladden, June 11, 1910, MIC 4, reel 9, frame 221, Gladden Papers; Gladden to Gilder, September 4, 1908, Century Collection.
2. White, *The Republic for which It Stands*, 21–22.
3. Washington Gladden, *Tools and the Man*, 187–88; White, *The Republic for which It Stands*, 230–31, 245.
4. Gladden, *Parish Problems*, 271–72.
5. Gladden, *The Christian Pastor and the Working Church*, 25; Gladden, *Parish Problems*, 274.
6. Gladden, *The Christian Pastor and the Working Church*, 32–33.
7. L. G. Herbert to Washington Gladden, March 31, 1905, MIC 4, reel 5, frame 200; R. W. Johnson to Washington Gladden, March 4, 1910, MIC 4, reel 1, frame 118, Gladden Papers.
8. Carter, *Union Made*, 10–11.
9. Gladden, *The Christian Pastor and the Working Church*, 29.
10. Washington Gladden to "Friends at Home," July 1, 1888, MIC 4, reel 2, frames 512–13, Gladden Papers.
11. Gladden, *The Christian Pastor and the Working Church*, 262, 268; on churches in this period, see Paul S. Boyer, *Urban Masses and Moral Order in America, 1820–1920* (Cambridge, MA: Harvard University Press, 1978), 137–39.
12. Gladden, *The Christian Pastor and the Working Church*, 34.
13. Gladden, *The Christian Pastor and the Working Church*, 428.
14. Gladden, *The Christian Pastor and the Working Church*, 430.
15. Roger Finke and Rodney D. Stark, *The Churching of America, 1776–2005: Winners and Losers in Our Religious Economy* (New Brunswick, NJ: Rutgers University Press, 2005), 206–7.
16. Washington Gladden, "Three Practical Questions," *Independent* 27 (November 4, 1875): 1-2.
17. Gladden, *The Christian Pastor and the Working Church*, 435–36.
18. Gladden, *The Christian Pastor and the Working Church*, 258.
19. Gladden, "The Christian League of Connecticut: I," *Century* 25 (November 1882): 50–51.
20. Gladden, "The Christian League of Connecticut: I," 52, 55.
21. Gladden, "The Christian League of Connecticut: I," 55.
22. Gladden, "The Christian League of Connecticut: III," *Century* 25 (January 1883): 349.
23. Gladden, "The Christian League of Connecticut: III," 343.

24. Richard W. Gilder to Washington Gladden, May 6, 1882, MIC 4, reel 2, frame 52; Ray Stannard Baker to Washington Gladden, October 7, 1907, MIC 4, reel 8, frame 130, Gladden Papers.

25. Alfred Williams Anthony, "The New Interdenominationalism," *American Journal of Theology* 20, no. 4 (October 1916): 494–96; David Mislin, *Saving Faith: Making Religious Pluralism an American Value at the Dawn of the Secular Age* (Ithaca, NY: Cornell University Press, 2015), 131, 140–41.

26. L. H. Ruge to Gladden, May 26, 1906, MIC 4, reel 7, frame 536, Gladden papers; for a detailed description of this effort, see Dorn, *Washington Gladden*, 354–69.

27. Washington Gladden, "The Anti-Catholic Crusade," *Century* 47 (March 1894): 789.

28. John T. McGreevy, *Catholicism and American Freedom: A History* (New York: W.W. Norton, 2003), 124–25.

29. Gladden to Richard Gilder, December 22, 1893, and January 11, 1894, Series I, Box 39, Century Company Collection.

30. Gladden to Gilder, December 23, 1893.

31. Gladden to Gilder, January 8, 1893, Series I, Box 39, Century Company Collection.

32. Gladden, "The Anti-Catholic Crusade," 792; Gladden to Gilder, January 11, 1894.

33. Gladden, "The Anti-Catholic Crusade," 792.

34. Gladden, "The Anti-Catholic Crusade," 792–93.

35. Gladden to Gilder, January 8, 1893; Gladden to Gilder, January 2, 1894, Century Collection.

36. Gladden, "The Anti-Catholic Crusade," 792.

37. Gladden to Gilder, December 22, 1893; McGreevy, *Catholicism and American Freedom*, 124.

38. Gladden to Gilder, January 2, 1894.

39. Gladden to Gilder, December 22, 1893.

40. Gladden to Gilder, January 8, 1893, and December 11, 1893.

41. Gladden to Gilder, January 8, 1893, and January 11, 1894.

42. Washington Gladden to R. W. Johnson, September 9, 1896, Series I, Box 39, Century Company Collection; Gladden, "Bishop Watterson" (April 23, 1899), MIC 4, reel 30, frame 536, Gladden Papers; Robert T. Handy, *Undermined Establishment: Church-State Relations in America, 1880–1920* (Princeton, NJ: Princeton University Press, 1991), 53–54.

43. Washington Gladden, "Ells and Inches," *Independent* 22 (June 16, 1870): 1.

44. Gladden, "Ells and Inches," 1.

45. Gladden, "Ells and Inches," 1.

46. Gladden, "Bishop Watterson," frame 537.
47. Gladden, *The Christian Pastor and the Working Church*, 467.
48. Gladden, *The Christian Pastor and the Working Church*, 471–72.
49. Gladden, "Bishop Watterson," frame 547.
50. Gladden, "Bishop Watterson," frame 548.
51. Allen Bower to Washington Gladden, August 11, 1913, MIC 4, reel 10, frames 440–41, Gladden Papers.
52. Gladden to Gilder, December 22, 1893.
53. Gladden, *The Christian Pastor and the Working Church*, 31, 337–38; see also David Mislin, "'Against the Foes That Destroy the Family, Protestants and Catholics Can Stand Together': Divorce and Christian Ecumenism," in *Faithful Republic: Religion and Politics in Modern America*, Andrew Preston, Bruce J. Schulman, and Julian E. Zelizer, eds. (Philadelphia: University of Pennsylvania Press, 2015), 9-21.
54. Gladden to Gilder, December 22, 1893; Gladden, "Bishop Watterson," frame 547.
55. See *Congregationalist and Christian World* 90 (July 8, 1905): 46.
56. Parley P. Womer to Gladden, November 29, 1909, MIC 4, reel 8, frame 972; James Hoye to Gladden, March 19, 1913, MIC 4, reel 10, frame 264; Louis A. Smith to Gladden, August 5, 1916, MIC 4, reel 11, frame 876, Gladden Papers.
57. M. D. Van Horn to Gladden, December 28, 1893, Series I, Box 39, Century Company Collection.
58. Gladden to Gilder, January 2, 1894; Dorn, *Washington Gladden*, 118–19.
59. Gladden, "The Foundations of the State," frame 283; White, *The Republic for Which It Stands*, 254, 472.
60. Gladden, *Recollections*, 246–47.
61. Gladden, *Recollections*, 316–17.
62. Washington Gladden to Theodore Munger, November 2, 1885, folder 49, box 1, Series I, Munger Papers.
63. Gladden, *Recollections*, 316; Dorn, *Washington Gladden*, 322.
64. Gladden, "Religion Vital to Democracy," 2908-2909.
65. Gladden, "Religion Vital to Democracy," 2909.
66. Gladden, "The Foundations of the State," frame 288; Gladden, "Religion Vital to Democracy," 2909.
67. White, *The Republic for Which It Stands*, 411.
68. Gladden, "Safeguards of the Suffrage," *Century* 37 (February 1889): 621.
69. Gladden, "The Fruits of Ignorance," *Independent* 29 (August 2, 1877): 1; "Safeguards of the Suffrage," 622.

70. Gladden, *The Christian Pastor and the Working Church*, 320; Gladden, "Safeguards of the Suffrage," 623.

8. CRITIC

1. Washington Gladden to Alice Kelton, October 24, 1914, MSS 900, box 1, folder 12, Gladden Papers; Dorn, *Washington Gladden*, 102.
2. Gladden to Gilder, December 7, 1908, and Gladden to Johnson, February 7, 1910, Series I, Box 39, Century Company Collection.
3. For more on the "tainted money" debate, see Dorn, *Washington Gladden*, 240–67.
4. See Lears, *Rebirth of a Nation*, 60–61.
5. Gladden, *Recollections*, 402, 406.
6. "The Tainted Money Issue," *Congregationalist and Christian World* 90 (August 26, 1905): 276.
7. "Topics of the Time," *Century* 70 (June 1905): 314; Graham Taylor, "Shall the Dollar's Pedigree Defeat its Destiny," reprinted in *Congregationalist and Christian World* 90 (September 16, 1905): 383.
8. Statement of a subcommittee of the American Board's Prudential Committee, quoted in "The Week," *Outlook* 79 (April 8, 1905): 867; "What Is Good Money for Missions?" *Congregationalist and Christian World* 90 (August 26, 1905): 281.
9. "Judge Not," *Outlook* 79 (April 8, 1905): 871.
10. Statement of the subcommittee, 868; "Mr. Rockefeller and the American Board," *Outlook* 79 (April 1, 1905): 767; "The Week," *Outlook* 79 (April 15, 1905): 923; "Judge Not," 871; H. A. Bridgman to Gladden, March 29, 1905, MIC 4, reel 5, frame 87, Gladden Papers.
11. "Mr. Rockefeller and the American Board: A Statement from Dr. Gladden," *Outlook* 79 (April 22, 1905): 985; Gladden, *Recollections*, 403–4.
12. Gladden, *Recollections*, 403.
13. Gladden, *Recollections*, 405–6; "What Is Good Money for Missions?" 281.
14. "Topics of the Time," 314.
15. "The Week," *Outlook* 79 (April 22, 1905), 967; Letter from Clinton V.S. Remington, *Congregationalist and Christian World* 90 (September 2, 1905): 334; Taylor, "Shall the Dollar's Pedigree Defeat Its Destiny," 384; Letter from Anonymous, *Congregationalist and Christian World* 90 (September 9, 1905): 338.
16. S. B. Stitt to Washington Gladden, March 27, 1905; MIC 4, reel 5, frame 35, Gladden Papers; E. O. Cornell to Washington Gladden, March 27,

1905, MIC 4, reel 5, frame 8, Gladden Papers; Letter from Emma C. Barrett, *Outlook* 79 (April 22, 1905): 988.

17. L. G. Herbert to Washington Gladden, March 31, 1905, MIC 4, reel 5, frame 200; George Knight to Washington Gladden, February 11, 1906, frame 244, reel 7, Gladden Papers.

18. Gladden, *Recollections*, 407.

19. Washington Gladden, "Shall Ill-Gotten Gains Be Sought for Christian Purposes," excerpts from address to the American Board, reprinted in *Congregationalist and Christian World* 90 (September 23, 1905): 411.

20. "The American Board at Seattle," *Congregationalist and Christian World* 90 (September 30, 1905): 446.

21. "The American Board at Seattle," 446.

22. Gladden, *Recollections*, 407–8.

23. Gladden, *Recollections*, 367–68; on the American Missionary Association, see Ralph E. Luker, *The Social Gospel in Black and White: American Racial Reform, 1885–1912* (Chapel Hill: University of North Carolina Press, 1991), 12–13.

24. Christopher H. Evans, *The Social Gospel in American Religion: A History* (New York: New York University Press, 2017), 41–43; Sehat, *The Myth of American Religious Freedom*, 124–32; Philip Gorski, *American Covenant: A History of Civil Religion from the Puritans to the Present* (Princeton, NJ: Princeton University Press, 2017), 119–24.

25. Gladden, quoted in Luker, *The Social Gospel in Black and White*, 215–16; Dorn, *Washington Gladden*, 298–300.

26. Gladden, *Recollections*, 370–71.

27. Gladden, *Recollections*, 369–70; see also Natalie J. Ring, *The Problem South: Region, Empire, and the New Liberal State, 1880–1930* (Athens: University of Georgia Press, 2012).

28. Gladden, *Recollections*, 371.

29. Dorn, *Washington Gladden*, 300–301.

30. Gladden, "The Southern Question," *Independent* 28 (September 7, 1876): 3.

31. White, *The Republic for Which It Stands*, 90–91.

32. Gladden, "The Southern Question," 3.

33. Gladden, "The Southern Question," 3.

34. Gladden, *Recollections*, 179; Gladden, "The Southern Question," 3.

35. Gladden, *Recollections*, 180.

36. Gladden, "Safeguards of the Suffrage," 621–22; Luker, *The Social Gospel in Black and White*, 203.

37. Gladden, *Recollections*, 374.

38. Gladden, "The Christian League of Connecticut I," 54.

39. Lears, *Rebirth of a Nation*, 207, 209; Andrew Preston, *Sword of the Spirit, Shield of the Faith: Religion in American War and Diplomacy* (New York: Alfred A. Knopf, 2012), 223–32.

40. Gladden, "The Nation's Opportunity," *Independent* 51 (January 12, 1899): 103.

41. Gladden, "The Nation's Opportunity," 103, 105-6; see also Ian Tyrrell, *Reforming the World: The Creation of America's Moral Empire* (Princeton, NJ: Princeton University Press, 2010).

42. Gladden, sermon preached December 18, 1898, MIC 4, reel 30, frame 82, Gladden Papers; Lears, *Rebirth of a Nation*, 215–17.

43. Gladden, "The Nation's Opportunity," 103.

44. Gladden, "The Nation's Opportunity," 104; Gladden, sermon preached December 18, 1898, frame 84.

45. Gladden, "The Nation's Opportunity," 104; on the broader context of this rhetoric, see Preston, *Sword of the Spirit, Shield of the Faith*, 191–92.

46. Gladden, sermon preached December 18, 1898, frame 91; "The Nation's Opportunity," 105.

47. Gladden, "The Nation's Opportunity," 103.

48. Gladden, "The Nation's Opportunity," 106.

49. Gladden, *Recollections*, 221–22.

50. Washington Gladden, *The Great War*, 6.

51. Gladden, *The Great War*, 4, 7.

52. Gladden, *The Great War*, 50; Irving Maurer to Gladden, October 24, 1917, MIC 4, reel 12, frame 266, Gladden Papers; on religious support for World War I, see Preston, *Sword of the Spirit, Shield of the Faith*, 253–74.

53. Gladden, *The Great War*, 16–17.

54. Gladden, *The Great War*, 30.

55. Gladden, *The Great War*, 45.

56. Gladden, *The Great War*, 47.

57. Gladden, *The Great War*, 14.

58. Gladden, *The Great War*, 9.

59. "A New National Hymn—America and Her Allies, by Washington Gladden," *Congregationalist* 102 (October 4, 1917): 431; on religious support for the war, see Jonathan H. Ebel, *Faith in the Fight: Religion and the American Soldier in the Great War* (Princeton, NJ: Princeton University Press, 2010); Ronit Y. Stahl, *Enlisting Faith: How the Military Chaplaincy Shaped Religion and State in Modern America* (Cambridge, MA: Harvard University Press, 2017), 15–23.

60. Gladden, "Do We Believe in God?" 87.

61. Gladden, "Do We Believe in God?" 87.

62. Theodore Halbert Wilson to Gladden, December 28, 1917, MIC 4, reel 12, frame 303, Gladden Papers.
63. Gladden, *The Great War*, 9, 35.
64. Gladden, *The Great War*, 52, 54, 57; Roger W. Babson to Gladden, July 17, 1917, MIC 4, reel 12, frame 190, Gladden Papers.
65. Gladden, *The Great War*, 49; on the rejection of militarism in the 1920s, see Michael G. Thompson, *For God and Globe: Christian Internationalism in the United States Between the Great War and the Cold War* (Ithaca, NY: Cornell University Press, 2015).
66. Gladden, *The Great War*, 35.
67. Gladden to Mrs. Jeffrey, April 11, 1918, MSS 900, box 1, folder 14, Gladden Papers.
68. Gladden, *The Great War*, 6.

AFTERWORD

1. . Evans, *The Social Gospel in American Religion*, 77–106; Matthew S. Hedstrom, *The Rise of Liberal Religion: Book Culture and American Spirituality in the Twentieth Century* (New York: Oxford University Press, 2012), 6–11.
2. . George B. Stewart to Washington Gladden, February 3, 1917, MIC 4, reel 12, frame 53, Gladden Papers; Marsden, *Fundamentalism and American Culture*, 118–23.
3. . See the discussion of James Fifield in chapter 1 of Kevin M. Kruse, *One Nation under God: How Corporate America Invented Christian America* (New York: Basic Books, 2015).
4. . Evans, *The Social Gospel in American Religion*, 10–11; see also Jill K. Gill, *Embattled Ecumenism: The National Council of Churches, the Vietnam War, and the Trials of the Protestant Left* (DeKalb: Northern Illinois University Press, 2011).

INDEX

adolescence, 6, 16, 139, 146

advertisements, 81
advice, 76, 100
advocate, 92, 124, 160; for friendship, 123; innovation as, 143; policies and, 114; for voting rights, 149; for workers, 107
African Americans, 29, 79, 160; education and, 159, 162; Jim Crow laws and, 151, 158; support from, 146; views of, 32, 79; voting and, 161, 162
agnostics, 102
alcohol, 117–120
alienation, 44, 131; urbanization and, 130
American Missionary Association, 159
American Protective Association (APA), 137; Constitution, US and, 140; opposition to, 140
amusements, 49; acceptance of, 123; the *Independent* on, 49; morality and, 50; rejection of, 52; writings on, 53
Andover Seminary, 17, 89
anti-Catholicism, 73, 138; denouncement of, 74; organizations and, 137; propaganda and, 138, 142
anti-imperialist movement, 164
anxiety, 103, 147
APA. *See* American Protective Association
apprenticeship, 5
articles, viii, 52, 123, 140

atonement, 46

Baker, Ray Stannard, 136
Bascom, John, 10–11
battlefields, 21; *See also specific battles*
Battle of Cold Harbor, 30
Beecher, Henry Ward, 9–10; influence of, 17; Tilton and, 63
behavior, 1, 2, 95
Being Christian: What It Means, and How to Begin (Gladden, W.), 91
beliefs, 35, 163; development of, 16; equality and, 147; humanity and, 166; knowledge and, 46; life and, 95; reinterpretation of, ix; rejection of, 51, 89
benefits, 60
benevolence, 76
bias, 165
the Bible, 101; conflict and, 142; public schools and, 67, 74; scholarship on, 87, 100; translations of, 88
bigotry, 139, 140
biographies, x, 82
Blaine, James, 147
blame, 110
Bowen, Henry, 58, 63; advertisements and, 81; conflict with, 81–82; reservations about, 59
Bowles, Sam, 59, 82, 85
Brooklyn, New York, 23

Bushnell, Horace, 42; influence of, 37, 47

California, 57
Calvinist theology, 72
candidacy, 145; letters and, 105
capitalism, 111
career, viii, 162; cultivation of, 7; at the *Independent*, 64; setbacks in, 34
Catholics, 62, 66, 144; hierarchy for, 75; immigration and, 137; the *Independent* and, 75; Protestants and, 62, 75, 137, 142; stereotypes and, 75, 138; sympathy for, 74; in United States, 75
Century magazine, 112; articles in, 140; short stories in, 124, 135
charity, 86; ethics and, 154, 156
Chicago Presbytery, 73
childhood, 2, 4
children, 3, 41; with Cohoon, 23; college for, 97; Daniels and, 4; nativism and, 144
China, 56; immigrants from, 55–57
Christian fundamentalism, 173
Christianity, 50, 113, 167; choices and, 94; community and, 122; conviction and, 9; corporations and, 152; economy and, 112; global context and, 66; hypocrisy and, 15; influence and, 142; mission of, 34; obligations of, 110; requirements for, 96; science and, 69; skepticism of, viii; society and, 12; standards for, 93; terminology and, 56, 96
"Christian League of Connecticut", 135–136
Christian Nurture (Bushnell), 37
church, 97, 125, 133; cities and, 98; class division and, 132; community and, 124, 131; cooperation among, 134, 135; denominations and, 136; dysfunction in, 25; finances and, 26; friendship and, 131; money and, 134; organizations as, 143; poverty and, 123; reverence in, 96–97; role of, 130; satellite locations for, 133; social services and, 122, 123; understanding and, 99; workers and, 112

cities, 62, 122; alienation and, 131; characterization of, 130; church and, 98; coffee houses in, 76; corruption in, 121; public safety/health in, 120–121; urbanization and, 61, 130
city council, 105–106
City Point (battlefield), 21
Civil War, 21–38, 166
class conflict, 131
class consciousness, 130
class division, 54; church and, 132; cities and, 62; New York and, 61; United States and, 63, 130
clergymen, vii, 169; defense by, 52; discussions with, 90; inadequacy among, 34; opportunity for, 113; propositions by, 67, 68; theology and, 36
Clericus, 52; on dancing, 53
Cleveland, Grover, 147
clothing, 54
coal, 98, 111
coalitions, ix, 141; respectability and, x
coffee houses, 76, 119
Cohoon, Jennie, 7, 18, 23, 151
Colfax, Schuyler, 64
colleagues, 91; disagreements with, 89
Columbus, Ohio, 97
columns, 72; "Religious Intelligence" as, 65; by women, 65
commitment, 141, 149; faith and, 65; to issues/causes, 18, 157
common sense, 76, 101
communion, 76
community, 129, 135; Christianity and, 122; church in, 124, 131; congregation and, 86; revivals and, 38; role in, 42; rumors and, 139; sin within, 76
Comstock, Anthony, 44
Confederacy, 31
conferences, 117, 124, 159
confidence, 34; in conviction, 22; as minister, 38; obstinacy and, 47
conflict, 63, 131, 151, 168; affiliation and, 146; the Bible and, 142; Bowen and, 81–82; message and, 170
congregants, 54; decisions and, 97; letters to, 99; response to, 92

INDEX

congregation: community and, 86; education and, 91; size of, 131
Congregational Church of North Adams, 38
Congregationalism, 90; merger with, 137; Rockefeller and, 152–155, 158
Congregationalist, 145
Constitution, US, 148; amendments to, 32, 67, 68; APA and, 140
conviction, 29, 113, 171; Christianity and, 9; confidence in, 22; evolution of, 45
cooperation, 116; church and, 134, 135; denominations and, xi; unification and, 143
cooperative enterprise, 116
corporations, 115; Christianity and, 152; influence and, 83; power and, 116, 153
correspondence, 19; Priest and, 14–15; with Tyler, 41, 97
corruption, 80, 167; in cities, 121; city council and, 105; government and, 116; morality and, 155; in New York, 121
cost of living, 106
coverture, 118
critic, 149, 151–171
Cross-Bronx Expressway, 26
Cuyler, Theodore, 52

dancing, 53
Daniels, Amanda, 3, 4
Daniels, Ebenezer, 4, 53
deaf, 86
death, 21, 61, 120, 171; at Antietam, 29; burial sites and, 31; of Cohoon, 151; of father, 3; of Jesus, 46, 47; war and response to, 30
debates, 87, 102
debt, 97, 108
decisions, 97; colleagues and, 91; government and, 106; principles and, 147
degrees, 145
denominations, 90, 93, 137; church and, 136; cooperation among, xi; Methodism as, 25; reform and, 90; rivalry among, 134; society and, 93
disagreements, 144; with colleagues, 89; Protestantism and, 65

diversity, 65
doctrine, 93, 100
documents, 138
Dodge, Mary Abigail, 65, 126
Dorn, Jacob, x
double consciousness, 159
doubt, 94; behavior and, 95
Du Bois, W. E. B., 159

ecclesiasticism, 143
economy, 108; Christianity and, 112; depression and, 62; economic inequality, 106, 109, 110; injustice and, 96; labor and, 109; New York and, 23, 25; socioeconomic status and, 130; workers and, 109
editorials, xi, 77, 156; on amendment, 68
editors, 152, 156; views of, 132
education, 22, 107; African Americans and, 159, 162; civics and, 149; congregations and, 91; disappointment and, 34; opportunity for, 6; women and, 126
Eggleston, Edward, 64
election, 98, 140; of 1860, 32; of 1872, 80–81; campaigns and, 146; city council and, 105–106; of Lincoln, 28
elites, 44, 114
empathy, 144
employment, 114
environment, 98, 121
equality, 79; belief and, 147; workers and, 115
ethics, 32; charity and, 154, 156; disparity in, 115; Standard Oil and, 153
Europe, 107; imperialism and, 165
events, 145
exclusivism, 76

failure, x, 148, 161; assumptions and, 149; of pastorate, 24; poverty and, 108
faith, 71, 169; commitment and, 65; decline of, 67; developments in, 66; government and, 121; rituals and, 93; in the Union, 31
family life, 3, 26; strain on, 19
fear, 69, 131; of consequences, 147; of infiltration, 139
Finney, Charles, 37

First Congregational Church, 97
First Congregational Church of Morrisania, 26
The Freedom of Faith (Munger), 88
free labor ideology, 115
friendship, 18, 64; advocate for, 123; church and, 131; Hamilton and, 8, 9; Matson and, 7; with Ward, 82
The Fundamentals, 88

games, 49
Gladden, George, 30–31, 108
Gladden, Helen, 120
Gladden, Washington. *See specific topics*
goals, 78, 142
God, 35; science and, 71
"Golden Rule", 58
government, 67, 120; corruption and, 116; decisions and, 106; faith and, 121; local government, 42, 120; morality and, 44; policies and, 114; public schools and, 75; role of, 123
grandparents, 4
greed, 62
Greeley, Horace, 78

habits, 43
Hamilton, Gail. *See* Dodge, Mary Abigail
Hamilton, Hattie, 7; letters from, 7–8, 9
harm, 51, 156; nativism and, 139
Hayes, Rutherford, 146
hell, 89
heresy, 45, 46, 133; Swing trial for, 71–73
historians, 168; history and, 75; on New York, 61; of religion, vii
Hocking Valley coal strike, 111
hometown, 1
honors, 145
Hopkins, Mark, 11–13; on humanity, 11–12; on slavery, 12
housing, 62
humanity, 6, 32; beliefs and, 166; Hopkins on, 11–12; optimism about, 33, 96; potential for, 46; view of, 168
humor, 16
hypocrisy, 50; Christianity and, 15; United States and, 68

ideas, ix, 142, 173; audiences and, 86; on conversion, 92; correspondence and, 14; exploration of, 72; intellectual development and, 70; Low and, 107; morality as, 13; revivalists and, 94; sermons and, 34; theology and, 45; vehicle for, 64
illness, 3, 31; exhaustion and, 13
immigration: Catholics and, 137; characterization and, 56; Chinese immigrants and, 55–57; issue of, 148; perspective on, 57; views on, 148; voting and, 148; wages and, 56
imperialism, 163, 166; Europe and, 165
inadequacy, 34, 42
inconsistencies, 165
independence, 14

the *Independent* (newspaper), xi, 43; advertisements and, 81; on amusements, 49; Catholics and, 75; hiring at, 63; politics and, 77–80; religious editor of, 58, 61–83; solutions in, 134

inequality, 79, 117; economic inequality, 106, 109, 110; recognition of, 111–112; riots and, 62
influence, vii, 16, 58, 123; Beecher as, 17; Bushnell as, 37, 47; Christianity and, 142; corporations and, 83; Du Bois as, 159; Hopkins as, 11–13; morality and, 121; newspaper and, 63; perspective and, 10; politics and, viii; of professors, 10; religion and, 119; of women, 126
innovation, 87, 143; religion and, 90; views and, 94; worship and, 45
intellectual development, 36, 174; ideas and, 70; pastorate and, 41; public intellectual and, 42, 43
isolation, 129
issues/causes, of Gladden, W., x, 113, 156; authority on, 107; commitment to, 18, 157; contentiousness of, 53, 54; immigration as, 148; labor as, 117; outspokenness on, 151; reform and, 119; sermons about, 124; society and, 76

Jesus, 93; death of, 46, 47; humanity of, 35
Jim Crow laws, 151, 158
journalism: interest in, 5; trend in, 77
journalist, 59; religious editor and, 58, 61–83
judgment, 95, 169; minimization of, 95

Knights of Columbus, 145
knowledge, 46, 91; fear of, 69; lack of, 122
Ku Klux Klan, 79–80

labor, 115; contracts and, 114; dispute, 55; economy and, 109; issues/causes of, 117; unions and, 110; wage labor, 108, 109; women and, 126
language, 87, 164; partisanship and, 147
leadership, 155; qualification of, 122
lectures, 43; content of, 11
lessons, 106
letters: candidacy in, 105; to congregants, 99; dictation of, 21; Hamilton and, 7–8, 9; from Matson, 1–2; mother and, 26; Priest and, 16. *See also* correspondence
lies, 138, 139
Lincoln, Abraham, 28, 30; impact of, 32; view of, 32
local government, 42, 120
loneliness, 131
Low, Seth, 107

marriage, 8; to Cohoon, 7, 18
Matson, Lewis, 1–2; friendship with, 7; on Hamilton, 8
McKinley, William, 141
memoir, 18, 89
memories, 21, 37
message, 91, 174; conflict and, 170; in context, 36; justification of, 101; loss of, 102; theological realism and, ix
Methodism, 25
Methodist Protestants, 137
militarism, 168
minister, vii, 25, 173; church and, 125; confidence as, 38; contributions from, 65; religion and, 125; role of, 124; Swing as, 71
ministry: providence and, 24; status of, 34. *See also* pastorate

models, 116, 135
moderation, 13
money, 26, 108, 134; alcohol and, 118; church and, 134; concerns about, 97; defense of, 154; morality and, 154
monopolies, 114
Moody, Dwight, 94
morality, 13, 120; amusements and, 50; corruption and, 155; government and, 44; influence and, 121; money and, 154; standards of, 49, 52
Moses, Robert, 26
multiculturalism, 56
Munger, Theodore, 88
municipal services, 106
myth, 102

national life, 61; conflict and, 63; deterioration of, 113
nativism, 139, 141; children and, 144
natural selection, 70
negotiations, 106
newspapers, 5; acknowledgment in, 59; influence and, 63; syndication in, 129; violence targeted at, 29
New Theology movement, 88; tenets of, 92
New York, 63; class division and, 61; corruption in, 121; economy and, 23, 25; national life and, 61
nicknames, 3
North Adams, Massachusetts, 41; Congregational Church of, 38
North Congregational Church, 85
Notre Dame, 145

observations, 55; Gladden, W., and, 1–19; on poverty, 111
opportunity, 14, 58; for clergymen, 113; education and, 6; scandal and, 77
optimism, 33, 47, 96
organizations, 136, 143; anti-Catholicism and, 137; ignorance and, 141
Oswego, New York, 19
Oswego Academy, 7
Oswego Gazette (newspaper): apprenticeship at, 5; contents of, 6; politics and, 5
Outlook periodical, 154, 157

outspokenness, 145, 149, 151

partisanship, 5, 78, 147; Chinese immigrants and, 57; language and, 147
pastorate, 41; failure of, 24; in Springfield, MA, 85–103; success of, 58, 83
personality, 23, 42; Hamilton and, 8
perspective, 53; changes in, 32; favor toward, 66; history and, 75; on immigration, 57; influence and, 10; reconsideration of, 108; of theology, 35
Plain Thoughts on the Art of Living (Gladden, W.), 43, 44
play and recreation, 50
Plessy v. Ferguson, 158
policies, 114, 157, 163; consequences of, 160; naturalization and, 149
politics, 98; corruption and, 80; identity and, 145–146; the *Independent* and, 77–80; influence and, viii; involvement in, 106; *Oswego Gazette* and, 5; religion and, 69; values and, 32
Pope Pius IX, 74
popularity, 110
poverty, 86; church and, 123; failure and, 108; observations on, 111
power, 68, 116, 153
Priest, Nancie, 16, 38; correspondence with, 14–15; on slavery, 15–16
principles, 147; Christians and, 113; models and, 116; reputation and, 81
professions, 24; status of, 34
prohibition, 118
propaganda, 138, 142
prophets, 103
Protestantism, 133; amusements and, 52; APA and, 140; disagreements within, 65; ministers of, vii; revivals and, 36; in United States, 66; women, 99
Protestants, 88; Catholics and, 62, 75, 137, 142
public safety/health: in cities, 120–121; corruption and, 121
public schools, 75; the Bible and, 67, 74
publishing, 63, 112
purpose, 44, 64, 151

racism, 79, 163
Rauschenbusch, Walter, 173

rebel, 41–60
Reconstruction, 160; violence and, 161
recreation, 123; religion and, 49, 50–51
reform, 119; denominations and, 90; public office and, 105–127
regret, 110
relationships, 1–2; with Bowles, 85; characterization of, 9; with press, 43
religion, 68, 135; development of, 92; doubt and, 94; historians of, vii; impediments to, 38; influence and, 119; innovation and, 90; life and, 51; ministers and, 125; other faiths and, 66; performance of, 67; politics and, 69; progress in, 70; prophets and, 103; recreation and, 49, 50–51; society and, 119, 125; terminology and, 35; *See also specific topics*
religious freedom, 141
"Religious Intelligence" (column), 65

the *Republican* (newspaper), 14

reputation, 53, 140; concern with, 59; insecurity about, 34; principles and, 81
resignation, 82
respect, x, 148
retirement, 151, 152
reverence, 96–97
revivals, 36, 38; burned-over district from, 36–37; critique of, 38, 87; revivalists and, 94; skepticism about, 34
right of self-determination, 164
riots, 29, 62
risk, 45; theology and, 49
rituals, 93
Rockefeller, John D., 152–155, 158
Roman Catholics, 73, 137
Roosevelt, Theodore, 153
rumors, 139

scandal, 54, 77, 141
science, 69, 71, 111
scientists, 69
scripture, 70, 101, 102
sectarianism, 163
secularism, 125, 142; content and, 64, 77
segregation, 162, 163
self-confidence, 14

self-control, 47
self-promotion, 42
sermons, 36; ideas and, 34; issues and, 124; publishing of, 112; syndication for, 129
Seymour, Horatio, 28
short stories, 124, 135, 136
sin, 76, 95
skills, 13, 98
slavery, 6, 79; Civil War and, 33; Hopkins on, 12; legality of, 16; Priest on, 15–16; status quo and, 28
The Social Gospel movement, ix, 173–174
socialism, 117, 174
social science, 111
social services, 122, 123
society, 131; Christianity and, 12; church and, 133; denominations and, 93; fragmentation of, 129; inequality and, 79; influence in, 123; issues/causes and, 76; prophets and, 103; religion and, 119, 125; theology and, 95
soldiers, 21
The Souls of Black Folk (Du Bois), 159
Springfield, Massachusetts, 85–103
Standard Oil, 152–153; ethics and, 153
standards: for Christianity, 93; of morality, 49, 52
status quo, 158; anxiety about, 147; slavery and, 28
stereotypes, 74; behavior and, 2; Catholics and, 75, 138; indulgence of, 141
stratification, 132; characterization and, 130
strikes, 55; coal and, 111; increase in, 111; shoemakers' strike, 57, 58
Strong, William, 67
success: of pastorate, 58, 83; professions and, 24
Sunday Afternoon (magazine), 85–86
Swing, David, 71–73
sympathy, 12; for workers, 112

Taylor, Graham, 154
teaching, 17
technology, 109
temperance movement, 117–120; suffrage movement and, 127
terminology, 29; Christianity and, 56, 96; religion and, 35
theological integrity, 47
theological liberalism, 65, 173; affirmation of, 77; Andover Seminary and, 89
theological realism, viii; message of, ix; proponents of, 103
theology, 35; clergymen and, 36; debates and, 87, 102; ideas and, 45; risk and, 49; society and, 95
A Theology for the Social Gospel (Rauschenbusch), 173
Tilden, Samuel, 146
Tilton, Theodore, 63
traditionalists, 101
training, 22
travel, 4, 107, 157
trial, Swing on, 71–73
truth, 45; denominations and, 93; lies and, 138
Tweed, William Macy, 80
two-party system, 78
Tyler, Moses, 17, 23; on Bowen, 59; on challenges, 42; correspondence with, 41, 97; recommendations by, 64

uncertainty, 94
unemployment, 109
unifier, 129–149
Union Relief Association, 86
unions, 110; support for, 112
United Brethren, 137
United States, 163, 166; Catholics in, 75; class division and, 63, 130; hypocrisy and, 68; industrialization in, 108, 165; open-air services in, 133; Protestantism in, 66; urbanization and, 130
urbanization, 61, 130

values, 32; perception of, 122; war and, 167
violence, 55, 62; Reconstruction and, 161; targets of, 28
Virginia, 21
virtues, 111
voting, 78; African Americans and, 161, 162; immigration and, 148; restrictions on, 149

wages, 111; immigration and, 56; wage labor, 108, 109
war, 30, 166; characterization of, 33; conscription and, 28; cynicism about, 33; response to death in, 30; values and, 167; *See also specific wars*
Ward, William Hayes, 64, 77; friendship with, 82
Washington, Booker T., 159
Washington Gladden: Prophet of the Social Gospel (Dorn), x
water supply, 105
wealthy, 44, 114
White, Andrew Dickson, 98
Who Wrote the Bible (Gladden, W.), 100, 102
Willard, Frances, 127
Williams, Asa, 118
Williams College, 10
Wilson, Henry, 64
women, ix; columns by, 65; coverture and, 118; influence of, 126; Protestantism, 99; relationships with, 1–2; view of, 126
women's rights, 148

women's suffrage, 125–127
Wood, Fernando, 28
workers, 107, 113; church and, 112; colleagues and, 89, 91; economy and, 109; equality and, 115; as partners, 116–117; sympathy for, 112; upward mobility and, 130. *See also* labor
Working People and Their Employers (Gladden, W.), 109
World War I, 151
World War II, 171
worship, 45
writing, viii, xi; on amusements, 53; authority and, 117; opportunity and, 14; skills and, 13

YMCA. *See* Young Men's Christian Association
Young Men and the Churches (Gladden, W.), 99
Young Men's Christian Association (YMCA), 53, 74

Zion, 96

ABOUT THE AUTHOR

David Mislin is a historian of religion and culture in the United States. His work explores the influence of religious liberals in shaping American political and intellectual life. He is the author of *Saving Faith: Making Religious Pluralism an American Value at the Dawn of a Secular Age* (2015) and a contributor to several volumes, including *The Lively Experiment: Religious Toleration in America from Roger Williams to the Present* (2015). He teaches in the Intellectual Heritage Program at Temple University.

www.ingramcontent.com/pod-product-compliance
Lightning Source LLC
Chambersburg PA
CBHW032042300426
44117CB00009B/1157